The easy-to-use strategies demonstrated in *Handwriting & Personality* show how to use graphology to discover the secrets of handwriting and reveal the meaning behind:

- *Wide or narrow margins on a page*
- *Where a signature is placed*
- *Heavy, light, or medium pen pressure*
- *Different types of slants*
- *The position of the cross on a "T"*
- *Combined print and script*
- *The look of the letter "I"*
- *And much more!*

HANDWRITING AND PERSONALITY

How Graphology Reveals What Makes People Tick

Ann Mahony

IVY BOOKS • NEW YORK

For Bobbie and Big Dad

*This book is also dedicated to world peace.
In every language, in every handwriting, let
us communicate with love.*

To the Reader:

To protect the privacy of any individuals other than public figures whose handwriting is analyzed in the book, the author has changed names and background information, and has also modified identifying characteristics that would personalize or permit identification of any individual handwriting by third parties. Any resemblance of a person to any individual discussed in the book is purely coincidental and not intended by the author.

Contents

Acknowledgments

I would like to thank Carol Costello for her initial push in getting me started on this project. Her organization, humor, and support were greatly appreciated. Thanks to Alice Martell for believing in me, and to Ward Mohrfeld, my editor, and Kathie Gordon, my copy editor, who kept me on track and helped me to clarify and refine what I was trying to say. To Debbie Boatwright and Judy Montgomery, who worked tirelessly to help me assemble the handwriting samples. They are not only skilled and professional graphologists but also loyal and supportive friends. And to Gwen Sampson, who opened my eyes to the world of graphology, and to graphologists worldwide who keep them open with their continuing research, study, and experimentation.

A final enormous and heartfelt thank-you to the countless number of people who have written to me over the years in response to media appearances and lectures. I'm unable to acknowledge each letter personally, but I treasure every one, for when you put a pen to paper, you are sharing a piece of yourself with me, your heart and soul. What a treasured gift.

Introduction

For as long as I can remember, I've been trying to figure out what makes people tick. As a child, I wondered why certain kids seemed self-confident in situations that felt uncomfortable to me. Were they bluffing? Were they just natural winners? I've asked myself, years later, where are these people now? Would they react with the same aplomb in a job interview or romance? And why is it that we wake up feeling like winners on some days but not others?

We've all experienced times when everything goes our way and other times when we can't do anything right. I've had these ups and downs myself, and hadn't a clue as to how I created my successes when on a roll or perpetuated disasters during one of those difficult days. I closely observed those who seemed to have the knack of being on top of things to see if I could learn the secret of their success. In the process, I discovered two things: Everyone has good and bad days, but some people handle it better; and, second, my own preconceptions about people interfered with my understanding of them. I was most attracted to those who appeared to be like myself (validating, of course that I was on the right track) and was wary of the exception, considering his or her consistent successes as flukes, not behavior I could emulate. I tended to ignore those who didn't *seem* to be on my wavelength, because I didn't understand them, but I began to suspect I was missing something.

In this ongoing process of wondering why we are the way we are and why we do the things we do, I discovered graphology, a fascinating tool that instantly records feelings, mood swings, even physical highs and lows. Although I studied avidly, I kept this newly gained knowledge to myself, assuming that others either weren't interested in this "mystical" science or that they already had found the answers I was still seeking. Later, I shared what I had learned with a few friends, and then I decided I was ready to begin teaching classes. It was clear that hundreds of other people were seeking, just like me, some organized method to achieve better understanding of their fellow human beings.

Few of us possess the skills of a trained behavioral psychologist, yet we all have to handle complex interactions with people every day. And we can't ask for twenty minutes of time off in the middle of a meeting with a client or a flare-up with a teenage child in order to assess motives and analyze behavior. Life doesn't work that way; it's immediate, it's here and now, it's unique for each person—and so is handwriting, which is why it is so important as a key to comprehension.

I came to the study of handwriting in a rather roundabout way actually, having first become a professional graphic designer, working in package design, museum exhibits, and corporate identity programs. While at the University of Cincinnati I had studied letterforms with professors from the School of Design in Basel, Switzerland. Having minored in psychology, I was also extremely interested in marketing techniques used in public persuasion. Working with marketing professionals, I often found myself on the hidden side of a two-way mirror, observing consumers respond to certain package designs. I learned quickly about the subliminal effect of graphic shapes and forms on consumers' desires to buy. I also watched their handwriting when they were answering questions and noted that surprisingly consistent patterns began to emerge. This had to be more than coincidence. I was hooked. I had to know more.

I began my professional training in Denver with the very distinguished graphologist Gwen Sampson. Her wonderful archive included such materials as thirty-three years of medical research from a doctor who had catalogued physical changes and ailments that surface in handwriting. I went on to investigate every class I could find across the country and every book published on the subject. In New York I met Felix Klein, a German-Jewish graphologist who survived the concentration camps during World War II by analyzing the handwriting of the Nazi guards in exchange for food, which he shared with the other prisoners. Felix generously shared with me his knowledge of the European study of handwriting, including the fact that many companies there won't hire people without having their handwriting analyzed first. My studies continue to this day as I try to stay apace of the new work of graphologists throughout the world. Handwriting is one language that's universal!

The study of handwriting has both simplified my life and enriched it with new depth and facets of meaning. Simplified because, without saying a word, I'm able quickly to comprehend the feelings of others, to understand what emotions trigger their behavior. I know what their reactions will be in a given situation almost before they know themselves. Enriched and complicated, because I can study many layers at once, like overlapping panes of colored glass, some transparent with joy, some clouded with criticism or fear. Never again will I make snap judgments about someone's behavior without analyzing its roots in personality. Now I understand that a boss's angry shouts may simply be the cries of a scared child.

Anne Morrow Lindbergh once sadly observed that "often in a large city, shaking hands with my friends, I have felt the wilderness stretching between us." Haven't we all experienced this void at one time or another? But the chasm isn't always between friends; it often lies within ourselves. Lindbergh also observed, "If one is out of touch with oneself, then one cannot touch others." Think about it. Graphology provides an invaluable tool for self-discovery as well, recording subconscious feelings about yourself and others more accurately than your conscious mind, which has too much invested in making you "right." If you often catch yourself saying one thing while really feeling something else, perhaps it's time to take a close look at your own handwriting.

Although the science of handwriting analysis is as contemporary as rockets in space, it is also as old as recorded history. We have systematic accounts of handwriting analysis dating from 1622, but only in our present age of "self-discovery" has its revival been embraced so enthusiastically.

Dr. Alfred Binet used graphology in his famous intelligence testing, and Dr. Albert Schweitzer was a member of the Société de Graphologie de Paris. Harvard psychologists Gordon Allport and P. E. Vernon, in their book *Studies in Expressive Movement*, support the theory of handwriting revealing character. Freud agreed—"There is no doubt that men express their character through their handwriting." Others who have contributed to the study of graphology include: Emile Zola, Elizabeth Barrett and Robert Browning, Sir Walter Raleigh, George Sand, Charles Baudelaire, and Thomas Mann. When painting portraits, Gainsborough was known to place samples of his subject's handwriting on the easel to give him a sense of their "inner" character. Carl Jung's Psychological Types have also been categorized graphologically. When studying this "new" science, you're in good company.

Graphology is as simple as walking or talking, and as complicated. To explain every nuance and subtlety would require a dozen books the size of the New York telephone directory, and would be about as interesting. This book is neither a quickie reference guide nor an encyclopedia on the science of graphology. I have tried to consolidate what's been said by graphologists, psychologists, theorists, physiologists, and teachers, and what I've learned in over a decade of analyzing handwriting for individuals, corporations, courts, government, and educational institutions. It's a workable, thorough manual that provides an overview of the salient characteristics so that you can start analyzing handwriting immediately.

Part One

The Public You

Reading People

The Dilemma

Haven't you ever wished you could read another person's mind and discover what he or she is really thinking behind the words that are spoken? What would you give to have this power? So many of my clients lament, "If only I had known before I married him!" (or "before I signed the agreement," or "accepted the job," or "started this romance"). Our lives may be filled with "if-only" hindsight and heartache. Confused by our own feelings and unable to get a handle on the other person, even the sharpest among us have found ourselves on occasion in a predicament similar to that of my friend Margaret. This was her story during a recent visit:

Imagine me, Margaret Bradley, in glorious Cancún! After Chicago's brutal winter, it was heaven to bake on the beach. Sure, I'd been skeptical when Cheryl mentioned Club Med—swinging singles, guys out for a good time. But she convinced me. So there I was, with high hopes, but realistic reservations.

Sure enough, we met the second night. He was bronzed and beautiful, from San Diego. But why would a Californian vacation in even sunnier Mexico? The archaeological wonders, he explained. My heart stopped. I majored in archaeology at Northwestern. Had I finally met my Indiana Jones?

Hold on, Margaret, I told myself. You're single, thirty-seven, and too eager. You'll just get used, and then it's back to Evanston and "Love Boat" reruns.

Over supper that evening, I tried to read his signals. Was

that a sincere smile as he gently kissed my cheek? Or a sly smirk at my naïveté? My heart ached. How could I be sure? He gave me a dozen roses with a love note. Everything happened so fast. Now it's been six weeks, and I'm still waiting for him to call. Will I ever learn?

We use every resource, every gut instinct, intuition, and past experience to get it right, and still get taken. Why? Because we're human. And subjective. We go with what we like and dislike, with what "feels" right. But what feels right may not necessarily be what's true. Watch yourself next time you're listening to a politician, a salesman, or a new friend. Regardless of what the person says, what you *feel* about what he or she says is what you'll believe to be true.

Communication experts have proven that most of us "half listen" or listen with our minds already made up. Psychologists call this "selective response." People find what they're looking for, not necessarily what's there. Margaret wanted to believe that this time she really had found Mr. Wonderful.

The truly successful communicators consider all possibilities. They don't kid themselves. But, like Margaret, most of us resist. We want to be right.

Sometimes we'll even intentionally cloud the issue. In trying to discourage a Chicago suitor, Margaret told him that this vacation was strictly for the girls—to get away and enjoy one another's company. Hmmm. Now she's on the *receiving* end of an unclear message. Is it surprising that someone who is less than honest with others can wind up confused and kidding herself as well?

There is an answer. There is a path that will lead you directly into the heart and mind of another, and you don't have to be a psychologist to use it. You'll have no more guesswork, crossed signals, mixed messages—just open, clear communication. Getting what you want from others. Now that's power.

The Solution

The solution bypasses usual modes of communication (spoken words, body language) and proceeds directly to the mind of the other person to read his true intentions. "But I'm not psychic," wailed Margaret. "I can't read another person's mind." She wanted my advice.

"You work with computers, don't you, Margaret?"

"Yes, a little," she nodded.

"Well, what if I could give you a printout of what's on Mr. Wonderful's mind? Actual black-and-white copy that recorded his feelings and emotions? Direct from his 'subconscious software,' so to speak."

"You're kidding!" she challenged.

"I'm dead serious," I replied. "Didn't you say he wrote you a note? Where is it?"

"But Ann," protested Margaret, "I've read the words. Over and over. I've interpreted them every way I can think of—sincerely, insincerely, the cad, the good guy, etc. How will you read them any differently?"

"I'm not reading the *words*, Margaret," I admonished. "He could write in Dutch for all I care. I'm analyzing the *patterns*—the energy, rhythm, passion, mood, temperament that formed the letters. It's quite a different thing."

"Handwriting analysis could help me?" she queried.

Handwriting Analysis?

Once, when I was analyzing a woman's handwriting, her husband, who happened to be a medical doctor, asked me skeptically, "Yes, but is it really a *science*?" Graphology, I explained, is an empirical science, just like medicine, psychology, and many other sciences that rely on observation and experimentation.

"I'll admit it sounds interesting," some people say, "but I don't think handwriting can reveal *my* true personality" because:

- I learned to write in school, and my teacher's particular style influenced me to write the way I do.
- I have arthritis (broke my wrist, wrote this on a window ledge, etc.), so my handwriting will be "off" a little.
- I have many different styles that change from day to day, so you can't analyze me. I'm too complex to be easily pigeon-holed.
- I print *and* write. Does that mean I have a split personality?
- I admired my aunt, so I copied her handwriting. You're really analyzing *that* person.
- I'm left-handed. I had to slant my paper the other way in school, and thus I have a left-handed slant.

- Men and women write differently. There is a "feminine" hand that will bias your judgment.
- Certain professions dictate a style—architectural printing, calligraphy, the doctor's scrawl.
- Handwriting depends on the person's strength and size. You can't tell me a linebacker for the Forty-Niners won't use more muscle than a thirteen-year-old girl.
- Handwriting is an acquired skill, like sewing.
- Handwriting is not really instinctive, not really a part of me.

As you will discover, handwriting is indeed a part of you—as much a part of you as your style of dress, manner of speech, eating habits, and the way you think.

Your John Hancock

Before we proceed further, why not jot down a few sentences and your signature on a piece of unlined paper to keep with this book for future reference. You may not wish to pause in your reading at this point, so you may use something you've already written, but remember, it's your last chance to submit a "virgin" sample before discovering the depths and secrets behind your script. Keep your writing free and natural. It's best not to copy anything, as the frequent stops and starts will interrupt your rhythm. If you have more than one style of writing, that's fine. Include them also, to enable yourself to analyze the total spectrum of your personality. You may wish to write a longer sample as well for more extensive analysis later.

What Happened?

What actually took place as you began to write your sample? Do you feel that the loops, swirls, and flourishes on the paper represent you? Did it seem like a projection of your personality in some way, or just some scratches on paper?

The Hidden Message

Look again. What does the arrangement on the page say about you? The wide, even margins, the tangled lower loops, the cramped scrawl? And how does the writing move? Is it natural and spontaneous? Exuberant? Constricted and repressed? How do you move through life in other ways, besides through the tip of a pen? Does the energy coincide?

Some folks may become defensive, claiming that they are more organized, more controlled, more dignified, even nicer than their handwriting portrays them to be.

A *B* Is a *B*

Maybe you're like Bailey, a friend of mine who felt that he was merely "repeating patterns" of letters he was taught in school. "Anyone could have done that," he claimed. "It's just a habit, just going through the motions. We all basically write the way we were taught. It's as nondescript as eating a bowl of cereal. A *B* is a *B*," he told me.

I decided to have a little fun with Bailey and prove my point in the process. I got hold of a petition that called for smoking to be banned in restaurants (Bailey is a smoker). I added my imitation of his signature and showed him a photocopy. When confronted with the document he argued, "But I didn't sign that!" "How can you be sure?" I queried. "That's not my *B*," he protested. "But Bailey," I smiled. "A *B* is à *B*, isn't it?"

Bailey still wasn't convinced. "Oh, Ann," he insisted, "a person's basic handwriting style just can't be *that* revealing!" Handwriting, I assured him, is as revealing as the disappointed slump in your shoulders and the shuffle in your walk as you quietly leave the boss's office. It's as revealing as that involuntary flush of surprise when you spot *her* across a crowded restaurant with someone else.

Handwriting, whether fast or slow, free or controlled, expansive or constricted, indicates how a personality propels himself through life. And each one adopts his own unique rhythm and style. I myself have done lengthy research on the handwriting of identical twins. I have found that, just as there are no two fingerprints alike, there are no two handwritings exactly the same. In fact, research has shown that the possibility of two writings being identical is one in 68 trillion!

What Is Handwriting?

When you directed your pen to move across the paper for your sample, you wrote not just with your hand, but with impulses from your brain. These brain impulses direct all your activity— walking, talking, sleeping, reading. They allow you to pick up a cup of coffee, hit a tennis ball, or drive a car. You're even holding this book with your brain—it directs each finger to curl just so, without your conscious awareness. Watch someone play the piano sometime and imagine the intricate computer guiding those ten fingers to operate independently, guiding one hand to play the melody and the other hand to play the chords while his eyes read the notes and translate them to the fingertips. Do you actually believe he is creating music with ten little appendages, or with complex messages from his brain? (Did you ever sit through a piano recital saying to yourself, If only I had *hands* as smart as that virtuoso on stage?)

Scientists estimate that we have between 100,000 and 1,000,000 different chemical reactions taking place in our brain *every minute*. Imagine! Centuries ago, when the great philosopher Aristotle was asked, "Where are your feelings located?' he gestured first toward his heart, then toward his stomach, because that is where his emotions seemed to live. But we know that, while fear may trigger neurological impulses that make the stomach feel "upset," attributing fear to the power of the stomach would be tantamount to attributing writing to the power of the hand. The brain, not the hand, directs the pen. In fact, a more accurate term for the phenomenon taking place would be *brainwriting*.

"Brainwriting"

Suppose you were in an accident and paralyzed from the neck down. Even the simple act of picking up a glass of water would be impossible for you. Without a message from the brain to pick up the glass, the limb is useless. The nerves that carry the message "Reach out, bend elbow, curl fingers" have been severed. No message, no movement.

So too with writing, whether the pen is held in the right or left hand, between the toes or even between the teeth (as is often the case with my paralyzed clients): the writing will still analyze the same. Why? Because it is the *same brain* directing the pen. The same personality and temperament are at work. With enough practice at controlling the pen, the same graphic patterns reappear—even when the writing is done with the foot.

Why is it that twenty first-graders who've all had the same instruction produce twenty different handwritings? Because twenty different brains are absorbing the material. Twenty different temperaments and levels of intelligence are at work, regardless of the teacher. She only provides the framework for learning a new skill. It's the power and force of the mind that dictates the power of the handwriting, not the strength of the person. That's why a determined ninety-eight-pound woman can write with the force of a leading executive, while Rosie Grier can "relax" with delicate needlepoint.

These responses are so complex that they occur beneath our level of conscious awareness. (When was the last time you consciously reminded yourself to inhale and exhale?) These impulses make us who and what we are. The neurochemical patterns from the brain are what gave Kennedy his charisma, Edison his determination, and Einstein his genius. They are what make Jimmy Stewart's h-h-hesitant speech so much a part of him. Handwriting, like the gait of our walk and speed of our talk, is another outward manifestation of this intricate computer that gives each of us personality.

The Mind/Body Connection

Dr. Bernie Siegel, author of *Love, Medicine & Miracles*, relates story after story of cancer patients who have altered the cellular structure of their bodies through the power of the mind. There is no doubt, claims Dr. Siegel, that "our state of mind has an immediate and direct effect on our state of body."

Dr. Hans Selye, author of numerous books on stress, has proven that suppression of anger or feelings of failure can literally make us sick. When we are under constant tension, our resistance to disease is lowered.

Now, do you honestly believe that a brain powerful enough to control our heart, liver, kidneys, lungs, and other organs on a subconscious level—and our running, swimming, singing, dancing, and other activities on a conscious level—is not directing our pen as well?

Handwriting is energy and will change to reflect *anxiety*, as you scribble phone numbers at the accident site, to *fear*, as you write directions to the hospital, to *relief*, as you copy the victim's address and number to phone his folks and say everything's fine. And watch your body: Its physical and emotional changes— tense stomach, tight shoulders, throbbing head—will affect your writing as well.

Different Styles

That's why your handwriting may look different from time to time. No one's moods remain constant. We may be tired, anxious, angry, happy, sad, or silly—but we're still the same people underneath. We may write differently when zipping off a grocery list or penning a love letter, when we have lots of energy or when we have none, but the same basic characteristics will surface every time we put pen to paper, because the patterns are coming from the same central source.

How Can I Use Graphology?

Because handwriting is a direct projection from the brain, it accurately reveals:

- what motivates people beneath the facade they show the world
- what they really think of themselves, both publicly and privately
- how they're likely to behave in any given situation
- whether they're likely to achieve their goals
- and much more

Through graphology you can sometimes know more about people than they know about themselves. You can know what makes them tick. That kind of knowledge about another, and particularly about yourself, is power.

Who uses graphology? Here are some specific applications: professionals faced with a career choice, personnel officers engaged in hiring, promotion, and employee relations, teachers assisting students in achieving maximum growth, psychologists who need immediate insight into a patient's problems, lawyers evaluating the sincerity of juries and clients, parents of troubled teenagers, and couples on the brink of matrimony.

Does It Take Special Talent?

"I don't know if I can ever develop a feel for handwriting," you may say. I think you can. Remember, we listen to our instincts every day of our lives, whether we realize it or not. We sense when not to ask for a raise, mention Donna's new hairdo, or kid Charlie about his weight. We respond to the behavior of other people, whether or not we are consciously aware of it. We sense their style or essence. We know whether we like a political candidate's style or "energy." We have gut feelings about people we date and marry. We know when people can't look us in the eye.

It's important to realize that you already have some of the tools to get you started: exposure to and experience with the human animal. Add to that a reliable, visual, concrete aid to chart and measure the subconscious "brain waves" of the mind, and any aspiring practitioner who *wants* to learn is well on his way to a whole new life-style of self-mastery, understanding, and power.

Touchy Subjects

There's a tendency to marvel at how accurate graphology is when applied to friends and business associates, but to scoff at it when we try to apply it to ourselves. Particularly when we run across something less than perfect . . .

When dealing with our imperfections, it's important to remember how to use graphology. Rather than concentrating on our "down side," graphology is here to point the way to insight and growth. (I'm reminded of the medical students who experience symptoms of every disease they study. You may begin to think you have every strange trait we mention.) I'm not interested in judging or criticizing. It takes a certain amount of courage just to look at yourself, especially in a mirror that tells the absolute truth. Give yourself some credit simply for doing that: looking. Be gentle with yourself, but also be honest.

A lot of people, having written a sample for analysis, say things like, "Oh, gee, I just grabbed a pencil and started scribbling. I usually never write on a scrap of paper like this, or use a scratchy pen. This isn't really me." Isn't it? One thing we know already about this person is: He doesn't plan ahead.

My friend Trudy was mortified when she went to the supermarket in curlers, wearing the dirty raincoat she was really taking to the cleaners, and ran into her boss's wife in the checkout line. "Oh, no," she winced, "I can't believe you saw me like this. This isn't really me!" Oh, yes, it is! It's Trudy on a bad day, maybe, but *it's Trudy*. And there's a part of Trudy that goes through life hoping she won't run into anyone in the checkout line. Graphology will tell you the truth, but you're in charge of how much truth you want to look at, and when.

Two Schools of Thought

When you begin to study graphology, you'll find that the science is divided into two camps or schools of thought. One is called *Gestalt*, one *Trait-stroke*.

The Gestalt school believes the writing must be judged in toto, never analyzing a single letter by itself. They consider the movement, form, and arrangement of handwriting as it interweaves to create a total personality picture.

The Trait-stroke school places great emphasis on individual strokes having a certain meaning. Each detail, the theory goes, tells us something about the personality. You might liken it to observing an individual's overall facial appearance as opposed to studying the individual features (eyes, nose, etc.). Both methods have merit, and when joined together, they provide the most thorough system available.

In Part One of this book, we'll adopt the Gestalt approach, observing the overall image the writer projects—if he's relaxed or nervous, energetic or tired, a participant or an observer. In Part Two we'll probe a little further, looking at *why* he feels relaxed or nervous, in control or at the mercy of the winds. We'll study each laugh line and facial twitch. We may even go back to childhood and see how the opinions of others helped shape the adult of today. In Part Three, it's your turn to try your hand, and realize just how quickly you've learned to analyze handwriting!

This Is Important

When I pick up a book, I'm often tempted to race through the chapter titles and read first the ones that fascinate me most. Or sometimes I'll jump ahead in an effort to get to the good stuff. Great care has been taken to arrange these chapters to build on one another so that when you're finished you have a total picture of the personality. Rushing ahead will only find you flipping back later to fill in the gaps.

2

Setting the Stage

The Dinner Party

In this book, you are about to meet eight very special people. Some are actual friends of mine, and some are composites of people I have known. They volunteered to let me put them together for an evening in some strange and even embarrassing situations so that you can see how their handwriting reveals their character. We'll look at samples of their writing before we begin and then watch them come to the party and interact with one another. We'll see what they wear, the image they project as they arrive, where and with whom they sit, what they choose to bring to dinner. We'll also explore some of the darker and more hidden sides of their personalities that gradually surface through the evening.

Once you have gained a working knowledge of these eight people and what is revealed in their handwriting, you will have the tools with which to analyze others'. You can apply the principles to people you meet—whether at the PTA, on the corporate jet, at the tennis courts, the bowling alley, or the bank.

Here's your invitation to the party:

> *You are cordially invited*
> *to a sumptuous potluck feast*
> *and the best of company at*
> *Nicole Chandler's*
> *1530 Chestnut Street*
> *November 14 at 6:30* P.M.

The only difference between you and the other guests is that you're in a special category: invisible. You can walk around, perch on a chair or table, and observe everyone without any of them seeing you. You can even take this book with you, so you can begin connecting people's behavior with their writing as the evening unfolds.

The Cast of Characters

This may be the most revealing dinner party you have ever attended. Here are the people you'll meet:

1. Dark, vivacious Nicole, who is head of marketing for a large, sophisticated shopping complex. Her beautifully decorated apartment has a gracious, open air. She sweeps in wearing a flowing white hostess gown, her manner outgoing and magnanimous; but you can't miss that beneath it all is a velvet hammer.

2. Her date, Bill, is a quiet, somewhat reserved physicist working in high-tech Silicon Valley. He's also an expert sailor. Dark haired and slightly built, he's quite handsome but appears almost shy in social situations. He arrives early to make sure everything's under control (he'll never learn that, despite the elegant externals, Nicole has a mind like the proverbial steel trap). Nicole has cleverly saved him some "detail work," folding the napkins just so, to keep him out from underfoot.

3. Monica is an executive secretary for a large land developer. She's disciplined, organized, confident, and capable, and has her job down to a system, so she can devote any and all extra time to her personal shopping and wardrobe service, Your Own Creation. She's just had a fashion tip accepted for an upcoming issue of *Vogue* and is on cloud nine. She throws her arms around Nicole even before she takes off her dripping raincoat, extending a smile and warm hello to all around her.

4. Blond, blue-eyed Joe produces a local morning talk show. He's forty and divorced, innovative and dynamic. He likes to buy old homes, fix them up, and sell them, and does much of the work himself. At five-foot-six, he wears a three-piece suit with a gold bar pin at the collar to command respect. He's a Vietnam vet, which has a strong bearing on the deeper aspects of Joe we see as the evening unfolds.

5. Silver-haired, elegant Toni is Nicole's aunt, a widow who's in the process of moving from residential to commercial real

estate. She's successful but lonely. She wears a safe, sophisticated Adolfo and pearls and remains rather aloof from the others at first. Clients don't warm up to her easily but trust her cool judgment and air of authority.

6. Michael is introduced as a part-time bartender at a local singles bar. (It is later revealed that he is an environmental planner working on his Ph.D. in sociology, and this dramatically changes the way people relate to him.) He's a gourmet cook and gives Nicole special instructions on how to serve the Greek casserole he's brought.

7. Connie is busy, busy, busy, with her two children, husband (even though he's out of town), ballet board meetings, and working as a travel agent two days a week. She has a million other things she'd like to do, like starting her own color consulting service, but where would she find the time? Fortunately, because she's always a little late, she's been asked to bring dessert.

8. James is the seventeen-year-old son of Nicole's neighbors across the hall. They're out of town and have asked Nicole to keep an eye on him. He arrives with quiches in pink boxes from the fancy deli because he and two friends ate the lasagna his mother had prepared for him to bring. He's going through changes and a little uncomfortable in this adult company, rolling his eyes heavenward and hanging back with an uncompromising yet noncommittal air about him. You get the feeling that he's nodding in agreement with you on the surface, but going his own way underneath.

Now let's look at a sample of each person's handwriting.

Poised, vivacious Nicole:

The Art Deco Party
should be an absolute
Did you know our Dien
modelling # 3-5 millio
worth of estate jewel

Disciplined, detail-oriented Bill:

Every 30 or 40 seconds we'd get su
I found that with care I could just
to clear the land. Trouble way, the sea
for careful sailing and we kept getting
always towards the beach, and always
when I needed every inch. When the .
us there was nowhere to go and only

Then a fishing boat appeared
line. He towed us all the way back t
I waded out to his boat, arms full of
a thank you gesture, the fisherman

Impulsive, restless Monica:

                                        relish
in the thought of sketching hoards of
my own personal creations, hand selecting
from the finest silks, wools, etc all
over the world, and having my very own
personal dress designer deal with the
finishing touches.

Since I thoroughly enjoy music, singing,
and all art forms (dance, drama, etc.) I occas-
sionally pretend to be a famous personality,
be it on stage or in a night club. Art has

Organized, logical Joe:

Thank you for giving
so much time this
afternoon. I am appre
of your comments both
personal and professi
Really looking forward
your appearance on 1
Are Talking!

Reserved, shy Toni:

Betty and I should like
thank you most sincerely
all the time and effort
you have expended in ou
and that of the hotel

Affable, pleasant Michael:

As for me, I've been on
a number of projects
much that I feel the
proverbial juggler, t.
keep several 'balls' in
simultaneously.
I saw Paul Daddino th

Gregarious, emotional Connie:

is progressing nicely & We continue.
and I love securing the national r
for these guys along as bigger and
I'm learning alot from all of these
personal Process is amazing when
step back and look   .

Reticent, aloof James:

You can include this Sam
my handwriting in the
shop exhibit. Its okay
to have it and

Thank you very much

Obviously, these people don't represent the entire human population, and we're not trying to divide all people into these eight categories. The idea is to give you some specific people you can get to know fairly well as they go through several hours together. This should make the connections between handwriting and personality real for you so you can remember them and apply what you learn to the people in your own life, whether fireman or fashion model, housewife or corporate executive.

3

Putting a Pen to Paper

Handwriting Pressure

In order for you to leave *any* type of mark on paper, you must exert pressure onto the writing surface. The amount of pressure you use indicates something about you and your state of mind. Whether the crayon scrawl of a toddler or the skilled stroke of a calligrapher, what we are witnessing is *energy* pouring forth from the individual.

The amount of pressure reveals how much energy, how much vitality and stamina you have available to you. Have you ever noticed that there are days when you can't seem to write through two layers of carbon and other times when, perhaps in the heat of anger, your writing could cut through cardboard? Ever experience a wobbly hand when recovering from an extended illness? Or observe the sudden angularity of a hand stricken with arthritis?

Envision yourself as a well of energy. Is it shallow or deep? Some folks seem to have a "bottomless pit" of energy—able to hold down two jobs, dance till dawn, or attend night school—while others can barely make it home to flop in front of the TV.

The more deeply the writing cuts into the paper, the deeper the reservoir of drive and energy the person has. Run a sample of handwriting between your thumb and index finger to see how "deep" or "shallow" it feels. You may wish to turn the page over and hold it up to window light to see the lines and ridges pushing through. (Felt-tip pens and photocopies cannot record this phenomenon as accurately.)

Don't expect the pressure to be completely even. There is a certain pattern of tension and release that flows through the writing in the up and down strokes. Just like the rhythm of breathing in and out, this reflects a healthy balance between tension and release. Children still mastering the neuromuscular skill of writing—or adults beset with physical or emotional problems—will not have this flow and rhythm to their pressure.

Types of Pressure

Handwriting pressure varies from person to person, but can be grouped into one of three categories: heavy, medium, or light.

Heavy Pressure

of graphology . Please include dai

you might have on the study of grap

dad how I might get started .

Thankyou for your time

I hope to be hearing from you s.

Just as heavy pressure leaves a strong impression on the paper, so too does the writer "leave his mark" on the environment! People who write using heavy pressure are usually forceful, dynamic, and productive. They possess great amounts of determination and endurance and rarely will they drop the ball or do something halfway. Their depth of emotion and aggressive spirit are well above average.

What keeps a Hatfield-McCoy feud fueled, or the wife of Odysseus waiting forever? Though they may try to conceal them, these people have strong, deeply felt emotions. If you know someone like them, check to see if the person uses heavy pressure in writing. He experiences joy from the toes on up, and anguish direct from the heart. Just as the writing cuts deep into the paper, leaving permanent "tracks," so too do sensory impressions leave deep tracings on the writer's psyche. The feelings of a heavy-pressure writer are more enduring than average. A heavy-pressure person may forgive an injustice or wrongdoing, but will never forget it. These individuals may sometimes be misjudged as carrying a grudge. Not so. The memory simply lingers on. Once they have experienced something—a breathtaking sunset, a bitter argument—it's "etched in stone" in their emotional memory.

There is a vitality and strength that underlies everything they do or say. This intensity of spirit requires release. Often they will be "outdoor" people, releasing pent-up energy through exercise or sports. The deeper the pressure, the deeper the passions—not just sexual energy, but passion for life, travel, challenge, adventure. It's the difference between those who "go for it" and those who settle for nine-to-five ho-hum living. The risk-takers, the movers and shakers, the leaders in their field—be it science, business, politics, or religion—will write with a force and dynamism that spells passion.

They have one funny little quirk: they tend to be set in their ways. They are averse to change they consider unnecessary. Once the furniture is arranged the way they like it, they'll want it that way forever. But don't fret. They usually stay in a marriage longer too. After all, they've invested all that energy!

Medium Pressure

Thank you for your recent inquiry about handwriting analysis.

Those who write with a medium pressure possess the same positive drive and determination as the heavy-pressured writer, but not in such great quantities that they relish burning the candle at both ends.

Energetic and resourceful, they have the ability to see a project through to completion. The writer who exhibits medium pressure may not want to run the company, but would be a great asset to any committee or team, as he can adequately shoulder his share of the responsibility. There is a vibrancy and dynamism to his spirit that, when inspired or motivated, says "All systems go!" Such people may "borrow from tomorrow" and operate on sheer willpower at times, but they know enough to rest and recoup their energies before the well runs dry. They recognize that body and mind work as one unit; rarely will they overextend their energies to the point of depletion or exhaustion.

Light Pressure

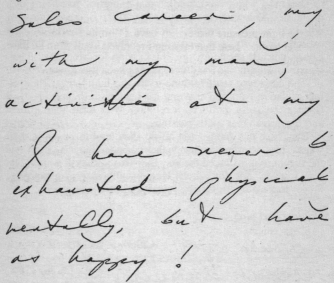

A hand that writes with less forcefulness is able to change direction easily. So too the writer who possesses a light, flexible script is more adaptable by nature. Not averse to change, he may switch jobs, living quarters or even college majors frequently!

Lighthearted and easygoing, he's quick to forgive your short-comings, flexible enough to accept a last-minute change in dinner plans, and accommodating enough to settle for franks and beans.

The down side? Although he is quick to adapt, this writer's energy reserves are short-lived. They quickly evaporate when he's forced into long-term or overwhelming projects. He may become moody or take shortcuts in an effort to see the task completed quickly. When forced to remain in a stressful environment, he may become tense or withdrawn. His gentle nature needs nurturing and care. The light-pressured writer has more mental energy than physical, is more of a thinker than a doer. You may find him curled up with a good book on a misty country weekend, against a background recording of piano or flute, while your heavy-pressure person is out tramping the woods with rambunctious dogs in tow and a thermos of rich Irish coffee in hand.

His flexibility and ability to accommodate other viewpoints, however, give him tremendous mental agility. Want to know just how mentally agile this type can be? I once said in class that the light-pressure writer *may* have a "limited endurance for physical labor." Late that evening I received a call from an irate husband.

"What do you mean my wife should have live-in help?"

I was astonished. This woman had translated my comment to her own liking, quoting me as the source for verification of her newfound need.

Note: Many folks stop at this point to check their own pressure and find they fall in the medium category. For some reason they equate medium pressure with being "just average" and are disappointed, wanting to be more than average—unique, special, even outrageous. But average is terrific. It indicates balance. Look what happens when you take things to extreme.

Extra-Heavy Pressure

While you may want all the gusto you can muster, extra-heavy pressure can be a sign of great emotional tension. Too much pressure on the paper means too much pressure in the individual. Strong feelings of fear, anger, or the stress of competition will put their resources on notice, ready to take action, even perhaps when none is needed. Impulsiveness and a wasting of vitality will take its toll on the health of one who writes with an extra forceful or domineering hand. When teenage bodies are going through the hormonal throes of puberty, handwriting often vacillates along with the surges of power and energy. But they usually stabilize by the time the child reaches eighteen years of age.

Extra-light Pressure

Due To a previous engagement
I have to change my appointment
to six o'clock friday

Extra-light pressure is evidence of anxiety—not to be confused with tension. Leslie King, a trained psychologist as well
as graphologist, makes this distinction in her book *Getting Control of Your Life*: Tension is positive in the sense that it arouses
a feeling of being ready to act and usually arises under the stress
of a deadline or important event (the swim meet, meeting your
future in-laws, etc.). Tension will subside, however, when the
circumstances causing it cease to exist (the recital is over, you
make the football team, etc.). Anxiety, on the other hand, is a
constant undercurrent of worry or apprehension—an edgy feeling of insecurity that interferes with concentration, yet isn't
pinned to anything specific. It never seems to let up, even when
the project is completed, the deadline met. Children who feel
they can't please a parent no matter what they do, or an adult
whose every effort fails to please the boss, suffer from anxiety.
Personally, I'd rather suffer from tension. At least you can work
it out with a good jog. Remember, tension=heavy pressure;
anxiety=light pressure.

Variable Pressure Patterns

Some writing may seem to have erratic pressure patterns that
jump from light to dark and back again. The writing appears as
if the pen were off-kilter, with the energy waxing and waning,
which is exactly what's happening. When the writer can't maintain a steady pressure, he loses motivation, succumbs to periods
of fatigue, and takes the path of least resistance. Physical and
emotional energy reserves work together in a delicate balance,
and the writer must plan for proper nutrition and rest to keep
his spirits positive and upbeat.

Do not confuse erratic pressure with the rhythmic pattern of
normal writing. Mature writing will exhibit a tension-and-release
pattern that produces a light upstroke and heavy downstroke.
This expansion and contraction, called sentence impulse, man-

ifests when fluid thought and muscular reflexes work together as one.

Normal Variations in Pressure

> Talking" this H.M.
> extremely interested
> handwriting analy
> discussed. It sou

Erratic Pressure Patterns

> This afternoon I went t
> town. The sun was shin
> There wasnt a cloud in
> sky.

Abrupt Changes

A change in handwriting may signal a change in physical or emotional balance. One December, I received a late-night call from Ruth, an energetic heavy-pressure writer. She had been asked to re-sign two charge slips while shopping that evening, as her signature wouldn't transfer through the carbon. She was concerned something might be wrong, and so was I, until I heard her day's agenda. She was up at 6 A.M. baking cookies, addressed and mailed cards on her lunch hour, went shopping after work, made dinner, did laundry, and was sewing angel costumes as she talked with me on the phone. Whew! And she wondered where her pressure went?

Writing pressure is extremely important to the graphologist, for it affects every other aspect of the analysis. All sorts of aptitudes and skills can surface in your writing, but without the energy to pursue them, you'll never get very far. We all know how much energy can affect our attitude or outlook. When we say "I'm not as young as I used to be" we're talking about energy, not age. When we're tired or sick, even the greatest party or most tantalizing job offer may seem like too much to handle. Keep an eye on your pressure. It's an accurate barometer of your energy level—both physical and emotional.

Everyday Examples

How can a knowledge of handwriting pressure help me in my everyday relationships with others? Let's take two examples, one romantic, one work related.

Randy, a college junior, came to me one day in anguish over a broken engagement. He had captured the sweetheart of Sigma Chi from a large midwestern university. Their June wedding plans were terminated when she told him she loved another. His heavy-pressure handwriting was hardly a match for her delicate script.

"I would have given my life for her," he sobbed.

Randy:

When I declare my love
forever, I mean forever.

Joyce's writing was open and honest. She had no intention of deceiving Randy, but her feelings were of a different intensity. When Randy said he loved her to the depths of his being, he meant it. When Joyce spoke from the depths of her heart, her depths were simply not as deep. She meant forever when she said it, but forever for Joyce meant until her feelings changed. Joyce was not being deceptive. She meant what she said at the time, but, like the wind, her feelings had a way of suddenly changing direction.

Joyce:

Call me if this is not the most convenient time for you.

A knowledge of handwriting can prevent you from judging others by your standards. Dave, a friend of mine, was astounded that a widower he knew remarried within six months after his wife of forty-six years had passed away.

"How could he do that?" asked Dave. "I thought he still loved his wife." Heavy-pressured Dave would have carried the torch forever.

"Of course the man loved his wife," I told him. "But his writing indicates that it's easier for him to 'let go' than it is for you."

I once knew a man who told his boss in the heat of anger just what he thought of his manipulative tactics. Later, when things cooled down, they had a long talk. The boss promised to examine his behavior and make some changes. Having gotten the problem off his chest, Hank, the light-pressured employee, promptly let go of the incident. Although the heavy-pressured employer forgave him, he never forgot the incident. He still feels a bit vulnerable when he has to deal with Hank. Hank's impulsivity in responding is also related to the slant of his writing, a subject we'll cover soon. The important thing to remember is that light-pressured Hank let go of the incident entirely and *assumed* his boss had done the same.

Width of Line Versus Depth of Line

In addition to handwriting depth, as seen in light, medium, and heavy pressure, handwriting also has a definite width, be it fat or thin. Handwriting depth records our depth of vitality and energy. Handwriting width, the richness of the line itself, reveals our ability to explore and appreciate these depths.

In other words, in addition to recording energy levels, handwriting also reveals just how *in touch* we are with this energy. A heavy-pressure writer may allow his deep feelings to pour forth in a rich, thick brush stroke of writing, or he may keep his wellspring of energy bottled up, only allowing it to trickle forth in a thin, pinched line of script.

Width of Line—Sensuality

Handwriting depth reveals the depths to which we plunge to gratify the senses, but the richness of the line itself will mirror how rich or starved are our senses. The same brain that transmits energy patterns also encodes messages from our senses of sight, sound, taste, touch, and smell. These neurological messages are transmitted through the pen, allowing handwriting to record our sensual impulses.

Many falsely believe that choice of pen determines line depth and width. Not so. The passion of the writer determines whether the line will be strong or weak, rich or sparse.

Full-Bodied Lines

The person who deliberately selects a pen to create a rich full-bodied line is expressing a desire for sensual pleasure. Fountain pens and soft felt-tip pens enable the writer to add force, vitality, and a shading effect similar to an artist's brush stroke.

There is a depth to the appetites and enjoyment of the person who writes with a full-bodied line. His idea of a terrific salad, for example, would hardly consist of a pineapple ring with a scoop of cottage cheese.

Dear Ann -
    Thank you for your en ment, support, and guidan this summer. Your effort: greatly appreciated by us.
    Would just like you

He would appreciate the nuances of texture and flavor in a perfect Caesar salad, savoring the blend of anchovy, egg, freshly ground pepper, full-bodied oil, and tart lemon juice. Often mis-labeled snobs, such people have expensive tastes, as their finely turned sense of touch can often distinguish a 100-percent-wool sweater from a blend—and of course they would prefer to have the former. They are drawn to the sensual appeal of silk, cash-mere, wool, leather, and pure cotton, although their budgets may not always allow them to indulge. They would rather do without than do with less, as they prefer quality over quantity.

Rich, clear vivid colors will be chosen over drab, muted tones. I'm not implying that their homes will be showcases for bright abstract art or red rugs. The idea here is richness. You might find a warm, walnut-paneled library with luxurious white silk sofas and a white rug. If the decor is monochromatic, look for *texture*.

And what about the truck driver with heavy pressure? White silk pillows? Come on, Ann. All right, look for the sheepskin seat cover, the cuddly soft flannel shirt, the bass turned up on his stereo tape deck. Follow his truck to the *best* roadside café for melt-in-your-mouth flaky-crust apple pie. And sneak a peek behind the seat for his favorite down pillow or a sensual paper-back. Never forget this group's capacity for absorption.

Once a friend with rich, sensual handwriting caught a whiff of nutmeg in my kitchen. Her olfactory senses kicked into over-drive as she spun and swirled tales for me of her favorite Christ-mas, 1945, when she "splintered and crunched" through crystal snow, lapped up eggnog with a "velvet tongue," and felt ec-stasy bursting at her seams in gratitude that the war was over. Whew! I felt the walls of my kitchen stretch to contain the depth of her imagination and feeling.

Joe, the recently transferred television producer of our dinner party in chapter 2, hadn't been in town two weeks before he took in a stray cat to stroke and cuddle. He also shipped in a few familiar antiques to feather his nest. Don't assume that all heavy-pressured writers lounge in the lap of luxury, however. Many direct their incredible energy into their professions, with time for little else. Nevertheless, even those who constantly travel need to feel their roost is cozy and secure. Woe betide the wife who discards her husband's "favorite" jacket he hasn't worn in twelve years! Even efficient and direct people like Joe will often surprise you by the sentimental items they cling to.

Joe:

of your comments both personal and professi Really looking forward your appearance on 1 Are Talking!

Joe writes with a wide-tipped fountain pen on 100-percent-rag-monogrammed stationery. Even with a regular felt pen, Joe's line still exhibits a thick-and-thin brush-stroke quality. When asked what he would bring to a potluck dinner, Joe quickly replied, "Pasta," and watched my face fall in disappointment. "Because you're just too busy with work to cook?" I asked. "Heavens, no!" protested Joe. "I would *make* the pasta myself. I really enjoy doing that. Then I'd probably make a marinara sauce or clams with capers." I could just see him gleefully churning out miles of noodles in his kitchen!

People with heavy pressure or a sensual line often have a sweet tooth or a weight problem (depending on the discipline in the writing). They usually have no problem eating ribs or chicken with their fingers—after all, food is meant to be enjoyed. Just say, "Mrs. Field's," and they can already smell the cookies baking.

In class I ask students to bring in any "exceptions" to the rule. After our class on pressure, Judy L. came up to me and asked me to look at the writing of her friend Karen.

Karen:

Romance seems to elude,
and heaven knows I'se bee
by interesting men. I I
though I'm always chase

"She has heavy pressure and a sensual, rich line," Judy told me, "but she's thin as a rail and eats nothing but cottage cheese! She looks like a model, and she is. Where does gratification of the senses come in?" Karen also had both vanity and low self-image in her writing (which we'll learn about later) but I was curious to meet her, so I said, "Let's all have lunch."

Judy was right: Karen was stunning, with a knockout figure and beautiful clothes. She knew a great little "diet" place where we could eat (groan). I was all set for the ground beef patty with cottage cheese. Instead, she took us to Jeanne Jones's Light Cuisine at Neiman-Marcus in Newport Beach.

"I'm ravenous," she exclaimed and ordered chicken breast in pink peppercorn sauce served on creamed leeks with herbed whole-grain pilaf.

Judy and I nearly dropped our iced tea! But the menu claimed it was all under 350 calories. The food was fabulous.

Gourmet Chef Jeanne Jones:

> *The quality recipe is too dependent on quality of ingredients.*

Later I interviewed Jeanne Jones, curious as to how she had developed such a scrumptious menu. Reed-slim Jeanne has written eighteen cookbooks and is a diet consultant for many chic health spas and hotels. "I believe in indulgence of *all the senses*," exulted Jeanne. "Everything should look, smell, taste, and 'feel' delicious. When you deprive the senses, there's only so much the body will take before it rebels." Imagine what happens to the poor folks with heavy and extra-heavy pressure. Their dieting bodies will crave sugar, salt, etc.—anything to satisfy the appetite. Smart Karen knew her "sensual cravings" and how to appease them.

Karen occasionally fasts. When she does, she said, she "feeds" herself in other ways—swimming, massage (touch), beautiful music (sound), a new dress (touch, sight). Jeanne would approve, I'm sure. Here's another funny quirk about thick-lined writers. They often enjoy mysteries and solving problems. They would probably rather watch a "Perry Mason" rerun or "Murder, She Wrote" than "Laverne and Shirley." And often the Orient holds an intrigue for them.

Reserve Judgment

Often when analyzing handwriting, people will jump on *one* thing I've said that they feel is not in keeping with their personality. Usually, it's the skeptic who rushes in to take things out of context before I've had a chance to finish my analysis. A case in point involved a man who had extremely heavy pressure and a rich, sensual writing.

"Rich food! Impossible!" he bragged. "I *never* eat rich food. I'm strictly a meat, potatoes, and tapioca man. In fact, I have an ulcer!" From his writing I could see why. He had strong feelings and emotions (pressure) and kept them all inside (repression). His wife assured me that he loved good food and at one time suffered from gout. Even now he refused to give up his Scotch, so he drank it with milk! Yes, indeed, a tapioca man, but he fit the sensual profile perfectly. She also told me he was a stereo nut and had *six* speakers in the living room. So ask your clients to reserve judgment until you've had a chance to create the total personality picture. One characteristic will influence another. And none should be judged in isolation.

Mr. Tapioca:

Pastosity

In fact, Mr. Tapioca's handwriting showed *pastosity*, a "pasty" or doughy appearance in the writing. The term was coined by Hungarian graphologist Dr. Klara Roman. Pastosity is sometimes an indication of overindulgence of the senses and can be good or bad depending on the form level of the script. Many gourmet cooks, artists, and fashion designers have this in their writing. Sensual sometimes to the point of overindulgence, the pastose writer reflects his feelings in his style of dress, speech, occupation, or hobby. His work stems from sensual gratification.

In pastose writing, the loops may look "flooded" or closed, and certain formations may look extra thick. In a negative writing, blobs, retracings, cross-outs, and smearing indicate an overindulgence of sensual gratification by people who have become totally absorbed in their own experiences. Their language is usually colorful too.

Positive Pastosity

tuings: Sister, lover, priest
woman, queen. Now in true
come to be wise-woman, a
may come when these twin
to be known. But in sober

Negative Pastosity

leadership. I'm talking here all
ways: I've never involved myself
it time to take
a stand.

Medium Line Width—Average Sensuality

the largest body of water close to Denv
wide and 20-23 miles long, and provides
for a 1000 miles in any direction. We

The writer with a medium width of line has all the sensual connotations of the wide-lined writer, but with more discretion and control. This writer might enjoy a sumptuous meal, but could say no to the rich dessert or cognac. He would enjoy as wide a range of sights and sounds as the heavy-pressure writer, but would be content to listen to a record or tape of his favorite artist, instead of attending the concert or lying immobile with supersonic headphones and a compact disc.

Thin Line Width—Moderate Sensuality

Writing that is finely tuned to a thin line indicates a sensitivity and refinement, capable of absorbing just so much and no more. The writer's need for sensual gratification is delicate and precise. He prefers a comfortable indoor concert to the damp grass or chill of an outdoor amphitheater. And sitting next to someone with heavy perfume or aftershave can make him dizzy or ill. As with a lighter stroke, the endurance and capacity is of a lesser degree.

I was once visited by a troubled newlywed couple. The wife had light, thin-lined writing, the husband heavy, rich handwriting.

"He hates my cooking," she lamented. "He adds salt, pepper, ketchup, and steak sauce to *everything*. And he plays that loud music he knows I can't stand." He, of course, thought she was overplaying the "delicate kitten" role. When I explained their different needs, they were able to compromise successfully.

Applying What You've Learned

We've just learned that handwriting possesses the depth and vibrancy of the person penning the script. Let's return to our dinner party and see if our characters' behaviors match their handwriting.

Cold sheets of rain slash across the windows, but inside Nicole's spacious apartment the atmosphere is cheerful and cozy, warmed by a roaring fire. The first to arrive is Bill. Nicole takes his coat and gives him a kiss. Self-sufficient Bill takes the dishes he's prepared to the kitchen. They're carefully wrapped in the *Wall Street Journal* to protect them from the rain. Since Bill will be host for the evening, Nicole sees to it that he is well versed in everything from chosen records and tapes to where to stash the extra ice. In her white silk hostess gown, she is now deliberating between a fabulous hand-hammered silver necklace to add pizzazz to a drizzly evening and a simple strand of pearls to set a warm and cozy mood. Let the candles set the mood, reasons Nicole as she fastens the silver collar.

Nicole:

Hope to see you th
The champagne bar, of c

Nicole is somewhat annoyed that Bill is underfoot while she's mentally reviewing her checklist of the overall plan. Quiet, polite Bill, who could be upset with him? But must he always be on time? Bill's offer to help is superfluous, as he quickly realizes. With Nicole you can always count on finding everything orchestrated and properly in place, from the brass umbrella stand outside the door to chilled plates for the salad.

No slouch on details himself, Bill has brought hors d'oeuvres that include tiny cherry tomatoes and Chinese pea pods, each individually stuffed with a cream-cheese-and-chive mixture. At this very moment, he is in the kitchen assembling his dessert of pears poached in wine.

Bill:

Then a fishing boat appeared
line. He towed us all the way back t
I waded out to his boat, arms full of
a thank you gesture, the fisherman

Joe, our producer, arrives next, removing his Burberry coat and scarf (purchased on his last trip to London to produce a special for the BBC). True to form, he's brought his pasta with clams and capers and a little surprise—beautiful fresh asparagus with thin strips of red pepper in a wonderful vinaigrette. "Here's a little something for color," he tells Nicole. "Use it for a vegetable dish or salad, whichever you need."

Joe:

so much time this afternoon. I am appre of your comments both personal and professi

Before he can move a step, in rushes Monica with a big smile and kiss for Nicole, and also a nice wet hug before she removes her rosy-pink raincoat (who wants to look dreary when it's already gray outside?). Monica has everything double bagged (Saks Fifth Avenue and Neiman-Marcus shopping bags) and has brought silver tongs for the salad and chopsticks for everyone. She swept through Chinatown on her way here and has an array of bamboo shoots, water chestnuts, endive, oriental lettuce, and a wonderful, tangy, light sweet-and-sour dressing. She's not only brought a large jug of wine, but a carafe with a bow tied around the neck for serving it. "More festive," she tells Nicole. As Joe moves toward the kitchen to see if he can help with anything, Monica checks herself in the mirror and straightens her red suede suit and raven black hair.

Monica:

my own personal creations, hand selecting from the finest silks, wools, etc all over the world, and having my very own personal dress designer deal with the finishing touches.

Michael is next to arrive. He enters with a warm hello, kisses Nicole, and quickly surveys the whole apartment to find a cozy spot. He's in a navy trench coat with a dark plaid cashmere scarf and carrying a black umbrella. Nicole graciously takes his dishes and sweeps into the kitchen as Bill takes his drink order. Michael orders a Perrier (he's seen too much drinking in his last thirty days as a bartender) and follows Nicole into the kitchen with a "Let me do that" as he wants everything just so. He's brought a Greek casserole dish much like moussaka, but he's added his own touches to make it totally vegetarian and not too heavy. Nicole, by the way, has prepared a lemon-roasted chicken. It's simple and light and should easily accompany any dish her guests bring. She reappears with Michael, and as they pass the hall mirror, he checks his appearance—dark hair, closely trimmed beard, corduroy pants, navy wool jacket, white shirt, and burgundy bow tie.

Michael:

Toni is soon at the door, bearing lovely cut flowers, croissants, and freshly ground coffee. Barely wet, Toni has sensibly cabbed it tonight, forgoing the hassle of finding a parking space. She seems to focus only on Nicole, as she is too uneasy to glance around the room at the other guests on her own. Nicole, who wants everyone to feel comfortable and at ease, takes Toni's hand and introduces her to Bill, Joe, Monica, and Michael.

Toni:

Hearing the festivities across the hall, James feels he can now slip in unnoticed and not have to converse if he doesn't want to. Having eaten the lasagna his mother prepared for him to bring, he sheepishly arrives with quiche in a pink box. Magnanimous Nicole has more than enough food, but graciously heats the quiche anyway. In truth, James's mother had asked him to arrive early in case Nicole needed help with anything—a promise he'd agreed to but had no intention of keeping. When he devoured the lasagna, he shortsightedly reasoned that this might give him an excuse not to go. Realizing his folly, he ran out and bought the quiche. Nicole wonders why he arrived soaking wet when he only lives across the hall, but says nothing.

James:

> *You can include this sam my handwriting in the shop exhibit. Its okay*

Bill has been so busy with wet coats and packages that some folks have yet to order a drink. Nicole quickly remedies the situation. Monica and Joe order white wine spritzers, and Toni has Campari and soda. James wants rum and coke. Nicole keeps a cool head with club soda and a twist. Connie won't be arriving for some time yet, so let's take a moment to step back and summarize what we've seen thus far. From food choices and drink orders alone, you might be able to surmise what our guests' handwriting pressure might look like.

Analyzing Pressure and Sensuality

Pressure patterns in handwriting need to be seen firsthand to be properly analyzed. Since all the samples in this book are reproductions, you're at a bit of a disadvantage, so I'll help you. Joe, Nicole, and James have medium-heavy pressure and are sensual, vital personalities. Michael, Bill, and Connie have medium pressure, and Toni and Monica have medium-light pressure. But you'll also notice that many of these people show pastosity in their writing. Monica and Michael, for example.

Let's analyze. Joe and Monica both order white wine spritzers—a very light drink of wine with soda. Why? Monica has never been a big fan of alcohol, noticing how it makes people loud and rowdy, and how it makes her too tired and listless the following day (light pressure). Although she loves to indulge in margaritas when feeling "festive," she lives to regret it later. Joe's reason for ordering a light drink is different. Knowing Nicole shares his rich tastes (heavy pressure), he's saving his taste buds for what he knows will be a wonderful dinner, accompanied by fine wine. Joe is abstaining so he can better savor the piquant flavors at dinner and indulge his appetites. Monica, with lighter tastes and a weaker constitution, is aware of her own impulsivity (which we'll discuss later). She knows she'll want to sample everything on the buffet, which will eventually make her sick if she isn't careful.

Monica's writing has pastosity (love of rich, sensual things like her red suede suit), but her light-pressured constitution can absorb only so much. Here is our first example of conflict in writing. Yes, she might enjoy a live concert, but only for so long. Her handwriting has the physical constitution of a light-pressured writer but the sensual tastes of a pastose writer. Her salad is rich and wonderfully appealing to the eye, with many textures and flavors, but the overall effect is still light.

Yes, Nicole prepared a neutral dish of lemon chicken, but she also has pâté encased in chilled consommé for an hors d'oeuvre, and handmade mints and Amaretto with whipped cream for coffee later. Heavy-pressure James couldn't let the homemade lasagna sit for even one day.

Medium-pressure Bill calls himself a meat-and-potatoes man. True to form, he's brought veggies for hors d'oeuvres and fruit for dessert. Michael's vegetable casserole has fabulous herbs and spices he's garnered from specialty shops to satiate his sensual nature (medium pressure, but with pastosity).

Toni's choices of flowers, rolls, and ground coffee indicate more about her desire to remain on the outskirts of dinner. We know from her light pressure that she'll probably sample everything, but is unlikely to overindulge.

Forty-five minutes into the party, guess who arrives? Connie. Remember she's on the ballet board and teaches aerobics one morning a week in Marin. ("It keeps me going," she says.) Connie is always on the go and *loves* giving that impression. She's in a yellow slicker, complete with hat and yellow boots.

No umbrella—her arms are too full of other things. Also, umbrellas are too cumbersome when you're trying to dash around. She has on a colorful wool challis dress (suits are too confining) and hangs up her own coat. As Bill reaches for her dishes Connie motions no thanks, I'm fine, and breezes into the kitchen with her homemade date bars and a salad. "It's just salad," she protests, but both Michael and Joe notice it's seven-lettuce salad with fresh orange and grapefruit slices, and a fabulous raspberry-and-walnut-oil dressing. Not too heavy, not too light.

Now that you understand a bit more about pressure, you'll probably never give light-pressure Aunt Jane musk or Opium perfume again. And when you have heavy-pressure Uncle Rick over for barbecued burgers, have plenty of fresh tomatoes, lettuce, onion, and pickles handy and make sure the baked beans have plenty of brown sugar.

But didn't we say that pressure reveals depth of feeling as well? Yes, and we'll touch on that aspect in our upcoming review. For now, let's cover one aspect of pressure and get it straight. Believe me, we'll see plenty of feelings surface as the night progresses. We already know that Nicole, James, and Joe have deep wells of feeling, while Monica and Toni are more the live-and-let-live type. Pressure, as we've said, reveals a great deal about our:

1. permanency of feeling
2. depth of emotions
3. enjoyment of sensory impressions

Review

Because you cannot see the actual samples firsthand, for now let's assume that the heavier the line, the heavier the pressure. (I suggest you keep your answers on a separate sheet of paper, so that others may use this quiz as well.)

1. Remember our friend Margaret Bradley in Cancún? Margaret is on vacation with her friend Cheryl and her new-found love, Roger.

• Who tries something new every day, from windsurfing to sailing to water skiing to climbing the pyramids to tennis to shuffleboard, and still has energy to dance half the night?

- Who might play tennis in the cool morning, followed by a short swim and perhaps a nap after lunch, or spend a quiet afternoon conserving energy for dancing that evening?
- Whose idea of a workout is finding an empty hammock? Who enjoys reading a book or writing letters in the quiet shade?

Samples

a.

Whatever the conseq
I hope you have

b.

It is next in order
on the Partmier List.

c.

would like to have
an analyses done.

2. You've brought gifts to Aunt Millie's afternoon tea and cousin Sara's sixteenth birthday.

- Millie receives an assortment of teas from chamomile to orange spice, soda crackers with mild cheese, and sumptuous yet delicate individual tea cakes. Her pressure is: light, medium, or heavy?
- Sara receives a romance novel, lily-of-the-valley perfume, and a lovely pink blouse. Her pressure is: light, medium, or heavy?

3. Paul has been juggling two romances simultaneously and has just been found out by the ladies in question. Which woman is more likely to forgive and forget?

Nancy:

I will receive medical be
and 60% of my salary
purpose will need to b

Phyllis:

I would like to know more
about Graphic therapy. No

4

Laying the
Foundation

Margins and Spacing

One day, Helen started for the grocery. On her way she stopped at the bank, picked up the cleaning, renewed the dog's license, ran her car through the car wash, picked up the kids, and headed home—*without* the groceries!

Certainly it's wonderful to have great reserves of energy, but how do you channel and direct this power? Are you disciplined and organized, or are you forever writing your To Do list on the back of an envelope and then mailing the envelope? Let's take a look at how you gather and focus your energy and incorporate it into the bigger picture of life.

Hold your handwriting sample at arm's length and drink in the energy. Does your writing appear clear, organized, and focused—or scattered and hopelessly scrambled? How much breathing room do you allow yourself when planning your day's activities? How much of the page is dark or ''busy'' and how much is blank or resting?

What you're viewing here is literally a picture of how you organize your time, framed by margins of breathing room. Whenever I explain this in class, inevitably someone moans, ''Oh, Ann, if only I had more time, I could get everything done.'' Yes, I know. But when we allow ourselves to fall into that trap we're forgetting one thing. The Henry Fords and Thomas Edisons of this world never had more than twenty-four hours a day, just like us. How was Donald Trump able to complete construction on a skating rink in New York's Central Park *ahead* of schedule?

Busy, disorganized Helen:

Busy but organized Ruth:

Margins

Margins create not only a frame of space around the writing, but also delineate a frame of reference for communicating with the writer. Some people crowd their lives like they crowd the writing surface, without an inch to spare. Others allow time for reflection, for gathering their thoughts, saving space in their lives (and handwriting) for additions or changes.

No Overall Margin

The person who utilizes every inch of available space wants to live life to the fullest. Quick to respond, he may become intrusive without meaning to. He simply hasn't noticed that you're not interested in the softball game or Marty's baby shower as he runs around the office with sign-up lists. Often people who don't leave themselves room to pause and reflect think that what *they* want is what *you* want too.

No
Overall Margin:

Broad
Overall Margin:

Average
Overall Margin:

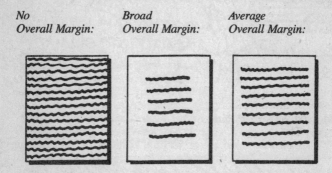

Broad Overall Margin

The broad-margin writer has allocated ample space for organizing his time and energy. This ability for discrimination and objectivity imparts a certain sense of refinement and poise to the writer. Pacing himself, he acts, rather than reacts. Spontaneous when he so chooses, he doesn't extend himself beyond what he knows he can handle.

Joe, from our dinner party, has this broad margin, and, although you might envision the life of a television producer as harried, Joe has *everything* under control. James, our seventeen-year-old dinner guest, has an extra-broad margin. Cautious and reserved, he refuses to extend himself beyond certain limits.

Average Overall Margin

Those who allow adequate room to tackle life's challenges establish average boundaries on their activities. They behave conventionally in involvements with others, being neither overinvolved to the point of intrusiveness nor aloof. They have a sense of order and control. Bill, Nicole, and busy, busy Connie all have average margins. Surprised?

*Narrow
Overall Margin:*

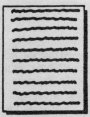

Narrow Overall Margin

This writer seeks participation and involvement. His full schedule requires that he check his calendar before accepting a luncheon date, but he's still in control of things. Whenever you don't see much breathing room (white space) in someone's writing, you wonder if he ever gives himself space to relax. Look again. The rest periods are usually scheduled right in with everything else—aerobics or "quiet time" is actually penciled in. He usually updates his calendar while waiting at the airport or at Susie's orthodontist. No sense wasting time! Michael, Monica, and Toni all have narrow margins.

Top and Bottom Margins

Top Margin Narrow: *Top Margin Wide:*

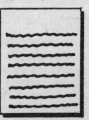

In Old English culture, the amount of blank space left at the top of the page indicated the rank of the person to whom the letter was addressed—a knight, a lord, etc. A letter to the king or queen might begin halfway down the page. Generous space at the top of the page indicates reserve, respect, and courtesy. Depending on other aspects in the writing, the person may be timid. In any event, the writer will defer to you, whether out of politeness of self-consciousness.

On the other hand, the writer who springs onto the page without pause adopts an informal and direct approach in work and human relationships. He may make his ideas known or feelings heard before stopping to consider just who is in the audience.

Bottom Margin

The longer a person stays with it when writing to the bottom of the page, the more he values productivity and accomplishment. Usually materialistically inclined, he values productivity in tangible, visible form. He is activity- and goal-oriented.

Bottom Margin Narrow: *Bottom Margin Wide:*

The less a person reaches for the limit (bottom of the page), the less inclined he is to value concrete, tangible productivity. He might prefer talking about it more than the actual doing.

Left and Right Margins

Margins can be narrow, average, wide, convex, concave, rigid, variable, increasing, decreasing—the possibilities are almost endless. Add to this the variations when combining right and left margins and it can be overwhelming. Let's simplify it this way: Because we begin writing at the left side of the page, graphological studies have likened the left side to origins, the past, security, and safety. This is where we begin and where we retreat to at the end of every line. Likewise, it has been determined that venturing across that lonely, naked page is quite a risk. Progressive movement toward the right has become synonymous with risk-taking, goal-striving, the future, and achievement. Margins that are left-oriented indicate a writer more security minded, while right-oriented margins signify a risk-taker.

And, since writing is activity, and space inactivity, putting a pen to paper indicates initiative, while continuing the line across the page is synonymous with perseverance.

Wide Left Margin: *Wide Right Margin:*

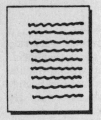

The person who allows an objective pause before initiating his writing stops to consider options and alternatives, not wishing to act in haste. He may feel a little unsure of his own abilities, or he may even be trying to separate himself from ties and traditions of the past.

A wide right margin approaches the future with trepidation (cautious space). The writer looks before he leaps. Uncomfortable in unfamiliar situations, he would rather avoid them than take an unknown risk.

Writing Extending Toward the Right:

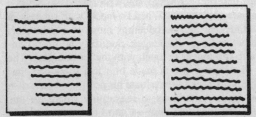

When margins increase or extend toward the right, the writer wants to get on with life. Enthusiastic about a project he's involved in, he hates to waste time dragging his pen all the way back to the left side of the page (back to safety and security). With initial doubt and skepticism overcome, his threshold for risk taking has increased. He no longer clings to the past.

Writing Retreating to the Left:

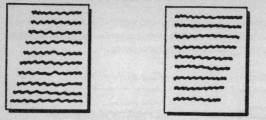

If, on the other hand, the margin clings toward the left side of the page, the writer values the familiar, the conventional. True, writing implies action, but left-tending writing implies introspective behavior that is more security- and tradition-bound. The writer needs reassurance that his decisions are correct. He will "back away" from future unknown risks.

Left Margin Concave: *Right Margin Concave:*

When the left margin is concave, the writer needs to begin a project feeling safe and secure. When he meets with success, it bolsters his confidence, and he becomes more of a risk-taker, reaching out to accept new challenges. Suddenly he finds himself out on a limb (no longer in touch with the left margin). The initial feeling of security, which made him feel grounded, has disappeared. He pulls back to reevaluate his position. Fools rush in, he reasons, as he withdraws to reexamine where all this headstrong behavior may take him—a good example of "cold feet."

When the right margin is concave, the writer impulsively embraces a new challenge. Once the activity is under way, however, he may have second thoughts and pulls back introspectively to determine if his initial decision was wise. (Can we afford this house? Should I go back to school?) When feelings of doubt are overcome, he proceeds full speed ahead with renewed enthusiasm and excitement toward his goal.

Most of us waver in initiative or enthusiasm depending on the task or project at hand, and our margins may change accordingly. Extremes, however, spell another story.

Extremes

Extremely Rigid Margins:

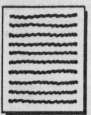

Compulsive Right Margin:

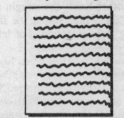

Extremely rigid margins indicate rigid unyielding behavior. People who are compulsively overcontrolled usually feel a need for self-protection. The writer trusts neither himself nor others.

A margin that won't "let go" signifies compulsive behavior. Here's an example: You could always count on Madeline to be at her desk working when other employees were putting on their coats to go home. She worked and reworked assignments. When time came for raises and evaluations, Madeline assumed she would be considered for a promotion. Imagine her surprise when she was terminated. Why? Madeline, her employer explained, didn't know when to "let go." She couldn't differentiate between essentials and nonessentials. At some point, it's more productive to move on to the next project. Rather than saving the company time, she was costing the company money. What Madeline viewed as an asset, her company viewed as a shortcoming. Perseverance is great—in moderation (witness the anorexic dieter).

Reserve Judgment

No handwriting can be judged from margins alone without analyzing the rest of the script. For example, you might assume someone who writes with a narrow left margin to be somewhat weak—traditional, conforming, security-oriented, even a "mama's boy." Not true. It can have one interpretation in a strong handwriting and another interpretation in a weak handwriting. We're simply gathering information at this point to observe general trends. No snap decisions, please; first appearances can be deceiving. Here's a case in point:

Paula:

Paula has a narrow left margin. She even signs her name to the left. Yet anyone meeting Paula would definitely describe her as a "go-getter." Her job experience runs the gamut from selling silver options to assistant television producer. Working for me, she appeased demanding trial attorneys on forgery cases, juggled speaking engagements and court appearances, interpreted "emergency" calls, and kept me sane to boot. Paula definitely has initiative and drive. She could have run her own company if she wanted to. But she didn't want to. In fact, she suffered a real internal struggle between embracing a full-fledged career and staying home to raise a family. Paula was extremely family-oriented. Although they lived from ninety to three thousand miles away, within five months I had met two sisters, a brother, and her mother, all of whom stopped by the office to say hello and share a hug. Paula's exterior was Esprit turquoise and black, but her interior was traditional all the way.

She abandoned a career in broadcast journalism, finding the sensationalism of TV news abhorrent. One incident in particular involved interviewing a teenager who had been raped and had both arms cut off by her attacker. "Leave her alone," shouted Paula as the cameras and reporters descended. She told her partner, "I can't handle this. It's not how *I was raised*" (home, tradition, left margin). She also stopped selling options, saying, "I can't take money from people when I can't promise the goods. It's not how *I was raised*."

Line Spacing and Alignment

After determining the overall framework within which we operate (margins), we place each line upon the page, one by one. Whether distant or tangled, orderly or confused, these lines represent our need for organization and planning. They also reflect our desire to become involved or remain aloof from our environment. Remember, the page itself represents our time frame; it is the world in which we operate. How we organize and fill that time is determined by how we space and pace ourselves.

Tangled Lines

Tight, overlapping writing can be difficult to separate and decipher. If your writing looks this way, you may not have organized or separated your activities. You may be so busy doing, doing, doing, that you find yourself spinning your wheels in a confusion of interests. Trying to accomplish thirty-six hours of activity in a twenty-four-hour day can sabotage success as quantity eclipses quality. Hating to stop and plan, the tangled writer would rather risk making a few mistakes than slow down.

This writer craves activity but needs to allow himself breathing room to regain his perspective and to concentrate only on those projects that are of true benefit. Otherwise he'll end his day feeling drained instead of satisfied and successful.

The crowded writer crowds his day and is often late for appointments because he fails to allocate time for emergencies—flat tire, etc. (You may notice your writing tangling when you are trying to take on too much.)

Average Line Spacing

> *both hands and it seems*
> *of my writing are differen*

Disciplined and organized, this writer has the ability to be observant and discerning. He can plan ahead, allowing himself enough time to accomplish his goals while keeping his schedule loose to allow for the unexpected. There is a sense of order, composure, and stability in his day-to-day operations. He feels more comfortable and in control when operating within some type of structure or schedule, but can be flexible and adaptable when an emergency arises.

Distant Line Spacing

> *many times. Several times*
>
> *write but work has alwa*
>
> *Now we no longer own ou*

At times, this writer can be almost too objective in his outlook, separating himself from spontaneous events and relationships. He values organization, structure, and planning, and would rather rely on himself than allow valuable time and energy to be misspent with a person or plan that is disorganized. Because he prefers to stop and give everything time for consideration, he may lose his ability to integrate and correlate ideas in a swift, fluid manner. Life can be unpredictable at times, throwing us a curve. When there isn't time to stop and plan, this writer feels uncomfortable winging it.

His equipment and work space will be organized, and woe betide the person who returns something to the wrong drawer. His boss may rely on him to lay out the objectives, timetable, and workbooks for the meeting, but may call on someone else for a last-minute welcoming speech or sales pitch to the new manager. In his desire for order and control, this writer sometimes sacrifices personal communication.

Utilizing Available Space

Many people feel that the way they write depends on the area they have to work with. "Of course it looks crowded," they'll protest. "Look at that itsy bit of paper you gave me to work with." Or "I didn't realize I was running out of room. I don't usually scrunch things up at the edge like that." Really? That may be true once in a while, but let's take a look at some typical examples—the postcard, for instance. You certainly know before you begin that you'll be working within a given space. Yet notice the different approaches of Debbie, Kay, and Nora to the same space.

Debbie:

Dear Mary and Tom,   September 2.
   What a nice surprise to hear from you. The pictures of the children were great. Clark and I have been busy this fall and winter with many new projects. We started remodeling our house and we are sleeping in the living room. We took a trip to Baja. Visited some of our favorite haunts. Clark picked up a few college units for the trip. He is starting his new book this fall. First draft is due to the publisher, isn't this great, by the summer of eighty seven. I'm busy getting my degree in Social Psychology. There are many more things to tell you. however I hope we can organize our schedule so that a visit will be possible in January.
                    Your friend always. Debbie.

Kay:

Dear John + Mary,   11-10-85

    Our trip has been wonderful. We have seen Jim, Karen + Jo. They all send their love. We are going to Boston on Thursday to see a play, on Friday we are going to the park, and on Saturday we are staying home. Love to all Kay

Nora:

Merry Christmas and Happy New Year to you. Your card was so beautiful and we were so happy to hear from you after so long. We especially wanted to invite you to call us anytime you're in the area and in fact, we'd just love it if you could try to squeeze in a visit to see us. But we know how busy your schedule is and just hope you can come. We have a

Nora:

Hope to see you soon!

Ann Mahony
PO Box 3218
San Francisco,
Ca. 94119

Debbie managed to convey a wealth of information in a limited, organized format. Kay was aware of the confines initially, but didn't plan accordingly. She just kept writing, adjusting as she went along. Nora rambled all over the card, front and back, oblivious to borders or boundaries. But is this really important? You bet it is. How would you like to be on the receiving end of a long-distance *collect* phone call from Nora? When will she get to the point? Like our friend Madeline at the office, Nora cannot differentiate between what is essential and nonessential. She doesn't know when to let go. Here's something else that may surprise you. Line for line, there is more information in Debbie's postcard, though Nora's appears packed with information; in reality Nora's is just busy. Remember, these are very real behavioral traits. How many of us fill our days with busy work, yet accomplish very little?

Word Spacing

Just as line spacing reflects a need for closeness or separation from people and things in our surroundings, so too, word spacing further delineates this very real need for contact with others. The amount of space the writer chooses to leave between words is a very real indication of the amount of space he requires to distance himself from others.

Psychological studies have shown that man subconsciously

surrounds himself with rings of influence. The first ring may have no outer limit and admit most anyone (e.g., airport crowds). The next ring is open only to those who appear to offer no threat (the store clerk, the mailman). The next ring includes acquaintances (friends at work). The next ring contains friends and relatives. And the closest ring (where you can smell, touch, and taste the person) is reserved for intimate relationships. You yourself have established a ''comfort zone'' that certain people are not allowed to cross. When it is violated (the shoe salesman who strokes your leg), you'll pull back to enlarge the space between you. So, too, word spacing in a love letter may be more intimate than in a monthly sales report.

Narrow Word Spacing

Everyyear donir theyTime passoss fastwhen you get older, it seemsor a
Dont misunderstand, I love being too, but I surely be missing privat

This writer enjoys a feeling of belonging, of being with people. He may even assume an ingratiating role, pushing others to include him, to avoid feeling lonely or isolated. The writer may offer advice or suggestions without being asked, filling his emotional need to be involved with people. He should take care that in his attempt to belong, he doesn't become too busy, busy, busy. This could destroy his clarity of thought and ability to discriminate between the important and the nonimportant. He needs time for selection and organization. Jumping at anything that comes along, he will soon find the tail wagging the dog.

Average Word Spacing

My husband is also
also like my (our) son

When it comes to interpersonal relationships, this writer has an adaptable nature that aids him in communicating and cooperating with others. His self-assured personality is neither intrusive nor timid. He can include others in his own affairs or offer them advice about theirs without interfering or overstepping the bounds. Likewise, he is able to withdraw gracefully, allowing others time and space to themselves.

Wide Word Spacing

I   want   to   learn
handwriting   analysis   and
that   you   would   be   c

At times, this writer may feel somewhat distant from others, either physically or emotionally. Even when truly desiring to build bridges of friendship, he may withdraw or feel uncomfortable when forced too close too soon. He's perfectly satisfied with minimal participation in a group and would never offer advice without being asked, respecting another's privacy as he wishes his to be respected. Rarely would he act impulsively or commit himself without first weighing the advantages and disadvantages—at least where dealing with others is concerned. Of course, it's wise to check to see if there's water in the pool before diving in, but by the time he takes the plunge the party may be over! He should force himself to take that risk when forming new friendships.

Naturally, it helps to understand the circumstances when you view this in someone's script. I once remarked to Larry, a warm and friendly student of mine, that I was surprised at his very broad line and word spacing, indicating isolation. He could barely speak as he told me he was just beginning to get physically close to others again, but still needed to maintain his emotional distance for a while. He had lost his only son in Vietnam two years prior and still couldn't talk about it. He was in tears. I felt terrible. I wished I had just kept still and trusted what I saw in the handwriting! He explained that he felt safe in my class and thus more comfortable expressing his feelings.

Time for Yourself

Now that we have learned how to judge the amount of time and space you allow for others, let's take a look at how much time you allow for yourself. The space *within the word itself* belongs to you. The space between the words is the space you share with others. How much space do you feel comfortable taking up for yourself? Do you scrunch your belongings in one teeny suitcase, or do you jump on the airplane and utilize the overhead compartment, space under the seat, and then some?

Squeezed Space Within Words, Wide Space Between Words

analyzed. Wald you tell me
charge, please? your, sequence
so interesting!

Susan is a nurse who never stops giving. She goes out of her way to give time and attention to others, even at the expense of depriving herself of adequate time to relax and unwind. Her constricted, inhibited script tells us that perhaps she truly believes others deserve more than she.

Expansive Space Within Words, Narrow Space Between Words

Last week I canned
peaches and part of the
jars turned out to b
too packed and expl

Celeste, on the other hand, would simply love to give you more time but she has to get her nails done and get to aerobics class and buy some new clothes and call about the job interview and watch her favorite TV show, and . . . Most of her free time is devoted to Celeste.

Average Space Within and Between Words

Thank you, Ann, for [
to speak to our emplo
know everyone will [
talk - finding it infor
entertaining. Hope to
in the future.

Chris rose early today to take in an exercise class and arrange the tray of food she'd promised to bring to the bazaar. After work she'll help with decorations and assist in a booth until about 8:00 P.M. Then she really needs to head home and tend to her studies. Chris allows adequate time for her needs and yours, sacrificing neither too much nor to little.

Prove It for Yourself

For those of you who still think that space is arbitrarily chosen, try this experiment. Sit in a totally darkened room and have someone dictate a paragraph to you. What happens? The margins are uneven. The lines and words run together. Everything becomes a tangled mess. Some will overcompensate and try to write larger in an effort to maintain clarity, but spacing patterns are totally lost. Why? Because, although many other characteristics in writing are performed automatically, spacing is deliberately and consciously chosen—whether it appears to be or not.

This may seem like a lot of information to absorb, but luckily it's pretty simple. Pretend you're viewing a work of art. You may stand back a few feet at first to experience the overall composition (margins). You then realize the painting contains certain patterns in its internal organization (lines of writing). Finally you move in closer to examine the details (word and letter spacing). Each plays a significant part in the final visual analysis.

Review

1. You need help with a project.

- Who is obviously too busy?
- Who is busy but might find a way to accommodate you?
- Who will ask for time to consider it while deliberating if this is really something he wants to spend his time on?

a.

I find the subject of graphology fascinating and in many cases beneficial. How may I obtain

b.

tho they have passed ann family there. This is w ould be exciting to know r ny roots.

c.

I am writing this letter for the "

___

show on "People Are Talking." I

years old, live in Cupertino, and

2. You're asked to share a small songbook at church. Which person would least object standing very close to a total stranger?

a.

There are many things that we need to get done before we can

b.

three mornings, browse all my magazines, going

c.

Dear Ann;

Please send all

3. You can usually find Marge giving her time to others—the PTA, Boy Scouts, United Way, etc. Last year she sold tickets for Sally's bazaar. Imagine her surprise when Sally said she was too busy to return the favor. Marge is upset. Sally always finds time for what *she* wants to do, but never has time left for anyone else. Which writing belongs to Marge? To Sally?

a.

Please send me more

b

your hand file

5

Personal Attitudes and Motivation

Size and Baseline

A knowledge of how the writer relates to the big picture of life (spacing) is important. But activity is one thing, channeling it into productive effort is something else again. Does the writer have the ability to stay on target and achieve his goals? And will his ego help or hinder him on the road to success?

The overall size of handwriting bespeaks a specific need for visibility and recognition. The line itself, progressing left to right across the page, will indicate whether the writer is steady or vacillating in achieving his goals. Is the writer determined and steadfast, or does he wander all over the page?

Both writing size and line consistency must be evaluated in conjunction with overall spacing patterns to arrive at a total TMR/0picture of the writer's organizational ability.

Writing Size—Large Versus Small

For someone whose writing is large, you may feel that a different standard should apply when judging margins and spacing. It may not seem fair that a person with large writing has to squeeze the same amount of information on a postcard as someone with a tiny script. Consider this: Who told the writer to write that large? And what does that tell us about him or her?

As you begin to examine how you utilize space, look at the overall size you've chosen for your script. Do you tiptoe across the page with tiny mouseprints, or sweep across with showmanship and vigor? Do you address the page extravagantly, or in a more modest, unassuming manner?

Large Writing

should be an absolute
Did you know our Brian

The person who challenges the page with a large, commanding script usually meets life itself with the same confidence and enthusiasm. Those who admire courage and boldness, who enjoy taking a risk, sticking their necks out, and being highly visible, will often have a script to match. (Remember John Hancock declaring independence from his mother country?) Self-confident and self-assured, these people are usually at ease both inwardly and with others. They often have high aspirations and ambitions and may seek responsibility or leadership. Magnanimous and outgoing, they enjoy public recognition and attention and have no doubts as to their own self-worth and ability to contribute to society. Others usually recognize their ability to influence and lead.

Small Writing

We were racing on Lake McCo
the largest body of water close to Denver
wide and 20-23 miles long, and provides
for a 1000 miles in any direction. We
under cloudy skys and a light breeze,
mark on the same side as our campsite

Small script, by contrast, is often indicative of a more introspective person. Although he may not be as open or communicative on first contact, he usually has a talent for detail and organization, much like his minuscule script. Often these people can concentrate for long periods of time on reading or study and possess an ''academic'' mentality. Do not assume, however, when you see writing that's tiny as a mouse that these people are shy or unassuming. Like the large-scripted writer, they have chosen to take a route off the beaten path and are often quite independent, caring little what others think of their behavior. The small writer, too, has confidence in himself and his abilities. Rather than seek the limelight, he may have more private goals that provide him with a sense of personal worth and self-satisfaction. He doesn't need public recognition for gratification. Comfortable working alone, he is self-motivated and directed and can concentrate on his interests, virtually to the exclusion of the outside world.

Average-Size Writing

To determine average size, we must compare writing to the norm taught in school. How far writing deviates from this standard in size will determine if it's large or small.

Initial measurement of writing disregards upper and lower loops (which vary enormously until a child masters small muscle control) and concentrates on the letters in the middle— $a,c,e,i,m,n,o,r,s,u,v,w,x$. Average copybook writing has middle case letters about ⅛ inch or 3 millimeters high. If your writing fits into this pattern, it is average in size and represents a person who has the ability to be practical, realistic, adaptable, and balanced in his approach to his environment, neither dominating nor shrinking away from people or events.

Let's peek back for just a moment at Nicole and Bill. Detail-oriented Bill had wrapped his food in the *Wall Street Journal* to protect it from the rain. Nicole, by contrast, subscribes to *Barron's*, companion to the *Journal*, giving her the broad overview of the financial world without all the nitpicky details. She loves it because she can throw tidbits to Bill and keep him going all night. "I read that soon all European cars must have catalytic converters," says Nicole. "And I understand they're made of platinum. Do you think we should be looking at platinum futures, Bill?" And he'll research it for days. Bill can put *Consumer*'s buying guide to shame when it comes to things like VCRs, cameras, and computers. Nicole was surprised to learn that Bill was a sailor, remarking that somehow he didn't seem the type. (She'd visualized sailors as being rugged, boisterous, and beer-drinking.) But Bill is an excellent tactician, computing wind speed and currents in his head and adjusting with split-second timing his execution (details, details).

We can tell from the size of their writing that these two will approach a project differently. They recently shopped for bicycles together (actually, the "together" part lasted one afternoon). Nicole's plan was to visit the three top stores, tell them her needs, budget, physical condition, get an overall perspective, and then *decide*. At the first store Bill got into a forty-five-minute discussion about derailleurs, bought two bicycle magazines, and nearly lost Nicole. They never made it to the second store. Realizing their differences in style, Nicole wisely gave Bill her list of needs and a two-week deadline to complete his research. Later that week Nicole did what she should have done in the first place. She spent a lunch hour on the phone with the three bike shops asking all the right questions and told Bill what she basically wanted. True to form, in two weeks Bill had all the info and a special price for partial self-assembly. While Bill spent Saturday morning in the driveway happily putting the handlebars, brakes, and seat on his bike, Nicole drove to the bike shop and paid someone to assemble hers. Nicole is interested in the total picture—the finished bike. Give someone else the instruction manual! While the shop worked on her bike, she bought some sexy blue spandex biking shorts and met a cute guy in the process—oops! She later rejoined Bill and they went off for an afternoon ride.

So when it comes to margins and spacing, it's true they are partially determined by the size of your writing. But *you* chose the initial size. You are in charge of your behavior, right down to how you approach a blank page. Once you begin to understand yourself and your handwriting a little better, learning why you do the things you do, you'll stop playing victim, blaming outside circumstances for getting you into trouble. No one forced you to start on your income-tax return too late, buy a house beyond your means, volunteer for one project too many, or run out of space on a written page. Once you take responsibility for your choices, you'll begin acknowledging the role you play in determining consequences that seem to happen without your conscious effort. All these choices are dictated by the same brain that directs the pen.

Line Direction

Another choice the writer makes is the actual shape and direction of the line itself. It may go uphill or downhill, may be concave or convex, or may seem to vacillate and wander. The direction of the line itself indicates whether the person is motivated from within or allows himself to be swayed by outside circumstances.

Keeping on Track

> *Let's plan to be at the theater early so we can get the best seats possible.*

Those who traverse the page in a straight line with determination and conviction are self-motivated. The writer who has straight baselines has the ability to plan ahead and exercise self-direction. Like a captain at the helm of a ship, he can stay on course through rough seas with no land in sight. He can be a reliable and productive worker, able to keep things in perspective and control. He may also be competitive and enjoy winning for the sake of obtaining a goal. A Yale University study found that only 2 percent of the population has well-thought-out and written goals—knowing where they want to go and how they're going to get there. It's a pretty safe bet that if your writing shows a straight baseline, you could join this rare 2 percent.

Vacillating Baseline

> When you called last Thursday, I
> was packing to leave early Friday for
> Honolulu — a quick business invitation
> to look over new hotels. I'd told Rick
> but maybe he didn't mention it. — I
> returned today I have an all day
> seminar Tomorrow

The writer with a vacillating baseline is more "outer directed" and responsive to his environment. People and situations can motivate, excite, or discourage him. Easygoing and adaptable, he sometimes alters his behavior to conform to outside circumstances or others' expectations. It may be difficult for him to make long-range plans, as he prefers to see what tomorrow will bring. He should take care that his sensitivity to outside influences doesn't leave him hopping from one project (career, relationship) to the next as he becomes a jack-of-all-trades and master of none.

Uphill or Step-Up Baseline Alignment

I'm always so eager to learn
I find graphology especially fo
I will turn 47 on Fri.! I am

I recently had a funny yet
frightening experience when
my shoe lace got caught
in an escalator.

Optimistic and enthusiastic, this writer has a naturally upbeat and buoyant outlook on life. Just as his writing climbs upward, so too his spirit reaches up toward new ideas, ideals, and untried frontiers. It's important to determine just how much of an upward climb the writing takes, as too much enthusiasm can indicate an over-responsive nature. Pie-in-the-sky dreaming can cause a person to lose sight of practicality in unrealistic goals that will never come to fruition.

Downhill or Step-Down Baseline Alignment

For People are Talki
a paragraph by a ~~By~~ left-hand
Incidentally, I have a
interest in handwriting analys
been intending to contact you

Yet another day downs
and we have the chance
to start all over again

When we feel discouraged or "down," our bodies reflect that sinking feeling in slumped shoulders, a shuffling walk, and a downcast glance. If you catch your writing slanting downhill, you're probably feeling temporary weariness, discouragement, or sadness; the reasons, of course, could be numerous. The important thing to notice is if the downhill trend is consistent or prolonged. Folks who habitually adopt a downhill slant are skeptical by nature. A negative outlook prevents them from pursuing alternative solutions, as they assume a perpetual attitude of Why try?

Note: Do not apply this interpretation to children or adults who normally write on lined paper but for purposes of the sample are writing on unlined paper. The hand has a natural tendency to pull toward the body and will automatically fall into a pulling-downward pattern when deprived of the structure of lined paper.

Convex Baseline

> Today is delicious for me. This is a normal work day. I am playing hookey The weather is beautiful and

The writer with a convex baseline often undertakes a task with great enthusiasm, but once things are under way, his energy peters out. Why? Perhaps he volunteered on impulse to do something (initial uphill exuberance). Later, that initial enthusiasm wanes (downward slope). Or perhaps he started the project expecting outside encouragement, and when it wasn't provided, he lost determination to follow through. He might withdraw from a commitment that seems too challenging or time-consuming. He needs to see immediate results, and have a little encouragement along the way. Take care if your script has this pattern. If you decide to drop a task when it's only half-finished, you're subconsciously conditioning yourself to give up, whether from fear of failure or lack of interest. You could develop a habit of procrastination to avoid completing an overwhelming task.

Concave Baseline

> through the university which would finance this type of research. There is always a light at the end of the tunnel if you're

What an asset this writer would be to any team or organization. Like the Olympic hopeful who rises daily at 5:00 A.M. to train outdoors regardless of the weather, here's a person who can attain a goal in spite of obstacles put in his path. It's all the more remarkable when you consider that he often approaches a new task with a feeling of trepidation or self-doubt. He may find it tough going at first, but once involved, he feels his confidence and self-assurance rising. Self-directed and motivated, he's a champion at pushing past his fear to grab the brass ring of success.

Lined paper

Those who prefer to write on lined paper are expressing a preference for structure, rules, and regulations. I myself prefer to take notes for any type of class on ruled paper. It seems to help me organize my thoughts. In personal correspondence, however, I dislike lined paper. It seems cold and businesslike to me; a free-form blank page seems friendlier.

Lined Paper Beneath Blank Paper

Some people will actually place ruled paper beneath blank paper before starting a note. This represents a covert desire for rules and regulations. Although wishing to appear independent and self-directed, the writer has an inner need to conform and wants the approval of others. He likes discipline, order, and often sets high, demanding goals for himself. He frequently expects others to live up to his high expectations as well.

Melanie:

> *I am most happy to b*
> *here tonight to celebra*
> *this tribute to my fath*

Melanie was a gorgeous woman of twenty-four who always dressed in the latest fashion. She appeared self-assured and independent. When I asked for a handwriting sample, I was amazed to see her slip a piece of lined paper underneath the blank paper I offered her. "It doesn't have to be perfect," I assured her. "I just need a few lines of anything." "She can't write any other way," her husband told me. As I got to know this couple better I was amazed to learn just how insecure Melanie was. What others thought of her was very important to her. Her sense of fashion, which I had interpreted as individualistic, was actually a slavish following of trends that assured Melanie visibility as being "with it" and "together." Few of her thoughts were original or creative, and she had a very conventional, conforming script.

Rigid Baseline

> After enjoying your man
> tne "People Are Talking" show, I
> write for your expert advice
> major importance to me right
> certain your experience has
> ject dozens of times, so I an
> in your thoughts & opinions.

Those who write with a ruler beneath their lines have an inordinate need to control themselves or their surrounding environment. We would have to look at other elements in the writing to determine why they feel they need to have so much control.

Internal Versus External Controls

Many will say, But I only like to write on ruled paper because that's how I was taught in school. It's a matter of environment. Or, I write a certain size because that's how much space was allowed on our ruled paper at school.

At a large electronics show at Macy's department store in San Francisco, I gathered a few samples of handwriting. Interestingly, even those whose native language was Japanese subconsciously maintained consistent spacing and size ratios, even when writing in a second language very different from their native tongue. Witness the small, disciplined, controlled script of Mark Hasegawa, president of Kenwood USA Corporation. He's a detail-oriented man who runs a tight ship. Compare it to the more expansive, outgoing script of Tom Yoda of Sansui Electronics Corporation. In his samples, Mark wrote about the yen, management policy, and the internal concerns of running a business. Tom wrote about service, sales, and the consumer, focusing on a more outer-directed approach. (The two contrasting styles are much like Bill's and Nicole's.) And their sizing and spacing remained consistent, whether writing in English or Japanese.

Mark Hasegawa:

The recent Yen situation has forced our Japanese manufacturer to change our basic management policy and sales activities.

最近のドル円事情は. 我々日本の会社に根本的な経営方針と販売活動の変更を余儀なくさせております.

Tom Yoda:

more quality and service to the consumer rather than more value with more discount by heavy sales pitch.

この内高下、顧客に
より素晴らしい品寅と
サービスを提供しようと

Review

1. You're a college counselor. Which student:

- Has his feet firmly on the ground, is motivated, and knows where he's going?
- May change majors from business to computer science to theater arts in the first semester?
- Is inwardly discouraged as he tries to please his parents and follow in his father's footsteps?
- Needs your encouragement, but will eventually overcome initial fear and succeed at his endeavors?

a.

I do Marketing Consulting.
Have a very good time ~~from~~ during
my sport car on the weekend.

b.

My friend, Mary, is leaving
for the West Indies this
week. It is sad for me. We
have always been close

c.

Please send me the pictures
of the class reunion. We
are planning to print them
in the next newsletter.

d.

Some people have all the luck.
I've never been one of them.
Maybe my luck will change
soon.

2. Both people have the ability to work on meticulous, detail-oriented projects. Whom would you choose to do research on a program of long duration?

a.

> Dear Mr. Mahoney:
>
> Was fascinated by your "People are Talking"
> program and would like more information.

b.

> My existence has been a bit more day
> the last three weeks. I am afraid I ......
> wrong decision.... not so much because of the

_____

Let's apply what we've just learned about ego needs and the ability to stay on target to our dinner companions. How will the size of their writing and baseline alignment affect their interactions with one another?

Joe:

> of your comments both
> personal and professi

Joe takes his pasta to the kitchen and disappears. This is his normal behavior, he claims, as he usually prefers to start in the kitchen and meet others who "retreat." With his broad margins and even word spacing, he allows himself plenty of room to stand back and take in the whole picture, working his way around the edges of a party before becoming too involved. Sure enough, he runs into Toni. But wait: Toni has narrow margins indicating initiative. Why isn't she right in the thick of things?

Toni:

> *Betty and I should like*
> *thank you most sincerely*
> *all the time and effort*

Toni has a reserved slant (which we'll get to soon) and wide word spacing. It's not easy for her to get close to others at first. She's in real estate but is certainly not a "hard sell" woman, allowing her prestigious firm's reputation to precede her. Many of her company's clients are quite prominent, and that makes Toni feel more comfortable. Is she a snob? No, it's just that she's uncomfortable putting herself on the line all the time, filling in conversation with lots of chitchat. When she says "Farnsworth Properties," in two words she's described her business and the clientele they handle. Recently she's expanded into commercial real estate, but only for her doctors, dentists, and professional clients—people she really feels comfortable with, rather than expanding her clientele by means of "cold calls."

Monica:

> *I apologize for taking so long to write.*
> *However, writing to someone who makes her*
> *living analyzing handwriting, runs a close*
> *second to baring one's soul at confession.*

Monica's narrow margins and spacing prompt her to greet everyone eagerly and get right down to partying. She heads for the comfy couch to get a good spot ringside. Bill, with his conventional spacing and margins, does the right thing and joins her to help form a nucleus and keep the party going.

James:

*[handwriting: shop exhibit. It's okay to hang it onby
Thank you very much]*

James, of course, takes the only single chair available. No one's going to corner him and monopolize his time with mindless conversation. If they try, he can simply scoot his chair farther away (very broad margins and wide letter spacing).

Michael:

[handwriting: As for me, I've been on a number of projects, much that I feel the proverbial juggler, t.]

Michael has narrow margins but somewhat wide word spacing. Yes, he wants to get involved, but he'll decide where and when. He's drawn to Monica's vivacious charm and beauty, but she's conversing with Bill. He gradually maneuvers himself around the back of the couch and quietly slips in on her other side (initiative) and waits his turn. Nicole has introduced her old friend Michael as a bartender who works at various establishments around the city, and everyone politely smiles. Michael allows this façade to pass through the cocktail hour, noticing that no one bothers to engage him in conversation, which gives him time to sit back (almost as invisible as you) and just observe and enjoy.

Toni and Joe eventually wander in from the kitchen, and Joe ushers Toni to another couch. Joe prefers to remain standing (apart) as long as he can, again, to just take everything in. Nicole sweeps in, happy to see no lone stragglers. She'd been about to corral Joe when the doorbell rings, announcing, at long last, the arrival of Connie. When she's finally unloaded everything, Connie comes right in and sits on the arm of James's chair (close word spacing), throwing her arm across the back. James continues to stare into his drink, hoping she'll somehow fade away. But good-time Connie soon has everyone's attention as she relates her hilarious adventures trying to find a parking space. Aloof James was going to make people come *to him*, and suddenly he's court jester to the queen of comedy. Connie even hands him her drink to hold so she has her hands free to tell her story.

Connie:

is progressing nicely (she continue, and I con securing the national re for those guys along al bigger and I'm learning alot from all of them pusonal process is amazing when step back and look).

Joe, the TV producer, remains standing apart as he observes the players Nicole has gathered. She's quite a little producer herself, he smiles, noting that Connie is only temporarily the star. Monica is already in the wings ready to tell a story of her own. Michael is admiring Monica's legs, Toni now looks more relaxed, and Nicole is purring like a cat. Joe turns for a moment to the bookshelf behind him to peruse Nicole's library when it suddenly hits him—her volumes were practically catalogued by the Dewey decimal system! "Nicole, good Lord, what organization," he whistles. "Actually, Bill did that," replies Nicole. "The books are mostly his. He likes to know where *everything* is." She rolls her eyes, remembering Bill's lecture when she once used a book and just tossed it back anywhere. Ask Bill where's the great book on wine and he'll tell you, third shelf over on the left. Ask Nicole and she'll answer, "Ask Bill." Nicole's expansive script takes in the overall picture, then delegates the details.

Bill doesn't actually live with Nicole, but her sumptuous, comfortable apartment (pressure) makes a much better place for reading than his sparsely furnished home. He's sensibly purchasing furnishings he loves piece by piece as he can afford them. His small, detail-oriented writing with orderly margins and disciplined baselines confirms that he'll achieve his goals on schedule.

Bill:

for a 1000 miles in any direction. We s
under cloudy skys and a light breere,
mork on the same side as our campsite

As Joe scrutinizes this perfectly orchestrated party, he continues to chide Nicole. "Come on, Madame President, I'll bet you've already finished your Christmas shopping." "Christmas!" yelps Monica, "I'm not even ready for Thanksgiving!" Don't you believe it. Monica has tiny, detail-oriented writing with narrow margins (signaling initiative and perseverance). Not only is Monica a whiz with details, she'll see to it that the job gets done. One reason she took the step as entrepreneur with Your Own Creation was that she had the support (including financial) of two top managers at work. They're allowing her to work part-time three days a week while she gets things off the ground. Why? "I know what I'm doing and I can prove it with my research. And I'm motivated. My bosses have seen me do the same for them." So why would Monica say she hasn't even begun her Christmas planning? If it's only in her head, it doesn't count. Monica needs to see tangible results.

Monica:

> *Dan left me a gift at my desk today. Don't
> the faintest reason why, but it was a nice s
> He never ceases to amaze me. I hope he enjoys my s*

Check the lines of her writing. Some are convex. Monica has probably already run a zillion ideas for Christmas through her head. When she's excited about something (lines), she gets so enthused that she spends her energy right away (light pressure) and winds up right back where she started—emptyhanded. In August she found the perfect Christmas present for her sister. She couldn't wait (convex lines, tight right margin), so she gave her the gift ahead of time. But don't worry, Monica loves a challenge and she'll work out great Christmas surprises right down to the custom wrapping paper.

Joe continues to kid with Nicole, knowing she always has goodies squirreled away—silver bookmarks, fabulous sachets— ready for any occasion. "I know you learned from the best," he says, drawing Toni, Nicole's aunt, into the conversation. Toni has narrow margins signaling initiative and perseverance. But her light pressure and somewhat aloof spacing indicate that it's quite an effort for her to get in touch with another's feelings and understand his heart's desire. Yes, her cards are ordered and the basics taken care of, but there are still a few special gifts she's searching for without much success.

Toni:

> *Betty and I should like
> thank you most sincerely
> all the time and effort*

"How about you, James?" quizzes Nicole. "Want to drop a hint or two for me to tell your parents? Have you bought them anything yet?" Very broad margins and wide letter spacing tell us that James distances himself from the needs of others. His somewhat erratic baseline indicates that he could easily succumb to those last-minute Christmas displays of perfume and ties. "Haven't begun," mumbles James.

James:

Thank you very much

On hearing this, naturally helpful Connie offers her assistance. Groan. James would sooner run a marathon on one leg than shop with Connie. Nevertheless, she persists, assuring everyone she knows a terrific woman in Palo Alto who can sweep you through fifteen fabulous stores in an afternoon, finding just the right thing! Connie offers to arrange a trip. Monica instantly responds, eager for new shopping sources and a good time. Monica and Toni should drive together, as they'll both begin to fade about halfway through the day (light pressure).

Michael agrees to go. His rather large and busy script tells us that he enjoys taking in the overall picture, covering a lot of territory in a short time. He'll probably get there on his own, however, as his word spacing indicates that he still prefers a bit of detachment. Sure, he'd like to see the sources, but please don't hover and chat as he's trying to buy.

Michael:

As for me, I've been so a number of projects much that I feel b

Joe's detached, disciplined, organized script says that he too doesn't need a lot of chatter and hand holding. Show him the goods, but he'll make up his own mind, thank you. Joe likes to plan and organize, then shop. If only he could peruse the catalogues like mad, then go see and feel the merchandise. The Sharper Image has come close to this with their catalogue/store combination, but they don't have enough "warm fuzzies"—children's gifts, gourmet foods, etc.—for all his shopping. Luckily there's a Neiman-Marcus and Nordstrom's in town, and he's hoping a Bloomingdale's opens soon.

And what about Nicole? If looks could kill, Connie would be tuning her harp. Nicole knows all about the personal shopper and has already contracted with her to work on her "difficult" list (including her aunt). Ah well, reasons Nicole, you do the best you can and that's that (large script).

6

Energy Unleashed

Handwriting Slant

If you were at a party and didn't know anyone, which person would you feel most comfortable approaching? Would you be drawn toward Connie, assured of a friendly greeting and easy conversation? Or would you stand quietly next to Joe and enter the party gradually, in our own good time? You are drawn toward certain personality types, but do you know why? Much of it depends on your need or lack of need for involvement.

Try this. Sit in a crowded restaurant and quietly people watch. Can you spot the couple in love? The couple having an argument? The group having a good time? It's pretty obvious, isn't it? What did you look for? Behavior. Visible signs. See the man eagerly leaning forward on the edge of his chair? You know he feels passionately about whatever he's discussing. Other people remain poised and in control, nodding intermittently, responding when appropriate. Still others lean back with arms folded, appearing aloof or skeptical.

Leaning Forward/Holding Back

Like facial expressions and bodily gestures, the slant of handwriting is an indication of emotional responsiveness and involvement.

How far forward or backward your writing slants indicates whether you release energy outwardly toward others, or inwardly toward yourself. Slant alone does not reveal what emotions you may be feeling (sadness, anger, joy) but rather *how quickly* these emotions will surface.

Slant is a terrific barometer to gauge how in control you are. Stop for a moment and reflect on your own behavior. In an emergency, although your heart may be racing, can you calmly lead others to safety? Or are you frozen in your tracks? How often do you find yourself purchasing electronic gadgets or a new outfit you don't really need? Do you think twice before spending your hard-earned cash?

Now look at your writing. Does it look like a racehorse dashing off the page or a car skidding to a stop at a red light? Maybe it's standing up straight as a tin soldier. Many folks respond, "But I write with several different slants. Does that mean I'm a multiple personality?" No, of course not. Some days our writing (like our life-style) seems to jump hither and yon at the slightest provocation. You might even unconsciously fall into a different slant once in a while. Why? Because, like your mood, your slant may shift when your feelings change.

Since writing is a progression from one side of the page to the other, the first word of the sentence you are reading was obviously written before the last. The beginning of the sentence is "older." As you leave the old (the left) and move forward across the page, you approach new frontiers—the unknown opportunities and risks. How will your love letter end? You may not know yourself until you write it.

The more your writing slants forward toward the right side of the page, the more you are "out there" in the environment, willing to take risks and make your emotions visible for all to see.

The more upright or left-tending the slant, the more likely the writer is to pull back, to resort to logic and control. Remember, any movement toward the left side of the page is a return to self, security, and safety. It's a drawing inward, staying close to home. Movement to the right involves venturing into the outside world, taking risks, and is action oriented.

If your handwriting slant is so extreme that it looks like saplings in a hurricane, leaning 45 degrees or more, you may have trouble keeping a lid on your emotions. If it's straight up and down, you probably take a more disciplined, analytical approach to life. If it leans backward toward the left side of the page, you're apt to be introspective, cautious, deliberate, even an enigma to friends. Any exaggeration in handwriting is an exaggeration in personality.

Measuring Slant

There are many ways to determine slant, from measuring 300 strokes per sample to just eyeballing a few lines. Slant is important, but it varies with our mood and emotions, so let's take a practical commonsense approach. It's fairly simple to judge if it's an upright, forward, or backward slant. Many schools will have you wielding a pocketful of transparent grids and magnifiers (it lends credibility). Yes, I do measure upstrokes and downstrokes in profusion both for forgery and fraud detection and detailed analytical work. But for now, you don't need it. Neophytes who get caught up in "measuring" handwriting often become confused, feeling the whole thing is beyond them. Nothing could be further from the truth. It reminds me of the man shopping for a birthday present for his wife. He doesn't know a size eight from a size twelve, but he quickly discerns which salesgirl closely resembles her "type" and proceeds from there. All the "types" are at our dinner party, so let's get started.

Types of Slant

There are several different slants, and we'll cover them all in just a moment, but first, here's a chart to visually assist you in our journey, and a brief description of each slant so you'll know where we're going.

If you moved into a new neighborhood, the A-slant person might just wait for you to make the first contact. The B-slant person would probably bring you some brownies and a smile, and leave you in peace to get settled. The C-slant person would mosey over, equipped with the names of good dry cleaners, markets, and veterinarians. The D-slant person would help you unpack and insist you come for dinner that night. The E-slant writer might bring his own sandwich, chat for an hour, and inquire how soon you'd be having your open house. The F-slant person would wait to meet you in his own good time, probably on his own turf.

A-Slant: Logic and Practicality

so much time this afternoon. I am appre of your comments both,

Handwriting with an A-slant is really writing with no slant at all. It stands straight up. Envision a person standing before you, tall and straight on the page. Does he seem in control, constant, and reliable—like a soldier at attention?

The person with an A-slant is in emotional control. He looks before he leaps. He considers matters thoroughly from a logical, analytical, and practical point of view. He examines the problem from all angles and makes decisions based on reason and impartial judgment rather than emotion or whim. He's cool and controlled, disciplined and objective—and great in an emergency.

I once knew a man with an A-slant who was having dinner in a restaurant with his wife and her mother, when the mother-in-law suddenly choked and fell to the floor, gasping for air. The emotional wife, who had a far-forward slant to her writing, fell on top of her mother, screaming, "Help, for God's sake!" The son-in-law quickly looked down at his mother-in-law and left.

His actions appeared cold and heartless until everyone realized he'd gone to get help from the maître d', who knew the Heimlich maneuver and saved the woman's life. The husband had calmly analyzed the situation, realized he could do nothing, and deduced that the most effective action was to go get someone who might have encountered these circumstances before and could deal with them. The wheels in his head never stopped turning. In this case, the A-slant person's way of being composed and aloof saved a life.

A-slant people can make life a little frustrating for those around them. One client came to me saying that she had nothing to complain about—she had a wonderful home, children, and everything she could want in life, including a husband who brought her flowers and took her out to dinner once a month. The only problem was that in eighteen years of marriage, he had never *told* her he loved her. It turned out that this man had a very upright slant, and even though he loved his wife a great deal and tried to show it with his actions, he had trouble verbalizing his emotions.

A-slant people may appear undemonstrative and noncommittal, even when the feelings are really there. If you're a fairly new acquaintance they aren't likely to come running up to you at a party, throw their arms around you, and kiss you on both cheeks. And if you come rushing up to *them* like that, they're likely to back off as soon as they can.

Dealing with A-Slants

Margo, a San Franciscan, was asked to be maid of honor at her best friend's wedding in San Diego. I immediately noticed the emotional, outgoing, forward slant to her writing as she sat in front of me in tears. "Help me, please," she begged. "The rehearsal dinner is Friday night, and I simply must have Friday off from work. You don't know my boss. He'll dock my pay or make me take a vacation day, and he'll think I'm not serious about my job." She showed me a sample of his handwriting.

As soon as I saw the upright slant, I explained that her emotional appeals were useless. She would get nowhere gushing about this fabulous wedding with all the old gang, and please, please couldn't she go early and stay over because she was *so* excited.

We formulated a plan. The next day, she calmly confronted her boss. "Mr. Philips, I need to attend a wedding rehearsal dinner in San Diego Friday night, so I'm going to have to leave work a little early. I realize that we have three clients in Southern California, and it gives them confidence in us when we make our presentations and follow-up in person. I've taken the liberty of going through their files, and if you'll just answer a couple of questions for me, I'd be willing to go down there early on my own time *for you* and service these accounts. We have another client in Los Angeles. I called, but he can't see me until Monday. I'd be willing to stay over and see him too."

After he recovered from his surprise, Philips arranged for the company to take care of Margo's airfare to San Diego. The presentations went very smoothly, and she had a grand time at the rehearsal dinner. Not only that, she met a man at the wedding who took her to the San Diego Zoo and dinner Sunday, then drove her to Los Angeles for the presentation Monday morning.

Her boss didn't dock her pay or make her take a vacation day, and when her six-month review came up she was cited for initiative, perseverance, and independence. She also got a raise. "And to think," quipped Margo, "all I wanted to do was go to the wedding."

Some people might call her behavior manipulative. I call it smart. You don't talk to a Spaniard in French. This woman talked to her boss in his own language, even though *she herself* was more impulsive and emotional (and had a forward slant to her writing); and she got what she wanted. He wasn't interested in what a beautiful wedding it was going to be, or how she and Sarah had been roommates in college. So what? He was interested in how it made sense for her to leave work a day early and stay over until Monday.

She appealed to his sense of logic, knowing that he would gather all the facts before making a decision, weigh the advantages, and not be swayed by her emotional appeals. She gave him logical reasons why she should indulge her emotional feelings.

Types of A-Slant

Poised, vivacious Nicole:

accommodations were elega

was fabulous . Tell Charles

Disciplined, detail-oriented Bill:

Every 30 or 40 seconds we'd get swep
I found that with care I could just m
to clear the land. Trouble way, the sea
for careful sailing and we kept getting
always towards the beach, and always
when I needed every inch. 'When the u

But wait! Bill and Nicole from our dinner party both have A-slants, yet they couldn't be more opposite in personality. Bill is calm and deliberate while Nicole is expansive, even flamboyant.

Bill seems to be more of a classic A-slant person. He's a physicist, tracking satellites for a major Silicon Valley firm. He's also earning a M.B.A. at night, tracking his expanding salary just as cautiously.

He's reserved and preferred to remain standing during cocktails rather than settling in with the others. Yes, I know he joined Monica on the couch, but this gesture was more an attempt to keep Nicole's party congenial than his own need to be gregarious. He assessed the situation and did the "right thing."

At the party, Nicole mixes and mingles. She seems outgoing, but, actually, none of her conversation is on a very deep level. She's too busy keeping one eye on the whole scenario. And let's not forget the logistics it took to put this party together: the invitations, the flowers, the canapés, and the elegant table.

Remember too, what Nicole does for a living. She's head of marketing for a posh thirty-shop center and coordinates deals with politicians, merchants, lawyers, the press, and customers. She manages a million details every day—and she is in *complete control*, cool and calm in the midst of chaos.

Other aspects of Nicole's writing (such as size and style) indicate that she's more expansive than Bill. She has all the emotional control that he does, but with a different style of living and relating to people. They may act differently, but you can bet that if an earthquake struck, both would know where the exits were and be in charge of the situation. (They would probably meet in the street—Nicole with a flashlight and blanket, and Bill with the ice bucket for drinking water and injuries).

Many, many types of personalities have A-slants. It's important not to categorize people when looking at *one* aspect of their handwriting. You need to get the whole picture before drawing any conclusions.

I once had an A-slant student who said I was all wrong about her. The tears welled up at sad movies, sunsets, and newborn babies—in short, she was extremely emotional. I asked her friend standing next to her, "How is she in an emergency?" Completely in control of everything, was the instant response. I checked her writing and found an A-slant with heavy pressure. She had very deep emotional feelings, but when the chips were down, you could count on her to keep it together. Her tears were simply a little closer to the surface than most A-slant folks, because her well of emotion was so deep.

A-slant people are independent. They don't feel compelled to conform or please others, because *they* are in control. At parties, they only seem to be wallflowers when they stand alone; they're sizing up the situation, deciding when and where they'd like to jump in.

B-Slant: The Emotions Emerge

As for me, I've been over a number of projects so much that I feel the proverbial juggler, to keep several 'balls' in simultaneously.

Remember, the more forward the slant, the more emotionally responsive the person. A-slant people seem poised and objective. B-slant people appear a little warmer, more friendly and sympathetic. It's not that they care more, it's just easier for them to show how they feel.

They might walk across the room and take your hand, and you might do the same with them. When people respond to you, it's easier to open up to them. B-slant writers are more outgoing and demonstrative, so they're easier to get to know.

They may also be a bit more conventional, because the B-slant is what is taught in most schools. People who retain aspects of school-model writing haven't deviated too far from the norm or experimented with different ways of expressing themselves.

The B-slant writer maintains a balance between emotion and control. He may seem a bit reserved at first, but he's fairly comfortable participating in activities and connecting with others.

Michael from our party has a B-slant. His profession requires a fairly rational approach (environmental planner, working on his Ph.D. in sociology), but he tempers too much academia with working as a bartender (where he can gather research for his dissertation). His gourmet cooking isn't "by the book" either; he lets some flair and creativity shine through.

He extends himself to others at the party without falling all over them. He's pleasant but not gushy; serious, but not entirely head-ruled. Michael, like Joe, decides when and where he'd like to expend his energy. He's more apt to get trapped by a long-winded conversationalist, however, as he doesn't want to appear rude or bored by pulling away too soon. (Conventional behavior—be polite.)

C-Slant: Getting More Impulsive

is progressing nicely. We continue, and I con securing the national is for those guys along all bigger and. I'm learning alot from all of them personal process is amazing when step back and look.

As the writing slants farther forward into the environment, we find the people who reach out to others.

The C-slant writer's emotions often influence his decisions. He may plunge into a situation without first counting to ten. This is the mom who volunteers to drive the Girl Scouts to the zoo on Thursday, and sure, okay, prepare the snacks, before she's realized that Thursday is Billy's orthodontist appointment! She automatically volunteered at the prospect of free admission and a day of fun. The more the handwriting slants to the right, the less control the person has over his emotions and responses. C-slant people tend to be extroverted, spontaneous, adaptable, and demonstrative. Eager and enthusiastic, they respond to people and events in their surroundings and may shed a tear with you over your troubles.

These people warm up to others easily, leaning forward to absorb every word. They can return from football games hoarse and exhausted, even though they were merely spectators. They might jump into a great-sounding investment, vacation, or used car offer without stopping first to think it over.

I know a woman with a C-slant who has been very successful selling medical supplies. She's fun-loving, athletic, outgoing, and swims in the chilly San Francisco Bay every morning. Her fortieth birthday party was in the Captain's Cabin at Trader Vic's, and after a lavish dinner she was presented with a double-fudge chocolate cake with gooey frosting.

As everyone sang "Happy Birthday" she blew out the candles, then enthusiastically plunged face first into the cake. When she sat up, grinning and blinking through a chocolate mask, she exulted, "I've *always* wanted to do that. And, God, I'm forty, folks. If not now, when?"

Connie from our dinner party is a C-slant person. She's late because she had to pick up her car and forgot about her ballet board meeting until the last minute, etc. Once she does arrive, she greets everyone as if they were an old friend—even people she's never met before. James is mortified when she meets him, hears his parents are out of town, and proceeds to take him under her wing like an orphan in a storm.

Connie is often late, but usually because she just can't say no, especially to an emotional appeal. She has her kid's PTA, the orphanage, volunteer work at the hospital, plus all her clubs, and her own part-time job, which takes more time than it might because she organizes her work emotionally rather than logically. She does what she likes to do first. That means shopping for a birthday gift while the laundry gropes its way to the ceiling.

D-Slant: Full Speed Ahead

> Since I thoroughly enjoy music, singing, and all art forms (dance, drama, etc.) I occasionally pretend to be a famous personality, be it on stage or in a night club. Art has

Restless, impulsive, strongly influenced by likes and dislikes, these people may argue with a police officer, hang up on their spouse, or quit their job, without giving the other person a chance to explain. When it comes to politics, they'll vote for the candidate they "like" and "trust" without really considering his platform. They have a tendency to plunge headlong into new ventures and activities, eventually exhausting themselves. They want to see results *now* and are better with short-term goals. They can become impatient and easily frustrated.

In relationships, they respond to what they want at that moment without stopping to consider if it's really what's best for them in the long run. They may be less discriminating, selective, or unable to judge when enough is enough.

Once, within the same week, I had two D-slant clients come to my office with broken hearts. The first client, a woman, was "hooked" on a man who never called until 5:00 P.M. Friday to ask her out for a date, and often didn't call at all. Yet all she wanted was advice on how to make it "work." She had no interest in rationally analyzing the relationship to see if it was right for her.

The other client was a man who had known a woman three weeks, married her, and a month later she had left him. He showed me her writing, which among other things was selfish and self-centered. "I'm curious to know, what attracted you to this woman in the first place, Kevin?" I asked. He got this funny look on his face and his eyes glazed over as he began a rapt account of how her hair shone in the sun when she tossed her head and laughed. Unfortunately for Kevin, she was laughing at him.

The D-slant person at our dinner party is Monica, who gushes warm hellos then cozies up in the middle of the couch to hold court. The minute she spies Joe, her eyes light up. When she hears he produces a morning talk show, she hands him her card and says, "You know, I have a great idea I think you should do for a Christmas show. Maybe we could have lunch." A-slant Joe politely smiles and says nothing. He'll decide what airs on the show, thank you. Poor Monica! In her exuberance and excitement, she pushed herself on him too soon, rather than stopping to reflect what approach might be most effective.

In all fairness to Monica, she truly has a heart of gold. In fact on her way to the party she stopped to lift a frightened, wet kitten into a warm apartment doorway, hoping someone would take it in. And with her detail-oriented script, she could probably coordinate a jam-packed, exciting TV segment. She simply needs to step back for a moment and slow down.

E-Slant: Hovering on the Brink

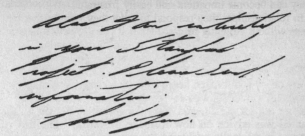

An E-slant writer is the extreme of emotional responsiveness. The writing, too, seems to rush forward, unable to stop itself. When these people feel strongly, they tend to lose perspective and react instantly, without considering the consequences. They can become thoroughly absorbed in the mood of the moment, taking on another's problems as their own, becoming targets not only for hard-luck stories but also for extremists, crusaders, and rebels with a cause, following them in blind faith. They tend to be unrestrained and impulsive, hurling themselves into their environment.

The classic story for the E-slant person is the man brought into the emergency room with blood gushing from gunshot wounds in his head and stomach. The resident doctor on call that night was an extremely competent black surgeon. When the wounded man saw this doctor, he propped himself up on the gurney and yelled, ''No minority's gonna operate on me!'' Being ruled by his emotions and prejudices nearly cost him his life.

These are the people who not only believe everything they read in the *National Enquirer* but run out and repeat it. They're the ones sitting next to you on an airplane who recount details of their gall bladder operation, their opinion on the economy, and whether Princess Di should have another child—before the plane has left the ground.

They remind me of the couple rushing down the highway on a long-distance trip. The husband is at the wheel and the poor wife, on ''navigation'' detail, desperately tries to catch the street names as they whiz by in a blur. ''Slow down,'' she admonishes. ''I think we may have missed our turn!'' ''Yeah,'' he replies, pedal to the floor, "but we're making great time!" This type of person is not really "in touch" with his environment.

F-Slant: The Poker Players

all the time and effort u
you have expended in our
and that of the hotel

As always, our rule is: Any exaggeration in handwriting is an exaggeration in personality. Remember the A-slant people, always in control? Well, exaggerate that characteristic one step further for people with an F- or backhand slant. They are extremely self-contained and rarely show at first glance what they are thinking or feeling. They like keeping to themselves, remaining anonymous.

They are likely to hold you at arm's length emotionally. This gives them a vantage point of control from which to operate. They need to get a "feel" for your personality before allowing you to advance too far into their world. You can't ever forget that they—not you—are in charge of whether or not you become friends.

As with other aspects of handwriting, movement toward the left symbolizes a return to safety, security, and the self, rather than an extension out into the world of risks and the unknown. The more the writing slants to the left, the more the writer is separated from his environment and the people around him.

People with an F-slant tend to be concerned about their egos and lack a certain naturalness or spontaneity; it's their way of protecting themselves. Their thoughts and energy often turn inward, which can lead to their seeming inhibited or repressed. All of this may sound less than positive, but the F-slant people tend to be individualists and act in ways that are unconventional and nonconforming. A certain amount of caution and skepticism can be healthy.

But isn't this slant only for lefties? By now you're well aware that all handwriting is governed by *the brain*, not the hand, yet I still get asked this question. Extensive studies have proven that the ratio of both right- and left-handed people with this slant is about equal. Surprised? Remember, handwriting is really brainwriting and a function of the psyche, not the hand. Years ago, lefties were singled out as being different—oddballs, southpaws. Many had their left hands tied down or pinned behind them in school in an effort to correct their "abnormality." If they developed a backhand slant, it reflected a need for self-protection and privacy.

True, the southpaw will find this slant more in line with the direction of his handedness and perhaps more comfortable. Nevertheless, both right- and left-handers who go against the grain of what they were taught express a streak of nonconformity and an inner desire to behave independently of society's dictates.

I knew a New York photographer named Steve who had a backhand slant and a reputation for being creative, aloof, and difficult to get along with. He rarely had much rapport with his clients, and if they tried to fraternize insincerely to get their jobs rushed through quickly, he turned to stone.

I too was a client, but maintained a polite distance, having seen his handwriting. By overhearing a conversation I happened to discover one day that he collected antique toys. Several months later I saw an article on antique toys in the Sunday paper, cut it out, and gave it to him. You would have thought I'd handed him the crown jewels. He oohed and aahed like a C-slant person, made sure I was on the mailing list for antique toy publications, gave me rush photo jobs without being asked, and underwent a total transformation—all because I knew from his handwriting not to try to be his friend before he was ready. I had to wait, find something that was important *to him*, and approach him on his terms.

Both Toni and James from the party are F-slant people. If you recall, Toni kept her attention glued to Nicole at first, afraid to look around the room for fear she'd catch other guests sizing her up. There's a bit of F-slant paranoia about Toni. She brought flowers and fresh coffee, giving "things," as opposed to the time and the TLC spent in preparing food. She aches inside from loneliness, but even a simple dinner after work with someone she's not totally comfortable with feels awkward. An exception to the rule might be a gallery opening where she could "float" and meet others among the artwork—a great prop and conversation starter when forced to be with strangers. She feels safe in her Adolfo and pearls. Remember, too, when others had wine, she ordered Campari and soda, thereby creating a statement of "I have a taste and style of my own" without having to create the same impression with unique conversation.

She finally warms up a bit to Joe, who has gone out of his way to talk with another "kitchen recluse," asking about trends in the real estate market. In other words, he's met her on her own ground, in her area of expertise. What a break for Toni! She can relax and converse for hours, appearing to become involved, without ever touching on her personal life, needs, and desires.

James wouldn't trust his emotions any further than he could throw them. Part of this is because he's seventeen years old; the situation may change as he matures. In fact, many teenagers temporarily adopt a backhand slant as they try to "pull away" from the emotional ties of childhood. You've heard "I can't talk to my kid anymore. He's in another world." Change in personality is almost always reflected in our writing. You may not write exactly the same way today as you wrote ten years ago, and you almost certainly don't write the way you did when you were a child.

Multiple Slants

The first thing I want to say about handwriting that contains two or more different slants is this: Most of us have them at one time or another. Our mood changes while we're writing grocery lists, love letters, business agreements, or exams. When you're addressing Christmas cards, the slant of your writing may be quite different by the time you reach the *w*'s than it was when you started the *a*'s. So if you see a little variance in your slant, it doesn't mean you're schizophrenic.

People with multiple slants are frequently versatile, impressionable, and lively. They have many interests and like change and variety. There are, however, some specific things to watch for.

Multiple slants can be a sign of wear and tear on the emotional system—pulling back and jumping forward—responses that vary dramatically from moment to moment. The more severe the slant, the more erratic the emotional control.

Multiple slants can also signal temporary lapses from reality. We all have them. Have you ever walked into a room and suddenly asked yourself, "Now what did I come in here for?" Or driven right past the exit you take every day on the freeway? Failed to get off at your bus stop? You want to pinch yourself and say "Wake up!" It happens to all of us. The simple truth is, our minds just aren't tuned in all the time. All activity, even physical, originates in the brain. Remember our example of the paralyzed patient who couldn't pick up a glass of water because the message couldn't get from his brain to his hand? Messages travel through hundreds of miles of nerve pathways via chemical synapses. When we're overtired, eating poorly, under stress, etc., our nerves can't function properly. Messages and signals become scrambled, and we experience a temporary loss of contact with reality. These temporary losses often surface in handwriting as multiple slants. Because of these losses, every day we lose fractions of seconds, minutes, or, in the case of extreme multiple slants, even hours.

The more severe the multiplicity of the slant, the more frequent the lapses. One woman with a severe multiple slant went downtown, had lunch, and bought a dress. When her husband asked her later what she'd done that day, she had no recollection at all. She didn't even remember where the dress had come from. As you can imagine, these lapses created quite a bit of wear and tear on her emotions, a push-pull situation that is reflected in handwriting.

Enclosed Is A Self Addressed Envelope, plea Send Further Information

Multiple slants are common in children's writing before the age of fifteen, partly because the extensor muscles in their hands aren't fully developed. Sometimes, however, multiple slants occur in the writing of children who are being emotionally pulled in two directions. They may have parents who are separated, divorced, or not in agreement with each other about how the child should be raised. The children play one parent off against the other, and the result is often a total lack of discipline.

Afraid of losing to the competition, each parent indulges the child. The child thinks, I can do anything I want and get away with it. That means that nobody cares. I don't know where I stand, and I'm not sure where to go or what to try next.

Remember, multiple slants that aren't too severe reflect changing moods and/or temporary fatigue, so be careful before you jump to conclusions.

Introverts and Extroverts

All the slants we've discussed can be gathered under two umbrellas—introverts and extroverts—but we're not going to use these terms in the classic sense. For our purposes, people with slants of F, A, and B are considered introverts. People whose slants venture farther right—the C, D, and E category—are extroverts.

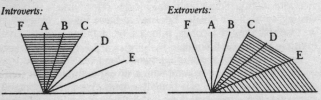

In graphology, introverts are independent, self-sufficient people who can live and work alone. They could be married or have business partners, but their relationships are through choice, not through the *need* to have people in their lives. They're discriminating, selecting a few carefully chosen people with whom to share work or love. They tend to direct their energy and interests toward themselves, rather than toward external objects and events, and are likely to find satisfaction in their personal world of thought, study, or fantasy. Many private school or "yuppie" handwritings are of the introvert variety, concentrating on "my" career, "my" success, "my" image, "my" goals, "my" needs, "my" wants, "my" investments, "my" biological time clock.

Extroverts, on the other hand, *do* need to be with people. They tend to be friendly, talkative, and dependent. They touch people and stand close by when conversing with you. They are more interested in events and circumstances surrounding them than in analyzing their own inner dimensions. They also tend to marry and divorce more often because they'd rather have a warm body—any body—than nothing at all. They are joiners (clubs, associations, etc.) and participate in their environment, whether politics or PTA. Their writing moves continually toward the right side of the page, the area of involvement and participation and risk-taking.

At this point a high-achieving entrepreneurial A-slant person may berate me for saying he's not a risk-taker. I didn't say that. If you look carefully at his risks, however, they're probably carefully thought out and have high personal rewards at the top of the list. Often when they join clubs, it's for the purpose of business networking, not social contact.

Slant may possibly be the most easily recognizable trait in handwriting. Let's combine it with what you've already learned to see how it influences the total picture. We'll return to the dinner party now, and I'll indicate the slants in our scenario to help you put it together.

Back to the Party

We left Connie extolling the virtues of her personal shopper. Michael speaks up. "Let me know when you're trimming your tree, Nicole, and I'll bring some of my homemade cranberry bread." Nicole has an annual tree-trimming party. It's a night for everyone to come in casual clothes and "take five" during the holiday rush.

"No tree this year," sighs Nicole. "We're leaving for a ski trip the day after Christmas, and Bill thinks leaving a dry tree in an unattended apartment is just too dangerous" (practical A-slant). "But I'm hanging angels everywhere, anyway. It has to *feel* like Christmas somehow." (Pressure and size of her handwriting verify a need for sensual and emotional gratification.)

"Oh, tell us about your trip!" chimes Connie.

"We've signed up for a time-share cabin for the season. It's in a great location and sleeps eight," says Nicole.

Cautious Joe, who thinks ahead, says, "But what if there's no snow? What if it's a short season and you can't get your money back?" (A-slant).

"Are you kidding?" replies Nicole. "Look outside at the rain. That means snow in the mountains [the overall picture], and I have an intuitive feeling that this is going to be a good season." Logical Bill, of course, is at the ready with antifreeze, good wiper blades, and chains.

"Sleeps eight, huh?" teases Michael. "So when are you inviting us?'' ''Name your date!'' prompts Nicole, always ready to organize another event.

Monica doesn't want to go alone, but she thinks it would be fun to go with a group (D-slant). Connie says she has skied everywhere, including Europe. Whenever they want to go, she's ready. She speaks before checking her calendar, of course, knowing that she can ''shuffle'' things around. We aren't too surprised to learn later that the trip presents a conflict in her schedule (C-slant).

Toni says, ''I don't know. All those people, the crowds, and waiting in line, and the cold! [light pressure—sensitive to extremes] and sharing bathrooms down the hall [introverted slant, wide word spacing]. I'm not too sure.'' She remains noncommittal (F-slant).

Nicole had chosen a cabin situated on the north shore of Lake Tahoe, to include gambling, shows, and fun. Nicole isn't always a night-life person. Her A-slant personality needs solitude and time alone, but she likes having plenty of options close at hand.

Joe adds that he would like to try cross-country skiing, as he understands it's not only invigorating and challenging (pressure) but allows one to commune with nature in a private, peaceful way (A-slant). Monica likes the rush, thrill, and challenge of downhill skiing (D-slant) but admits that on her last trip she tired quickly (light pressure) and enjoyed a few cozy afternoons in the lodge.

James finally shows a spark of life as he speaks up. ''Wow. Sounds great!'' He asks Nicole if the cabin's available the last week in February. This is break time for northern California schools. ''The slopes will be packed with kids and families. Not really a good time to go,'' he assures Nicole. ''The lines will be horrendous.'' Nicole watches the little wheels turning in his F-slant head (What's in it for me?), realizing that James would love to take his entire senior class to a cabin that sleeps eight. ''I'll check,'' she promises tentatively.

Review

1. Slant measures the degree of emotional responsiveness in a person. Match the following descriptions to the appropriate slant:

- responsive, outgoing, compassionate
- loss of perspective, reacts impulsively

- fair, objective, emotions under control
- eager, enthusiastic, subjective viewpoint
- introspective, cautious, evasive, private
- crusader, extremist, rebel

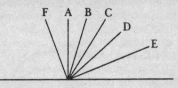

2. The cocktail hour was so lively no one noticed something burning in the kitchen until too late. Smoke billowed into the living room.

- What emotional individual screamed "Fire!" and knocked over a drink while running to the kitchen?
- Who reasoned "Panic serves no purpose?" and remained calmly seated and outwardly poised?
- Who grasped the overall situation, took control, smothering the flames with baking soda with one hand while dialing the deli to order replacements with the other?

a.

Betty and I should like

b.

should be an absolute

c.

and all art forms (dance, drama, etc.) Soccer-

3. After dinner, Nicole brings out coffee and Trivial Pursuit. Match the handwriting with the description below:

- What logical, detail-oriented person brightened at the thought of rustling his memory for seldom-used facts and figures?

- Who immediately pulled up a chair, ready to join *any* activity?
- Who yawned and leaned back in his chair, feigning boredom and indifference to hide his true feelings and conceal his fear of appearing ignorant on geography, politics, etc.

a.

my handwriting in the

b.

for those guys along (a) bigger and I'm learning alot from all of them

c.

I found that with care I could just

7

Physical, Emotional, Intellectual

Life's Balancing Act— Handwriting Zones

Linda is busy climbing her way up the corporate ladder. Most evenings she's attending workshops or reading books on business strategy. But she's so immersed in the psychology of corporate gamesmanship that everyday matters tend to bottleneck at her desk. She's busy spinning new management strategy while current work is being neglected.

Jack, on the other hand, is a pragmatic, results-oriented guy. His contracting schedule is booked solid for weeks. He doesn't have time for management workshops and ''feedback'' from his staff. Imagine his surprise when he hears his top foreman is leaving to head his own firm, taking most of Jack's best men with him!

Even the Bible reminds us, ''There's a time to plant and a time to reap.'' But as Linda learned, when you're too busy planting there's never time to harvest your crops, and as Jack discovered, you've got to get off the tractor and sow a few seeds (inspiration, future growth) or soon you're plowing an empty field.

We all need *balance* in our lives—physical, emotional, and intellectual. When one aspect suffers at the expense of another, our lives become lopsided. Witness the workaholic who awakens one day to discover that his tiny children have grown into young adults.

Thinking, feeling, and acting are separate and necessary aspects of living. Hopefully, we have a balance of all three, but

I'm sure we've all encountered exaggerations in each category—
be it Mr. Intellectual, Ms. Congeniality, or Mr. Achievement.
How can we maintain a healthy balance and pinpoint areas where
we might be going overboard?

Zones

Handwriting itself is divided into three distinct zones, which
separate and illustrate the mental, social, and physical aspects
of personality. Below is an illustration of the word *boy* next to
a picture of a boy. Notice that each letter falls into one or more
of three zones—upper, middle and lower. Your writing and your
body can be divided this same way. (Here's a good example of
why I love this science so much. It's incredibly complex, yet *so
easy* to learn.)

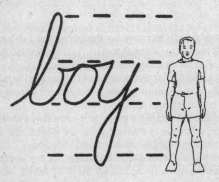

The upper zone corresponds to the head, the intellectual re-
gion of the body. The middle portion of the handwriting corresponds to the area of the body involved with social interaction.
You might visualize the boy shaking hands with another. The
lower zone relates to biological drives and the need for material
and sexual gratification.

Upper Zone—The Intellect

The time has come to tell
all you know about this
situation, to tell what
you learned from this

The upper portion of writing contains loops or extensions that correspond to the upper portion of the body—the head and all it contains. The more space the writer allocates to this zone, the more room he allows for activities of the mind. This is where we find broad- or narrow-mindedness!

I sometimes compare upper loops to cartoon "balloons" containing dialogue. The bigger the balloon, the more space to develop ideas. Your mind is a container for all realms of thought—philosophy, psychology, dreams, plans, hopes, ideas, ideals, religion—the *intangibles*. So let's call those upper-loop formations containers for our thoughts.

Upper Zone—Average Width

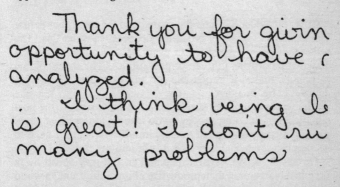

Thank you for givin
opportunity to have
analyzed.
I think being l
is great! I dont ru
many problems

An average upper zone is one that is neither too broad nor too narrow in relation to the rest of the writing. Upper and lower loops are compared to the letters in the middle zone (*a, c, e, i, m, n, o, r, s, u, v, w,* and *x*). In conventional script, an average middle zone letter is 3 mm. wide and 3 mm. high. So an average width would look something like this:

An average-width upper zone indicates resourcefulness and the ability to consider new ideas. The writer enjoys a good mental challenge or intellectual discussion and appreciates the imaginative powers of the mind that foster creative ideas and dreams.

Wide Upper Zone

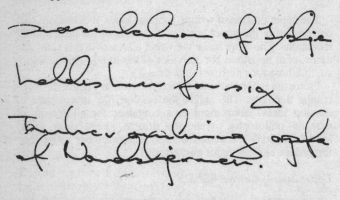

True, the wider the loop the more open the mind, but before you extoll the virtues of broad-mindedness, consider this: The writer can be *so* responsive to every new idea that comes his way that he drowns in a sea of possibilities. The sheer volume of options makes it impossible for him to be specific or specialized in his thinking.

The writer delights in stretching his mind to explore the possibilities, but in doing so may try to take on too much at once. He might pause a moment to ask himself, "What do I need to accomplish today and how will this fit into my plan?"

He has an active, fertile imagination, but may spend more time in daydreaming than productive effort, substituting a world of fantasy for a world of reality. He should try to harness and channel this energy. One ray of sunshine focused through a magnifying glass has more power than ten rays reflected off the broad surface of a pond.

Inflated Upper Loop

I have no problem with a blue background but I let the decorator

What began as a genuine thirst for knowledge has become exaggerated out of proportion. When the writer tries to include every idea in his storehouse of knowledge, he loses the ability to discriminate and be objective. A realistic approach to any new learning process requires selectivity. Graphologists believe that a bloated upper zone is actually a sign of "overcompensation for feelings of intellectual inferiority." In other words: bluff.

I once met a man with this handwriting trait who had studied all the great religions of the world—Buddhism, Taoism, Islam, Catholicism, Judaism. He professed to embrace and practice all religions, though many held tenets and beliefs that were diametrically opposed. When questioned about Krishna, Buddha, Jehovah's Witnesses, Mormons, the Torah, he could talk himself into circles of confusion with a contradiction at every turn. He equated selectivity with inflexible, biased judgment. Clear thinking, however, requires discernment and discrimination at some point.

Narrow Upper Zone

Well I finally made a big decision — I will be official retired as of June 30th. Boy do I feel brave! Part of my

The writer with a narrow upper zone is a selective learner— narrowing his viewpoint to opinions and sources that agree with his own. Undue skepticism or fear of the unfamiliar may lead him into patterns of rigid thinking and behavior. This limits his growth, creativity, and resourcefulness. He may be complacent or lazy in his learning, assuming most situations can be resolved with the same old answers or explanations, so why tax himself? Depending on education and experience, this may work for him, but no one is so wise that he can afford to put a lid on learning.

Retraced Upper Zone

A zone that is retraced inhibits and represses influence in that area. As my Aunt Mary B. from Oklahoma used to say, "His mind is so narrow, his ears are stuck together!" Perhaps the writer is closing himself off from ideas he finds painful or hard to accept.

This is why there are lots of lovely things, all of them placed within sight, and budget priced for

Do not make the mistake of equating a narrow zone with lack of mental ability. The writer simply may have chosen to direct his focus elsewhere. He may be more focused on productivity and accomplishment than on planning and conceptualizing. Also, once in a while, if we're on a mental vacation our handwriting can look like this.

Chronic retracing, however, does indicate a certain amount of rigidity and fear. Check to see that adolescent handwriting does not adopt this limited and unreceptive attitude.

Nicole, Joe, Michael, and Toni don't have any width at all in their upper zone. Does this mean they're narrow-minded? No, their writing style includes a combination of both printing and script, and needs to be judged in a category by itself. It's called "printscript."

Printscript Upper Zone

however, your thoughtful ideas
will be taken into consideration
and I'll do my best to put

Writing that eliminates loop formations altogether, or that incorporates printed forms in the body of the script, adheres to a philosophy that is rational, pragmatic, and get-to-the-point. Sure, they appreciate brain-storming sessions and think-tank enclaves, but only if they produce workable solutions and viable alternatives, not wild speculation and fanciful theories. They have pared down both their writing and their thinking to the essentials.

Thrusts into the Upper Zone

Sometimes stroke formations seem to "jump" into the upper zone. These connections are usually rhythmical and legible, not tangled. Again, this upward striving is evidence of mental activity and creative imagination. Often people who are brilliant and clever possess these formations.

Kenn:

I'll be around later and I
in the evening to say hello
life is going well I wish mo
But if things are not peac
I wish great changes sho

An illustrator and art director by trade, Kenn writes incisive copy, coordinates sound mixing, and supervises television commercial "shoots." His perception is razor sharp and he wrings more ideas from people watching than anyone I've ever met. He once combined his shrewd power of observation and penetrating wit to produce a hilarious article that compared dating to hunting—snake, rabbit, fox, etc. The fox hunter, for example, enjoyed the chase itself (flirting), never intending to take his prey home. Kenn's favorite was pheasant hunting, where man's best friend flushes out the prey, picks her up, and brings her to you. In other words, Kenn had a pal out working the room while Kenn remained cooly at the bar waiting for the girl to be delivered to him. Yes, his mind is working all the time. Joe and Michael have thrusts in their writing.

Upper Zone Height

In addition to being wide, average, or narrow, the upper zone can be tall or short. For simplicity's sake, let's maintain an average width while we explore the possibilities.

Tall Upper Zone

The taller the loops, the higher the person will reach to obtain knowledge. He will go to great heights to seek answers, whether through classes, private reading, or associating with those from whom he hopes to learn.

B. J. Stanton:

I am very happ
Ann. And I am a
to be here today in
my mother — we had

B.J. Stanton is an aerobics teacher and more. Whether leading classes on the *QEII* or working with private clients, she strives to achieve an integration of mind and body. She has studied counseling and has been asked to teach San Quentin inmates "A Course in Miracles," which she describes as a "spiritual path to inner peace." According to B.J., "Exercise alone is not enough. If you release stress from the body and not the mind, tension remains in the muscles. My goal is to make people more conscious and aware of the mind/body connection. Exercise," she affirms, "is a form of meditation."

Notice the reaching for new insights in the height of her upper zone. The letter *h* in particular reflects metaphysical and spiritual aspirations.

Short Upper Zone

If you think this makes sen
then go ahead with this p
or call me if you want t

The shorter the loops, the less the person will stretch to obtain this knowledge. Learning and growing may be part of the intellectual makeup, but the writer tries to satisfy his desires easily and simply. Yes, archaeology might interest him, but he would prefer to learn about it through an educational TV series or a book, rather than a trek across some desert wasteland.

Middle Zone

Although each zone plays its part in balancing the personality, you need to pay special attention to the middle zone, as this area demonstrates our actual behavior with people.

Thought and behavior are two very different things. I may say or do one thing while I'm thinking something entirely different. I may pretend to be interested in listening to your vacation plans while I'm actually worrying about a problem at work, or about Johnny's surgery tomorrow, or perhaps I'm indulging in a sexual fantasy. You may notice I'm distracted, but you won't know *what* is holding my attention. And how do you determine I'm preoccupied? By my outward behavior—vacant stare, fidgety movements, etc. My thoughts are not visible to others, but my *actions* sure are.

Actions, behavior, communication, social interaction, these things are revealed in the middle zone. Do you recall how word spacing demonstrated a desire to remain aloof or come closer to others? That behavior was located in the middle zones too. This is the area of people-to-people communication.

Just as the upper zone reflects future plans and dreams, the middle zone concentrates on the here and now, the present—where you spend the majority of your time. The middle zone reveals how you translate your ideas into tangible behavior. You may have grandiose plans, but can you put them into action? What we'll examine in the middle zone is self-confidence and self-assurance, as well as expansion and contraction in your writing—where you allow yourself to stretch, and where you bind and limit your growth.

Middle Zone Height and Width

As with all zones, the middle zone has height as well as width. The graphologist Leslie King observed that the height of the middle zone can be compared to "how tall you feel in a crowd or how much visibility you seek in public." In other words, it relates to a need for recognition. The width, she observed, is related to your self-assurance, your ability to accept yourself and be "open," relaxed, and at ease.

Middle Zone Average Height and Width

There is so much to tell
about but I hardly know
where to start. I'll hope

Writing with a middle zone that is balanced in height and width shows evidence of a healthy attitude about self, of an inner security, a willingness to share and communicate. This person can relate to people, places, and events in his environment, and appreciates the exchange and feedback that communication offers.

Expanded Middle Zone

> *my handwriting r*
> *to you the kind*
> *person to whom*
> *could open and*
> *I would be deligh*

This writer enjoys the day-to-day contact that communication brings, and he'll cast his net far and wide to include a variety of personal encounters and experiences. He likes to expand his sphere of influence and involvement and will make attempts to keep abreast of the latest happenings in his world. He likes to "be there," whether as a spectator or a participant.

Joe:

> *afternoon. I am appre*
> *of your comments both*
> *personal and professi*

True, Joe's A-slant leaves him viewing from the sidelines, but he loves people watching. As in a two-way mirror, you can't see in; but he hasn't missed a trick. When he does decide to reach out to you, he can be direct, warm, and instantly involved—no empty small talk. He has paid attention to what interests and moves you and tunes in on your wavelength. His mind isn't far off in the clouds somewhere, he's right here, right now and you have his full attention. He does enjoy expanding and reaching out to others; he simply needs to be in control of when and where.

Compressed Middle Zone

Dorothy:

> I am a photo journalist, have experienced
> Life and Love from infinity to the microcosmos
> — music is an important Spiritual vehicle as
> is the church to which I belong and the fellowship
> therein ...

This kind of writer may value interaction with others but at times feels himself holding back. This could stem from many sources—a fear of not being accepted, needing to be perfect, or a fear of intruding where he hasn't been invited. Or it could be a holdover from having been squelched or stifled in another business or social relationship. He loves being included in the party, but may sit out every dance—just waiting to be asked, afraid to take the initiative. He may withdraw or avoid committing himself in a social situation. This is a defense mechanism he has built up to protect himself against criticism. At times he may appear tense or retiring, as he tends to feel uneasy in unfamiliar situations.

Notice Dorothy's handwriting above. Her word spacing tells us that she wants to be close to others, yet inner tension, fear, and stubbornness (which we'll learn about soon) hold her back. I told Dorothy that she put a lot of restrictions, a lot of "shoulds" on herself. She smiled and said it was true, but that I didn't understand the many hardships she had endured in her life. In other words, *they* (outer circumstances) and not *she* were responsible for her behavior. Every time I told her she could change the situation, she interrupted to tell me that I didn't understand. I understood only too well. I myself bought all the "shoulds" and "don'ts" of Catholic school training until my middle zone looked like a closed accordion. I still have to remind myself to let it expand so I can "hear the music."

Large Middle Zone

> I am sixteen years
> old and going to be a
> senior in high school
> I was also wondering
> how you learned to
> do this or was there
> special classes you
> took to learn how

If the middle zone is large in relation to the rest of the writing, the writer embraces life and lives it to the fullest. He's usually up on the latest, whether restaurants, plays, politics, publishing, fashion, or gossip. He's aware, alert, and in touch with his environment. The drawback: He's so busy with the here and now that he tends to let tomorrow take care of itself. He may be overly concerned with the social at the expense of the intellectual. He must guard against becoming overly concerned with his own little world, overemphasizing things that are not of great importance in the grand scheme of things.

This type of writing indicates someone who is absorbed in the present rather than planning for the future, so it's often characteristic of adolescent girls whose whole world revolves around themselves. They are going through tremendous physical, psychological, and emotional changes, trying to cope with the world outside as their world of childhood crumbles around them. Where do I fit in? How am I supposed to act? I look funny. Everyone is watching me. Their major plans for the future may consist of what to wear—acceptable behavior for an adolescent, but not so rewarding for a woman in her forties.

I once had a friend whose sole mission in life was finding a husband. I included her in parties and social events to help her along. On one occasion, a group of singles had a series of symphony parties, with cocktails before each performance. I noticed her heading for the door after intermission. "Katie," I exclaimed, "where are you going? This is a fabulous performance." "Home." She sighed. "I didn't meet anyone at the cocktail party, and I didn't meet anyone at intermission. Those were my only two chances. Everyone goes home after the symphony anyway, so I may as well leave now." Talk about focused on the here and now! No man—therefore no fun!

Katie:

I just realized I never
wrote you to let you
know how impressed
I was with your party
The event was super.

"Gee," I can hear you say, "Nicole's writing has an emphasized middle zone and I thought she was pretty nifty!" Here's
where discernment comes in. Notice how Katie's writing
seems almost "curled" and self-contained, with lines doubling over
themselves, knotting, twisting, and retracing? Like a newborn
who can't see past his own fingers and toes, she's all wrapped
up in herself. Nicole, on the other hand, has a middle zone that
is expansive, clear, and uncluttered. Her writing is also a form
of printing (which we'll discuss soon). Yes, she's a bit too concerned with the here and now, but she makes each day exciting
and fun. She doesn't wallow in self-pity about the past or waste
energy fantasizing about the future. She doesn't wait for things
to happen, she *makes* them happen.

worth of estate jewe
Hope to see you th
The champagne bar, of e

Michael, too, has a middle zone that says, Don't tell me all
your grandiose plans, show me what you've done. I want to
enjoy life and live my dream, not talk about it.

proverbial juggler to keep several 'balls' in simultaneously.

Small Middle Zone

In relationships, whether personal or professional, this writer may tend to withdraw or underrate himself. His ego could use a little stroking from the outside world. He tends to succumb to feelings of inferiority or feel uncomfortable when placed in a social situation and expected to make small talk. He's most comfortable with those he already knows well and prefers to expand his social sphere quietly at his own pace. This is the person who may have put his Volkswagen image into a Porsche, but still can't let it go over 55 mph.

Note here (and I hope this doesn't sound sexist) that many male handwritings will have a dwarfed or compressed middle zone and an inflated upper or lower zone. You would never know to meet them that they feel inwardly ill at ease in social situations; there is too much bluff and smokescreen.

really have to admit a taste I just can't see myself women are just

Do not make the mistake of judging a small middle zone in an overall small script the same way. Both Bill and Monica have a small middle zone, but both have strong independent egos.

> *I checked patients in and out, set up surgery schedules, did medical transcriptions and occasionally translated for spanish speaking patients.*

When necessary, they can isolate themselves in their own little worlds to concentrate and get things done. Even D-slant Monica has tremendous capacity for concentration and control.

Vacillating Middle Zone

> *the several symbols are learned and, therefore easy to use — even a tyro in astrology with more sen*

When the letters in the middle zone jump from large to small back to large, the writer exhibits bursts of self-confidence and high self-esteem followed by moments of self-deprecation or doubt. There is no stabilized behavioral response in social situations. Often, outside events or people determine the writer's behavior, and he may vacillate from feeling accepted, to undervalued, to bluffing in an effort to hide fear of failure.

Lower Zone

Just as the middle zone depicts our present activity, the zone beneath it represents activity *below* this level of conscious awareness. Our biological drives and instinctual urges are housed here. The expressions ''head in the clouds'' and ''feet on the ground'' apply to handwriting as well. The lower zone is concrete and material, as opposed to spiritual or intangible. You can feel it, not just imagine it. Some compare the line on which we write to a horizon, separating the lofty heaven above from the rich, fertile earth below. Like a tree lowering its roots for life and support, our physical needs (food, sex, material desires) are answered here. Projects with visible, tangible, concrete results take root in the lower zone.

As the upper zone reflects plans and dreams to be realized in the future, and the middle zone registers activity in the present, the lower zone represents memory pictures from past events we draw upon for support.

The zones in handwriting have been likened to the levels of a home. The upper story (bedroom) is where we go to refresh and restore—to think, dream, rest, and retreat. The main floor of the house contains activity and interaction—talking, playing, learning by example—life in general. The basement is the underground room where we store things we have consciously forgotten. We reach down for these objects, memories, and lessons as we need them. The writer reaches down and back to encircle and enclose those experiences and ideas that are now behind him. Ideas he wishes to save. The lower loop contains a composite picture of past experience.

Another quick memory tip for lower zone study is what I call the three F's—Funds, Friends, and Fantasy. Remember, we're talking concrete, material results.

- *Funds*—survival needs, materialistic instincts, and a desire for the things that money can buy are revealed here.
- *Friends*—a need to be with people, perhaps not as much from a social aspect as from past needs for security and a feeling of belonging, also learning from past experience with others. The size of the ''circle of friends'' needed is depicted in this zone.
- *Fantasy*—by fantasy, I mean imagination. Not the upper zone thirst for new philosophy, but memory pictures from past events and an imagination that delights in producing tangible results. Inventors, engineers, and architects will often have an active lower zone.

In other words, by remembering the three *f*'s, you'll call to mind all the different aspects the lower zone encompasses—material desires, ties to the past, need to belong. The larger the loop, the more these needs will surface.

Lower Zone Length

The length of the loop indicates the length to which the person will go to achieve what he needs. Do you recall aerobics teacher B. J. Stanton stretching to gather new ideas as she pushed her upper zone higher and higher? The same criterion holds true in the lower zone. The further the person stretches downward, the further he is willing to reach, expand, and grow in this area.

Short Lower Zone

why they were showing I was wondering if yo my handwriting. Everyone says I have sloppy hand printing isn't very neat & any exercises I can do t writing?

When the writer makes no attempt to stretch the lower zone to greater lengths, we know he prefers to achieve the results he seeks with minimum exertion or inconvenience.

Depending on the form level of the writing, the writer may be independent, preferrig not to get too encumbered with all the instinctual and material drives of the lower zone.

Long Lower Zone

Those who possess a long lower zone often exhibit a restlessness and inability to sit still. Variety and change are important prerequisites for any project they undertake as they become easily bored with routine.

If you have a long lower zone and are desk-bound in your job, you'll find that your performance may improve if you work in concentrated spurts, get up, move around, and then return to your work. Have pictures on the wall so that you can escape mentally for a few moments even if you can't physically—this way you won't feel so trapped. I know of one extended-lower-zone employee, Frank, whose boss always found him at someone else's desk and misjudged him as goofing off. Frank craved variety and change, and was actually offering valuable tips to at least half a dozen other employees on how to do their projects more effectively. He had heavy pressure (energy and drive), close word spacing (people contact), a magnanimous and expansive middle zone (interpersonal communication), and a long lower zone (restless spirit).

This is an area ∆ *a. interested in.* ∆ *have always* ∩ *for the field of Psychology & relai* ∆ *hope to discover some traits about myself. Thanks for your*

When Frank was transferred to another department, all his creative ideas went with him. Productivity went down as well as the boss learned that Frank had been the general cheerleader of the group, actually checking up on others' progress. How did he ever get his own work done? He carried it with him! This never came out until months after the transfer, when he admitted, "I hate being cooped up in an office. It makes me restless and I can't concentrate. I work better on the go, thinking on my feet." Frank was moved back to his old department, allowed to resume his work style, and the boss gave him a pair of welcome-home roller skates! If only they had checked his handwriting at the start.

Here's something fun. Remember we said that the lower zone applies to the material aspects of life? Peek at your friend's lower zone before you accompany her shopping. Why? Lower-zone folks go to *great lengths* for what they want, be it the best bargain or the most unique item. They'll often frequent many merchants, buying their meat at one market, their vegetables at another. The short-looped writer would rather find everything at one shopping mall or do without. The long-looped writer will drag you across town and spend fifty cents in gas to save thirty-five cents on strawberries!

Below is a visual representation of what happens in the lower zone when you reach into your past. The pen "reaches down" into the depths of the subconscious (all those memory pictures from the past) to draw upon past events and experiences. The pen then forms a "container" for these ideas and brings them back to present reality (middle zone) to assist in living, working, and dealing with people.

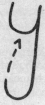

Incomplete Lower Zone

If the lower loop remains unfinished, the writer has failed to integrate past learning experience into present-day reality. In other words, he hasn't learned from his past mistakes and is likely to repeat them.

Kitty, a client with unfinished lower loops, had many unresolved learning experiences from her past. She was continually attracted to the same type of man—handsome, suave, sophisticated—and was forever getting burned. She would fantasize about these men, totally ignoring their true behavior. Her loops remained dangling in the sensual, material, physical lower zone without any grounding in reality. Her loops are "stuck" in the past (old behavior), never surfacing to the cold, hard light of day (the here and now of the middle zone).

If writing has unfinished lower-zone formations, the writer may remember past events with little effort, but will infuse them with his own interpretations and feelings. Things are always much better or much worse by his estimation than they were in reality. Rather than reviewing situations honestly, he views them through rose-colored glasses or filtered through layers of pessimism and resentment (the loop does not "let go" of the past). He thus reduces his ability to learn from past mistakes.

Have you ever met someone who's still reliving his great football save from '57? Someone bemoaning the refusal of a marriage proposal? Or talking about the ocean-front property he once could have had for nothing? These folks are still hanging onto yesterday. They need to integrate past situations into their present life as learning experiences.

Michael has formations like this, and there are probably a few mistakes in his life that he is still not looking at realistically. Note, however, that Michael's writing is a combination of printing and writing (something we'll get to later) with many letters in printed form, thus we would not judge his writing as harshly as we would writing that was totally cursive sytle with unfinished lower loops.

Weak Follow-through

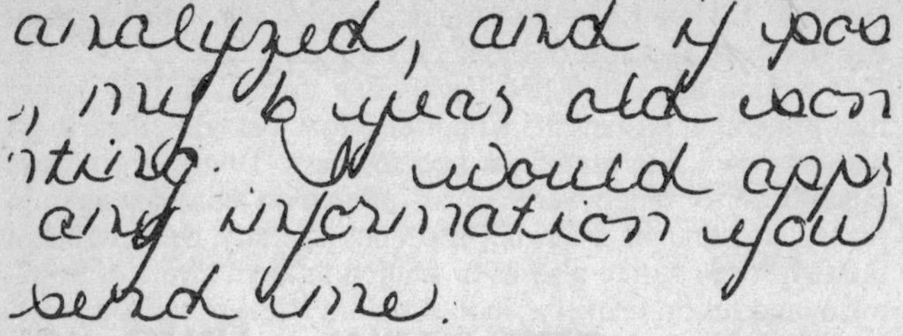

[handwritten sample]

Remember that the downstroke initiates action into the lower zone. The upstroke implies follow-through. This handwriting has strong initial determination, but weak follow-through.

Selective Lower Zone

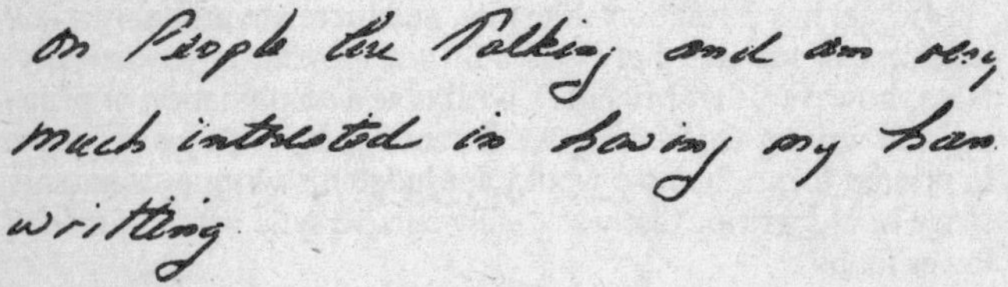

[handwritten sample]

When the loop is closed, but fails to return to the middle zone, the writer retains a memory picture, but fails to integrate it with present learning experiences. Although the writer can visualize and review past events, there's no guarantee that he'll transform his observations into practical applications for daily living. He may or may not integrate lessons he has learned. Selective by nature, he prefers to choose which circle of persons and events will influence him.

A selective lower loop that cuts off short of the baseline represents a person who has ''cut'' his circle of friends to a select few. The size of the loop represents the size of the group. Those with an average loop may always hang out with a certain crowd. Those with a very small lower loop might prefer to associate with only one or two good friends.

f training, acquiring knowledge towards

to have my handwriting analyzed and to learn more about Graphology Could you

You're not really surprised to learn that James has this in his writing, are you? His F-slant personality withdraws by nature, and his uneasiness in unfamiliar surroundings prompts him to seek out a special group he can feel comfortable with. We see here that the group is rather large, and could possibly consist of all high school seniors in general. After all, don't seniors know everything?

You can include this sam my handwriting in the

Lower Zone Width

In addition to various lengths, the lower zone can also adopt a variety of widths. We'll explore those next.

Average Lower Zone

Active and alive, the writer with this formation has the energy, drive, and inner resources to achieve what he sets out to do. He draws on past learning experiences to assist him with future success and he wants to see tangible results in projects and undertakings. He enjoys the physical aspects of living—work and recreation—as well as its material rewards—comfort and success. He wants to see, touch, and experience. He has the imagination and resourcefulness to produce concrete results and the spirit to pursue his goals.

I'm especially enjoying the memory of yester-

Narrow Lower Zone

I liked it, especially because very consistent; its ordinary t/particularly graceful.

This writer may be interested in a variety of topics, but when it comes to deciding and refining—experiences he allows himself, ideas that influence his actions—his selection is exclusive and restricted. Rarely will he deviate from familiar patterns and methods, feeling more comfortable and in control doing things his own way. He has chosen a select framework in which to operate.

Retraced Lower Zone

Thank you for a thoroughly delightful and enjoyable evening.

It's been proven that learning from mistakes can increase chances for future success. Still, this writer has a tendency to get locked into certain methods for problem solving. He limits his own resourcefulness when fear or insecurity prompts him to adopt the familiar, tried-and-true solutions. He'll then rely on limited resources and ideas to accomplish his goals. He has placed restrictions on his power of choice that can eventually kill his enthusiasm. he has some doubt with regard to his own performance and may adopt an authoritarian attitude as a defense—if no one is allowed to question, then no one can criticize. But this leaves him unable to receive positive feedback as well. (There may also be repression of past traumatic events, as well as unacknowledged sexual repression.)

Single Downstroke Lower Zone

This writer needs to balance time with family and friends with periods of solitude and privacy. He might sometimes prefer to see a movie, solve a problem, or take a minivacation all by himself. To him it is more important to be his own best friend than to be submerged in a whirlwind of casual acquaintances.

Please note that a single downstroke has a very different interpretation from a retraced one. The person who determines when and where to limit influence is self-directed and independent. The person who retraces takes great efforts to cover over, conceal, and close out the past—but it is still there.

Isn't it interesting that both our backhand-slant writers, Toni and James, prefer to be with a select group of friends (James) or alone (Toni) when given the choice? In Toni's case, which came first: the chicken or the egg? Does she find it difficult to warm up to others easily at first (slant) and thus decides it's safer and easier to remain alone? Or does she value her privacy and solitude to such an extent (lower zone) that she "pulls back" from people and situations until she's given them the once-over to determine if they're worth her time?

We'll have to study all aspects of her writing to get the total picture, and even at that we may never get to know the many layers of elusive Toni.

Large Lower Zone

If your lower zone looks something like this, so many things interest and arouse your imagination that you want to do it all. The result could be poor concentration, loss of objectivity, or dissipated energy. This formation is typical of a physical, sensual person who appreciates pleasure, enjoyment, and the things that money can buy. Because of all the energy he puts behind it, his active imagination can get carried away! He enjoys a variety of people from all walks of life and hates to limit his options on anything. He should focus on harnessing his energy reserves into productive endeavors, as he has enough inspiration and drive for three people.

is progressing nicely (the continue, and I con securing the national 1 for those guys along all bigger and. I'm learning a lot from all of them personal process is amazing when step back and look)

Well, look who's here. Busy, busy Connie. She's reading three books at once, teaching aerobics (physical), attending board meetings (active imagination creating tangible results), shopping, meeting new friends, and warming up to young and old alike. If anyone can melt ice-sculpture James, it will be Connie. Naturally her extra-long zone directed her to the travel industry, satisfying her desire for variety, change, and wanderlust. She takes at least two trips a year physically and takes dozens mentally.

Careful, though: Connie's loops are tangled, indicating a confusion of ideas and interests. She's trying to do thirty-six hours in a twenty-four-hour day—something's bound to suffer. Connie's writing looks like this all the time, but your own might look like this when you've taken on one project too many. Supermoms often go through this syndrome right before they throw in the towel. Before you get to this stage, you might want to research opportunities in job sharing or companies that have daycare centers. By the time your writing reaches the tangled stage, you usually can't see the forest for the trees and may make poor short-term decisions. Connie's disciplined baseline and margins tell us she has incorporated this whirlwind syndrome comfortably into her life-style and can juggle more options than the average person. Still, she could get more done if she would limit her options a bit.

Review

Our dinner companions are now deep in a discussion of Christmas shopping and presents.

1. Whose extravagant imagination and love of material things carried her to new heights of spending as she bought "a little something" for all of her many friends?

a.

second to baring one's soul at confession.
Alas, friendship withstanding, here's proof I'm

b.

accommodations were eleg

c.

is progressing nicely. We continue
and I can securing the national

2. Which gentleman declared, "I buy for my family and that's it?"

a.

Thank you for giving
so much time this

b.

my handwriting in the
shop exhibit. Its okay

c.

the largest body of water close to Den
wide and 20-23 miles long, and provid

3. Which woman stayed sensibly within her budget, stating, "I
always invest my IRA allowance the first of each year to earn
as much interest as possible. I've got to think of the future,
you know."

a.

The Art Deco Party

b.

ely (The continue to grow steadily
ring the national recognition
eg, of bigger and better projects.

c.

term goal then I would normally strive for,
but one with a lot of possibilities. What the

4. If you were given a three-day holiday, with whom would you
choose to see and do everything and why? (Each person
reading this may have a different answer.)

a.

accommodations were eleg

b.

great food and maybe even a to
shopping . and days of walking —

c.

As for me, I've been
a number of projects
much that I feel

8

The Face You Show the World

Your Signature

I know from experience that several people who pick up this book will immediately turn to this chapter first, under the misconception that the signature—your "trademark," so to speak—must reveal the "real you" because it is unlike anyone else's script. After all, we can sign our name ten or twenty times in a row, often in less than a minute, and every signature is similar. Who can match our fluid letter formations in that amount of time? Indeed, signatures are accepted as *legal representation* of who we are on checks, wills, licenses, contracts, etc., every day in countries all around the world. They must reveal our most unique selves, right? Not exactly.

A Common Fallacy: The Signature Represents the Total Personality

Were I to try and evaluate your personality from your signature alone, I would be getting only half the picture. After all, when you write a letter to someone, you do much more than sign your name. And a note left on your lover's pillow might say something entirely different from a birthday greeting to your brother.

The personal and spontaneous aspects of your writing reveal secrets about the private you. The signature, stylized and practiced, reflects the public you—the persona you wear for the outside world and the public personality you slip into as easily as

143

you glide into your signature. You don't, after all, greet the stranger at the bus stop the same way you greet your lover.

What's in a Name?

Although we may be unaware of how or when our handwriting style began to emerge, most of us can remember some time in our lives when we made a conscious effort to create a signature. It usually began during the teenage years, when we were trying to establish our own identity—when we practiced loops, swirls, underlining. We may have even copied letter formations from someone we admired.

Now here comes that old argument again: "But, Ann, I write just like my dad, so you're really analyzing *his* personality, not mine." Not so. You may have incorporated some of his patterns into your own personal style, but nonetheless you are still you and unlike any other. If you think your writing is identical to another's, try forging that person's signature sometime.

Remember when I said you could sign your name identically ten or twenty times in a row? Try it. Then trace a few of your signatures and lay them one over the other. You'll see that each is a *little* different—in size, expansion, length of lower loop, etc. (Even if they appear the same to the naked eye, I could show you how they're different.) Studies have shown that the chance of your writing your own signature the same way twice is one in three billion. In fact, one criterion for forgery detection is if all the signatures are *too* identical—indicating that they've been traced from a single original. And, considering that the possibility of your writing matching that of another person is one in sixty-eight trillion, do you see how unique your writing is?

Indeed, you've developed a "trademark" at some time in your life and probably practiced it until it felt right. Whether it's flamboyant or retiring, meticulous or illegible, it's a "face" you've chosen to wear for the world. Its position, style, size, etc., all scream the needs of your ego, of how you want others to see you.

Signature Placement

Obviously, if you're confined to a tiny space (postcard) you'll have less freedom to write your signature at its normal size. You'll really need a sample with two pages of writing to adequately determine signature placement.

Vertical Signature Placement

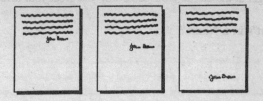

The body of writing may be likened to activity—people and circumstances in the outside world. A writer subconsciously chooses a distance that feels comfortable for him when he begins to position himself in the outside world. Whether he remains closely aligned to those around him or chooses a more independent role will be revealed in the position of his signature—where he chooses to place his trademark, to establish his identity.

What we're discussing here are behavior patterns a person has established for his *public image*, for his family, job, etc. Privately he may have very different wants and needs.

The more closely the signature is juxtaposed to the body of writing, the more the writer feels tied to his outside group or surroundings. The writer whose signature remains closely aligned to the body of writing might introduce himself to you at a party by saying, ''Hi, I'm with First Financial, my name is John Jones''—identifying his group association before he identifies himself as an individual.

When the signature begins to move away from the rest of the body of writing, the writer is indicating a desire for separation, for individuality apart from the world of involvement with family, office, clubs, etc. He's aware that participation must be balanced with privacy. Committed to neither dependence nor independence, he'll adapt according to circumstances. He may have visibility as an individual while working within the context of a group. Many leaders in business who are also ''team players'' have adopted this strategy. The farther removed the signature, the more individual recognition the person seeks.

If the separation is exaggerated, the writer may be trying too hard to avoid being submerged within the group identity. He is standing apart to say, ''Notice me as an individual.''

If the signature position varies a great deal, the writer is sensitive to outside conditions, and his reactions may vary with the situation at the moment.

Notice Me

> When was the last time you heard anyone say anything about high interest rates? True, they've wreaked havoc for borrowers. But for savers they've created a bonanza — the money-market fund, a low risk investment currently paying about 14 percent a year on money that may be withdrawn at any time.

Eydie Takahashi

I once worked with a young television producer, Eydie, whose signature was miles from her handwriting and extremely different in style. Her writing was open, responsive, and somewhat conventional. Her signature was very tall (high visibility) and extremely compressed (sacrifices for others). This was many years ago, and she happened to be Asian and female, which was considered a ''double minority'' at that time, giving her some advantage in job openings because of the pressure from the unions to hire minorities. Eydie was adamant that others recognize she had been hired on talent, not on minority status. Just as her signature demanded recognition on its own, so did she. When told her talents were indeed recognized, she countered that women and minorities have to work twice as hard. ''We've been given a chance, but it really isn't equal opportunity. They're just waiting for me to trip up. I can't let down my guard for a minute.'' I couldn't convince her otherwise.

Both vertical and horizontal placement reflect a need for self-expression. The vertical placement is concerned with the *image* of individuality—a desire for visibility and recognition. The horizontal placement takes direct *action* on these feelings—with the writer either sticking his neck out or playing by the rules. (Remember: The left carries connotations of conformity, while the right exhibits risk-taking behavior.) Eydie wanted visibility, all right, but how far out on a limb was she willing to go to get it?

Would she stay within a structured framework of rules and regulations, or break from routine and be a maverick working on
her own? We'll soon see.

Horizontal Signature Placement

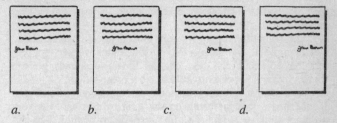

a.   *b.*   *c.*   *d.*

Just as with margins, left-tending formations indicate a desire
for safety, security, the known, the familiar.

Tradition, the past, and a sense of belonging are important to
people in this category. They tend to rely on the known, the
familiar, and might forgo a risk that would leave them out there
without a safety net.

Note: This criterion does not apply within the common business format wherein everything adopts a flush-left margin. We're
referring only to personal letters and correspondence.

If the signature zings way over to the right (sample *d*), extending beyond the handwriting itself, this person doesn't wait
for anyone or anything. He may be imprudent or impatient. But
he's also willing to stick his neck out and take responsibility for
his actions. Does this mean he refuses to cooperate with others?
Not at all, but he does expect each person to be judged on the
individual merits of his own work as it contributes to the group.
Most important, if he makes an error, he'll accept responsibility
and not bury the mistake in someone else's department.

A signature that moves somewhat toward the right (sample *c*)
adopts a balanced and adaptive position. Neither a coward nor
a risk-taker, the writer adopts the conventional signature placement taught in many schools. He does nothing to rock the boat
without good cause. His choice to accept responsibility or remain anonymous will vary as he appraises each situation and
reacts accordingly.

If the signature is centered (sample *b*), the writer positions
himself beneath the protective umbrella of the group. He won't
get wet when the rains of criticism come pouring down. These

folks avoid individual risk by utilizing the corporate "we." Shirley is standing there by herself when she tells the boss, "But *we* thought you said it was okay to use the petty cash for Chuck's going-away party." Even if it was her idea, somehow the group takes the rap. These people don't feel comfortable in a leadership role. When it comes to independence, their answer is "Yes and no."

If the signature remains safely tucked toward the left-hand side (sample *a*), the person may be a fabulous worker, but prefers that someone else take charge. If you've already got too many chiefs, this person would make a great Indian.

Guard against forcing your personal opinions on an analysis. I once had a student bring handwriting to me that was very ordinary-looking, with little ambition or determination. The signature was fairly close to the left-hand side of the page.

"Figure this one, Ann," my student demanded. "Alex works for the government, makes forty-thousand-plus a year, and is in a position of high seniority. He's lazy and admits it. He's bored in his job, but has no ambition to do anything else and has no intention of leaving 'Uncle Sugar' [Uncle Sam]. He doesn't have the aggressive writing or signature of a leader, yet he's a top manager. So how did he get there?" She had jumped to the conclusion that a leader should have a leader's handwriting. Many people rise to the top in an organization by virtue of seniority. Alex had been in his department seventeen years. He did what he was told to do and was promoted on a regular basis. I wouldn't classify him as a leader just because he held a management role.

Again, it's very important not to read more into handwriting than is there and also to remember that you can make a determination only about the current sample you are viewing. Don't fall into the trap of predicting future behavior from a present situation.

Amelia also had a signature that seemed "safe" and secure, not that of a risk-taker. Yet she plans to open her own jewelry store someday and has a five-year plan. She has worked in jewelry stores for the past ten years, learning the business and making her mistakes on someone else's time and money (safe and smart). Currently she works in a bank during the day (secure), saving every dime, and free-lances at home in the evening.

Amelia:

I have a five year plan that if I work as hard as I can and save as much money as I can - I will open a store in five years - I have been in Jewelry stores for 10 years And I have a lot of Jewelry experience in all different kinds of Jewelry.

During the day I work in a bank. During the night I work freelance at home.

Amelia Zeidman

When the time comes for her to take the plunge, I'm sure she will have calculated her odds for success, including contingencies for errors, emergencies, and seasonal shifts in the business. Her signature may move forward a bit as well, as she takes progressively higher risks.

Putting It Together

This may surprise you. As we saw on page 131, TV producer Eydie's writing was almost dead center, although it was scraping the bottom of the page. Yes, she desired high visibility, but she strove for it within the context of the group. She felt "different" enough as it was, an outsider by virtue of her ethnic origin. So she wanted support and encouragement from others. Running a successful business would have been a hollow victory without the recognition from others in her industry.

Contradictions in handwriting usually signal conflicts within the person as well. Many job seekers have come to me with highly individualized writing but with a signature that straddled the fence in the middle of the page. These people valued the security (benefits, paid vacation, steady paycheck) in working for an organization, yet desired independence too. They wanted freedom to work in their own department without interference from above. I had to remind them that they were playing with "above's" money and resources.

Vacillation

What if the signature is here today and there tomorrow? Obviously, the writer vacillates in his need for risk-taking versus security, for belonging versus independence. We might have to check other things in the writing to see why this is so.

Signature Size

Large

When a signature is larger than the rest of the writing, the person has a lot invested in the image he projects to the outside world. He hopes others see him as more confident and self-assured than he actually feels. He may resort to bluff in times when his self-image could use a little boost. Perhaps if he were more in touch with the positive, talented side of his personality, he could rely on inner strength and resources, ignoring outside criticism. (Of course, if your own signature looks like this, I wouldn't expect you to admit that any of this description is true—even to yourself.)

Small

When the signature is smaller than the rest of the writing, the writer may be too modest, underestimating himself or his abilities. Not one to actively seek the limelight, his talents and accomplishments often go unrecognized, even by him! Perhaps he's accepted a backseat role to someone else at sometime in his life, neglecting to take stock of how valuable he truly is. He would do well to accept praise and compliments, realizing that perhaps others can judge his talents and abilities with a more honest eye.

Depending on other aspects in the handwriting, a person who deliberately fashions a small and insignificant signature when the rest of the handwriting is bold and forceful may be deliberately calculating a façade of false modesty. Judge carefully whether this apparent modesty is genuine or fabricated.

Signature and Handwriting Similar Style

I've been really busy planning our 25th anniversary party.

Judy Houston

When the signature is congruent in size and style to the rest of the script; the writer exhibits the same personality in public as he does in private. There is little pretense or veneer, as he is comfortable with who he is and feels no need to create a façade for the benefit of others.

Signature Different Style from Handwriting

The children were nestled all snug in their beds while visions of sugarplums dance in their heads.

Beverly King

Some people have two different and distinct styles—one for their signature and one for the rest of their writing. Their writing appears to have been done by two different people. In a sense it was—the public person and the private one. (Consider the submissive, dutiful secretary who becomes a powerful, authoritative parent at home). The writer reveals himself slowly, preferring to adopt a different personality for his public image.

Illegible Signature

The writer of an illegible signature remains an enigma, and that's just fine with him. Close friends get to know the real person only after time and effort, and even then he keeps certain facets of himself secret. He wears a mask in public. He may fear being misunderstood or not accepted for who he is. By creating distance, he is able to control the acceptance or rejection.

Some will protest, "But I'm in such a rush." How long can it take to sign your name? How much longer would it take to sign it legibly? Three seconds? The illegible writer is showing a lack of interest or desire to communicate clearly. This inordinate need for self-protection inhibits effective communication. Have you ever become involved in one of those "but I thought that you thought that he said that I meant" situations? You may find yourself in a similar conversation with the illegible signer.

In fairness to those who sign their names many times a day (approval forms, stock certificates, medical prescriptions), these people will often develop a certain trademark for the sake of repetition and efficiency, so we need to make allowances. But it still inhibits communication and makes an easy target for the forger.

The forger? Many who advocate ambiguity assure me it's for protection. "No one can forge that!" they'll declare. On the contrary, one of the easiest signatures to forge is one that's illegible. This book doesn't concern itself with forgery, so without going into great detail on the subject, let me assure you that a busy bank teller comparing a scribble to a scribble will more often than not consider it authentic. After all, what is she supposed to look for? You haven't made it any easier. When a forger has to copy loops, strokes, and angles, specific lengths and widths, it's difficult. Tremor, hesitation, patching and retracing occur, giving him away.

Suppose I were to ask you to try and forge the following two signatures. Which one would you attempt first? Which one looks easier to execute?

Paul Mann

People reluctant to sign contracts or petitions may purposefully fashion an ambiguous signature, so that they can later deny it is theirs and thus not be held responsible.

Mr. Evasive:

Sincerely,

Peter was a master of "dodge and weave." He cleverly delegated his own work to others and successfully buried many of his mistakes in the shuffle of paperwork and other clients' budgets. A student of the Harvard Business School summer session, his résumé was carefully worded to imply that he was a graduate of their regular two-year program. He could talk smokescreens around clients when selling feasibility studies, product awareness, and expensive ad campaigns. You couldn't understand Peter any more than you could understand his signature, but his confident air of authority and the implication that he grasped things "beyond" you prompted clients to offer their support. Peter was highly intuitive and told clients what they wanted to hear instead of what he was really thinking. You could never get close enough to Peter to know what his feelings were.

The Spectrum

Suppose your name is John Jacob Brown. You could sign your name one of many ways.

John J. Brown

"John J. Brown" is the conventional form of signature and would indicate a personality that conforms to social customs, that does what is expected.

Don't forget, we're talking about the public persona. You may be an underground renegade, but to the public you're "Father Knows Best."

John Brown

Assuming that the person has a middle name, a simple "John Brown" would be more direct, outspoken, and less conventional. It shows a bit more individuality and a streak of courageous spirit. "I'm John Brown, take it or leave it," as opposed to resorting to the formalities of John J. Brown.

J. J. Brown

This writer is a get-to-the-point person. Concerned only with essentials, he is bored by lengthy discussions and elaborate explanations. Many high-energy, impatient executives have this in their writing. If you can't state something in a few sentences for them, then you haven't clarified your idea. Come back when you've reached a decision and have something to present.

People who sign in this manner often keep their true emotions and feelings under wraps. They don't like a fuss made over them and have a certain reserved shyness. (Check the size of the signature before you make a determination on this.)

J. Brown

Those who want to go along with the crowd or who desire to escape notice often sign with only one initial and last name. Petition signers or women wishing to avoid job discrimination may also adopt this style.

In 1924, Oklahoman J. Selby applied for and was accepted in the position of secretary/treasurer and later business manager of the Yale Medical School and Hospital in Chang Sha, China. Several years later, when it was time for Selby to return to the states, the president of Yale told his secretary to ask for a picture so they could put Selby in their Hall of Fame at his welcome-home party. The secretary quietly corrected him, "You mean 'her' picture, sir. J. Selby is a woman." "You mean to tell me a *woman* has been running our medical school?" he yelped. "Yes, sir, and according to the records, doing an excellent job." J. Selby achieved anonymity through her signature, applying for and winning many positions that might have been denied her had they known she was a woman.

J. Jacob Brown

Those who utilize the signature format above like to stand out from the crowd and are unlikely to underestimate their abilities. Individualistic, they have flair and style in the way they do things. It may be personal style or risk-taking on the job.

W. Foster Ferris Jr.

W. Foster Ferris, Jr., is a graphic designer who has done everything from marketing a cotton T-shirt in the dead of winter (and netting well over six figures) to designing and manufacturing children's games, packaging for Clairol, as well as theater costumes and sets. He personifies the individualistic, entrepreneurial spirit this signature typifies.

"Fos" was given his nickname by his parents. His father's name is William Foster Ferris, and they call him Bill. To avoid the confusion of two Bills in the household, they called Fos by his middle name. Well, then, you may protest that "this format wasn't his choice, it was his parents' doing." True. I've taken this into careful consideration in my research, and all I can tell you is, whether the person himself made the decision to adopt this style or whether it was somehow given to him, the results are the same. It's somewhat like stage mothers: Did their kids become stars because they were pushed, or because they wanted it themselves? Either way, they became stars.

John Jacob Brown

The person who writes every word of his name in full seems to naturally accept the limelight. Rarely will he shy away from public speaking, and he tends to make a good impression on others, which in turn bolsters his ego to accept new and more highly visible challenges.

John Brown

When the family name appears larger than the given name, the writer may rely on the family for support. This can occur for several reasons. Perhaps family ties are important to him. He appreciates the feeling of belonging to something greater than himself. There is something about strength in numbers, stability, background support, or even tradition that appeals to him. This can also be found in the writing of people who have been taken into or expected to continue the family business; they feel that their support lies therein.

Mary Brown

Often when a married woman depends on her husband for support, her signature adopts a pattern of having the last name stronger than the first. This support could be financial, social, or emotional. If a signature of this style belongs to a single woman, she may still rely on the family for some type of support. If not financial, perhaps emotional. Whether or not she lives at home is irrelevant.

John Brown

When the first name is emphasized, the writer has an inner feeling that he can survive and make it, even in the worst of times. He prefers not to rely on the family for support, deriving satisfaction and a sense of accomplishment from doing it himself. Not that he doesn't value teamwork, he simply realizes that a chain is only as strong as its weakest link and he prefers to rely on himself. He looks to his own inner resources for strength and support.

Mary Brown

A female whose first name is large and strong exhibits self-confidence and self-reliance, preferring not to accept help from the family either financially or socially. If the woman is living at home, she is still independent and standing on her own two feet. She probably has a job of her own and may be paying part of the rent. If married, the woman would not expect her husband to answer all her financial and social needs.

A woman who signs in this manner needs recognition as an individual and appreciation for her own accomplishments. She may belong to groups, clubs, or associations where she feels she can make a valuable contribution through her efforts.

Mary Smith Brown

A married woman whose maiden name is emphasized will usually check with her father or someone in her own family before making a major decision. I once saw a signature like this in the handwriting of a couple who had turned to handwriting to help dissolve a communication barrier. A few months prior, they had been in the process of buying a new home. The husband had researched several promising options, but when it came down to making the final decision, Fran always asked her father what he thought and would abide by his decision, often overriding her husband's judgment. This had happened in other areas as well, where Fran was reluctant to break her ties (which were both financial and emotional). In fact, Tom later learned that one of the reasons Fran had married him was that her father had approved of him!

Underscoring

Mary Edwards

Adele Kennelly

Hubert Alston

If the signature is underscored, this represents a further show of independence. The person is adding an extra "grounding" and strength to the self-image. The underscore will often have a certain flair or curve to it. The person may strive for recognition or achievement in a profession or endeavor he has chosen. Take care that the flair doesn't become too involved or decorative. The person would then be exhibiting an inordinate need to be seen as special and might pout, retreat, or bow his neck when he fails to receive the attention he feels he deserves.

Regressive Underscore

Charlotte Edwards

If the stroke pulls back toward the self or past, or if it vacillates back and forth, the person exhibits indecision with regard to personal independence. He wants it, or the underscore wouldn't be there, but perhaps he experienced unhappiness, doubt, or failure when he reached for it before. (If a single underscore, check to see if the person is left-handed, as this directional formation is more in keeping with the natural direction in which the hand moves.

Overscoring

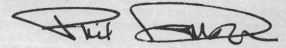

I once was in a television studio in San Francisco where Buster Crabbe was being interviewed about his role as Tarzan. He happened to have his adorable four-year-old grandson with him. When the host wanted to bring the little boy onstage, too, Mr. Crabbe became very protective and politely but firmly said, ''Please, no.'' He wanted the boy to have the privacy he deserved. When the taping was over, he swooped his grandson up in his big arms and planted a tender kiss on the little boy's forehead. Notice the protective umbrella stroke over the family name Crabbe? These shielding strokes symbolize just that—shelter and safekeeping.

Encased, Sheltered

A person wishing to hide his true identity from another will often ''hide'' behind a protective shell or shield. The signature above represents the writing of a man who would talk to you all day about himself, but never cross the line into discussing family affairs. He had been divorced long ago, and his former wife had not allowed him to see his son for years. There was great sheltering, hiding, and sensitivity to criticism with regard to the family picture.

Notice how Carol Burnett shelters and protects her family name. I'm certain it was extremely difficult for this brave lady to confront the *National Enquirer's* accusations of drinking and clear her family name. Her protective instincts led her to sacrifice personal privacy in attempting to shelter her family from further damage from the press.

Crossing Out

Sometimes whether a signature is clear or ambiguous, you'll find crossing out of one name or the other, indicating that the person is not happy with the image as it stands and would like to make a change.

Edouard is an intelligent, self-reliant young Frenchman I met while he was traveling around the United States in his quest to "see the world." Only twenty-one, he was wise beyond his years, possessing the poised and self-confident demeanor of one who has experienced a great deal of life. He returned to the States several times to work during summer breaks from business school. I admired his independence and adventuresome spirit, but his family viewed his peripatetic education as wasteful wanderlust. He was constantly compared to his older brother, an attorney—a man sensible and dependable. Although Edouard loved his family, he needed to negate their conforming, conventional influence, which he knew would stifle his real education.

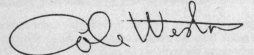

Cole Weston is a photographer, filmmaker, sailor, and world traveler. He is also the son of renowned photographer Edward Weston. Yet you can see by the size of his first name, as well as the cross-through of the last name, that Cole wants to be recognized on *his own* merits. His mother, he claims, wrote with flair, and he feels he got that quality from her. (We now know, of course, that any element you incorporate into your style, you incorporate into your personality.) Trained in theater, he became a photographic assistant to help his father, who had developed Parkinson's disease. He has always photographed in color, however, breaking from his father's traditional black and white. And his photos have a brilliance, depth, and energy of their own.

When the 1960s heralded the escalation of the Vietnam War, heavy drug dealing, and the hippie scene, Cole gathered his wife and five children onto a fifty-foot ketch to "escape to reality," as he called it, and headed for the South Seas. "I wanted to give my children a chance to enjoy life, learn about the sea and the rest of the world. We gave up everything, and I guess it appeared to others as if we were dropping out, but I felt we were dropping into the real world." Could his confident, self-reliant self-image have responded any other way?

Now that you have a general idea of the way a signature can speak to you, I hope you'll use your good judgment and instincts and not resort to go-by-the-book analyses. For example, many celebrities and others in the public eye sign with a large last name. Does this always mean a family dependency? I know one famous actress who has a friendly, open first name and a rather ostentatious last name. She is "herself" with her friends and has a public personality when she is performing. Interestingly enough, in one interview she gave recently, she said, "I would be *nothing* without my public. They made me what I am today. I value and appreciate their support." So her image, in fact, does have a certain emotional dependency linked with her source of outside support. Her stage name is different from her given name, which she uses for checks and legal documents. Her "real" name has the first and last names the same size. (Her name is withheld to protect her privacy).

Mary Private Person

Mary Actress

Conflicting Slants

Bear in mind that the signature is the personality we have chosen to wear in public; it is the body of the writing that tells us of the person's true inner nature.

across the country, and won't be seeing most of you for a while!

Hilary Allen

Hilary is gorgeous, vivacious, and wealthy. You name it, she has it. She is also intelligent, well read, articulate, warm, friendly, and a joy to be around. At parties, when she sweeps through the door she instantly has everyone basking in her warm glow of friendly energy. I once watched a shrewd realtor "work" her at a social gathering, describing a perfect investment—a small six-unit apartment complex on Russian Hill that he said was a "steal." Hilary said it sounded marvelous, and he thought he had her sold. "Like candy from a baby," I heard him whisper and wink to his partner.

He was in for quite a shock the next day as he took her for a tour, extolling the virtues of the lovely brick pathway, flower boxes, and brass hardware, while her A-slant logical personality remarked, "Cosmetics, cosmetics. What about the building? The electricity needs rewiring, the west end has settled a good six inches below the rest of the structure, tile is rising around several toilets, and the pipes are leaking in the first-floor garage." Whew! Our realtor had assumed that the responsive, impulsive exterior image (signature) bespoke what lay beneath. He learned his lesson.

* * *

Jennifer, a product of private schools and family wealth, is pulling away from a marriage that she feels is beneath her station in life. Her husband, a skilled physician, has turned to holistic medicine. He has abandoned the wealth commensurate with his former position, works two days a week in a free clinic, and spends many days on the road lecturing to clubs and corporations about preventative medicine. Jennifer worries about her children's college education and the loss of her former lifestyle. She's embarrassed to have rows of corn growing around the swimming pool. She and Tony are no longer on the same wavelength. In fact, she has filed for divorce. She berates (and negates) herself for having such poor judgment in choosing a marriage partner. No, you couldn't read this entire story from the handwriting—but you could discern that something is going on, and that she is pulling away.

Dinner Party Signatures

We'll rejoin our dinner companions later; I'm withholding their last names for the sake of privacy. But I can tell you this: Every one of them not only has a legible signature, but one consistent in style and size with his or her overall writing. This is one of the reasons they were chosen for the book. I knew they would allow you a glimpse into their real personalities. These people project to the world exactly who they are, faults and all. With Joe, James, Toni, or a few others, you're going to have to work to get to know them. But you're aware of that right up front (slant, spacing). At least you don't meet Mr. Congeniality in public, then have to deal with Mr. Aloof in private.

Review

Because we often have to base decisions on first impressions, let's see how we do from observing people's public behavior.

1. You need someone to mastermind the publicity and PR for your fundraiser. You have three willing participants. Who best understands the importance of good "exposure"?

a.

Laura O'Conner

b.

c.

Christine Williams

2. You're tired of playing the dating game, yet your best friend assures you that after the first date, you'll feel like you've known Johnny all your life. Johnny Who?

a.

b.

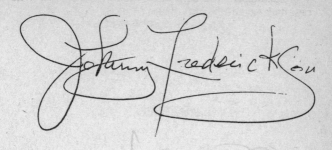

Johnny Fredsick Cou

c.

Johnny Cummings

3. You're hostess at a party that your friend's niece will be attending. You've been told she's painfully shy, so please help introduce her around. You forgot to ask her name, so you scan the guest list, then look for the name tag that says:

a.

Dianna Osborne

b.

Judy Montgomery

c.

Joan Corege

d.

Amy Black

e.

Bobbie James

f.

Laurie Martinson

4. You're about to sign papers for a business partnership. When problems arise, which partner will be the most willing to put his ego aside, sit down, and discuss things clearly?

a.

Carol Adams

b.

c.

Before we continue, I'd like you to try this exercise to test your judgment.

From surface exposure, how well do you feel you know our dinner companions? Do you think you could seat them in a compatible arrangement for dinner?

Below is a diagram of the dinner table with accompanying place cards. Feel free to seat our guests in any order you wish. There is no right or wrong answer; your table setup may be completely different from mine and that's fine. Remember, during cocktails our friends could move away from a boring or undesirable partner. At dinner, they're trapped. Also, there will be plenty of wine, which tends to loosen tongues and inhibitions.

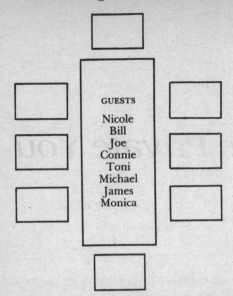

GUESTS

Nicole
Bill
Joe
Connie
Toni
Michael
James
Monica

"Why not a round table?" you may ask. Life doesn't always present the perfect solution. We usually have to do the best with what we're given.

Go ahead and try this exercise. It will help make this knowledge a part of you, so don't be a spectator.

Part Two

The Private You

9

How Does Your
Mind Work?

Are You Logical,
Intuitive, Analytical?

In the first part of this book, we approached handwriting much the same way we might first approach a person—from outward appearances. Does he eagerly lean forward or withdraw? Does she allow herself breathing room or tangle everything together?

Handwriting, like body language, is highly visible and strongly reflective of habits, patterns, and personal behavior. But what is it that makes one person respond while another holds back? What goes on *inside* the mind to trigger such behavior?

Seven-year-old Rita sits there with arms folded across her chest, refusing to get dressed, eat, or go to school. We can easily observe her outward behavior. But what motivated it? Perhaps she's a slow learner and fears looking foolish in front of everyone. She may have a stern teacher who rockets Rita's anxiety level whenever the teacher enters the room. Maybe she took Janie's cookies at lunch and Janie promised to return with her big brother today. And so on. What determines this behavior? What inner forces are at work?

In Part Two of this book, we're going to probe, prod, and put handwriting under the microscope. We're going to peel back that smile on the boss's face to see if it stems from genuine warmth or sarcastic humor at your naïveté. We're going to X-ray the mind to see what makes those little wheels turn, something you rarely if ever have the opportunity to do.

So set the handwriting in front of you. You can recognize if it's tense or relaxed, but look further. Examine the handwriting this time from the inside out. Take each word apart. Every letter, every curve has a life of its own. Even the tiny connections between the letters are important. Are they fluid? Awkward? Different every time?

Do you think the way you connect your letters bears any resemblance to your skill in connecting in other areas of your life? Connecting ideas? Connecting with people?

For the next two chapters, we're going to concentrate on how you form connections in your life, both intellectually and emotionally. At times you may connect on only one level, either intellectually or emotionally. You may admire Bert's grasp of complex chemistry formulas and his easy tutoring style, yet are immune to his romantic overtures. Or thoroughly enjoy someone's social company while strongly opposing his political beliefs. In fact, whether or not you even *attempt* to make connections in your writing is one indication of how you mentally connect and process information.

Let's examine for a moment how you do process information. While reading along, have you felt a need to reread certain sections, slowly and deliberately, to retain the material? Or perhaps felt bored by information that seemed obvious? Maybe you even wished you could have probed further in certain areas. Perhaps you made associations between the material here and people you know, or with other areas of study that fascinate you.

So how *do* you connect with information in your world? Are you the intuitive type who just "sees" an answer? Or are you the logical, analytical type who wants to write it down, recording findings as you go?

Connected Writing

Those who automatically connect their letters in a logical, systematic progression will usually connect their thoughts in the same manner. As children, we learned to write each letter separately. Only gradually did we connect these letters into words and finally ideas. Even once we had the basics of handwriting mastered, if we had to copy lessons from the blackboard, we did so in phrases, a few words at a time, or as much as we could comprehend and remember at once. Eventually, as writing became a mastered skill and our learning advanced—so that we developed continuity and fluency both in thought and handwriting—the teacher could express an idea without writing it down, and we could take notes "from memory."

Those who connect their writing in a fluid, logical, and systematic progression usually find it easy to connect ideas and arrive at a sound conclusion. Their reasoning is deductive from cause to effect, and their thinking style is more constructive than creative. When ideas can flow freely without interruption, this encourages good memory retention.

Because this pattern is more deliberate than creative, rarely will the writer impulsively embrace a new philosophy or theory that has no basis in sound constructive reasoning. Connected writers are good at slowing others down and "filling in the gaps" for them, particularly those who seem to operate on instinct or intuition and haven't stopped to consider the consequences. Don't expect the connected writer to jump at the chance to drive four hours to a ski resort on your hunch that there's going to be great snow. Better show him the weather reports to back up your claims.

Just as the writing moves along in an uninterrupted fashion, so too does the individual's mind appreciate tackling problems from start to finish. Don't have him completely packed for a Florida business trip before reminding him that they've had a cold rainy spell and did he bring a sweater, raincoat, and umbrella? Likewise, if you've given your employee the final copy and photos for the annual report, don't ask him to please squeeze in another eight paragraphs somewhere without fair warning.

"Sounds great!" said Wendy, in one of my classes. "I wish I had a drone who could ignore distractions and plow right through the workload." Perhaps not. If a writing appears *too* connected, in a monotonous, repetitious pattern (try writing "antidisestablishmentarianism" without pausing), the person may get so caught up in the doing that he misses the overall pattern of where he's going. I once witnessed this on a highway in Southern California. The man who was painting the line down the middle of the road became either mesmerized or so hypnotized by the rhythm of the dotted line that he let his machine veer off into the left lane. He wasn't looking at where he had been, just where he was at the moment.

Monotonous Rhythm

You might assume that those who have an uninterrupted flow would flow into personal connections with people just as easily. In some instances, this is true. But visualize a pattern of waves endlessly hitting the shore without interruption. The consistency comes from momentum and repetition, not through any power of choice. Connections that are reduced to machinelike consistency lock the writer into repetitive patterns. This blocks creativity. Sometimes, in interpersonal relationships, he fails to stop and take notice of what is going on *right now* so he continues into the future with old patterns from the past.

*Mary had a little lamb
fleece was white as s
everywhere that mary
lamb was sure to go. It
her to school one day*

Disconnected Writing

*The Art Deco Party
should be an absolute*

The disconnected writer has less need for attachment or continuity. He separates himself from routine patterns and predictable behavior just as he separates his letters. Unencumbered by connections, he creates a space where he can remain detached, accessible to surrounding stimuli without becoming tied down.

The openness in the writing leaves him more open to stimulation from his external environment. Rather than attempt a laborious, systematic approach to problem solving, he may rely on impressions or observations, assessing a situation quickly and formulating an answer on gut feeling. In these breaks between the letters, the flow of the pen (and the mind) is interrupted, allowing a flash of insight to enter and influence conscious thinking.

These people are usually very quick and may begin an idea orally, finish it in their mind, and move on to the next idea. Once the idea has been completed in their heads, they see no need to keep on talking about it.

I have a friend whose mother operates this way. Once while I was visiting Sandy at home, her mother asked for help with a party. She wanted us to get candlesticks and decorations out of storage in the garage, arrange them in a centerpiece on the table, and polish certain serving pieces. She knew exactly what she wanted, which pieces of silver polished, and had visualized the finished table in her head in the twinkling of an eye.

But here's what she said: "Girls, could you go out to the garage, third shelf over? Ann, honey, you can arrange those on the table while Sandy does the silver." Period. Those were our instructions. She said them as she was flying down the driveway to the store for some last-minute things. She was more than surprised when we didn't have everything finished as she had visualized upon her return.

Quick and intuitive, the disconnected writer often just "sees" an answer, inductively jumping from cause to effect. Socially, he may appear uncooperative. Why? His thoughts and ideas often leap without transition, but because *he* can see the continuity, he fails to elaborate further to establish a clear connection for the listener. He wishes that others would simply understand as he does, without having to go through the process of explaining everything.

These people sometimes appear disorganized, but they have an individuality that lends itself to inventive and imaginative thinking. How often have you found yourself struggling with a problem, only to see the answer in an intuitive flash when you took a break to let up and let go of it? (In other words, you created the "space" for new insight to enter.) You're in the shower or driving along in your car, and bingo, it just pops into your head.

Experts who study communication, perception, and thinking claim that, consciously, we learn through one sense at a time.

Sometimes we're so tuned in to what's happening across the room that we fail to hear what the person next to us is saying. Sometimes we're so absorbed in our feelings that we don't see what's going on around us and cross the street against a red light.

But subconsciously, all the five senses (sight, sound, taste, touch, and smell) *are* tuned in all the time, computing and storing information. That's why under hypnosis the gas station attendant can remember the license plate number of the holdup car. Although he doesn't consciously remember seeing it, it has been recorded and stored in the subconscious.

Experts explain this complex process through a familiar analogy. Imagine that the human brain resembles a television set that can pick up five different stations. One station transmits sound, another pictures, another aromas, the fourth touch, and the last taste. The conscious mind has only one screen, and continually switches from station to station, sometimes seeing, sometimes hearing, sometimes tasting. It's happening so fast that all senses seem to be consciously tuned in at once. In reality, only one sense is in command while the *subconscious* is busy absorbing and recording information on the other four channels. And we're not even aware of it.

Our conscious decisions are subtly affected by all the information our other stations are receiving. We consciously hear the politician's promise, but there may be something about his body language, voice inflection, or subconscious intent that doesn't feel right and we sense it. Many of our perceptions are unconscious, but they affect our conscious behavior. In other words, we know more than we think we know.

Call It Intuition

The intuitive person constantly has information streaming through these subconscious gaps and artfully draws from numerous sources for his reasoning. These are the people who can somehow sense the danger of an impending plane crash and change their reservations, or simply know when the phone rings that it's Aunt Mary.

You and a friend meet movie star Jason Wonderful at a party. You are entranced, your intuitive friend doesn't like him at all. "Why?" you'll ask, demanding logical facts to support his decision. "What did he do? What did he say to prompt this response?" "I can't put my finger on it," he replies, "but I just *know*. Call it a hunch, but there's something about him I don't trust.'' Your friend has instantly subcoded, rearranged, regrouped, and compiled all past messages he's ever received from friends and co-workers that spelled ''dishonest''—tone of voice, body language, shifting eyes, actual shift in body temperature signaling distrust, defensiveness, etc. He puts it all together from all his different sources (this happens in a matter of milliseconds) and he *just knows*. Here's the real clincher: He's usually right. Don't try to lie or be evasive with a disconnected writer. He can pick up on your deception before you've finished your sentence. He may not call you on it, but you've lost his trust.

All this happens on a subconscious level. The disconnected writer may have a hard time filtering out all this information. Sometimes he may feel too sensitive to his surroundings and may become moody or reclusive, in an attempt to withdraw. He needs to maintain a certain distance to be able to integrate all these messages into the bigger picture.

He operates from sensing and feeling, not reason and logic. He knows without understanding how he knows; and he thinks more in conceptual terms than in a systematic process.

Roger von Oech, founder of Creative Think, a company specializing in innovation and creativity in business, claims that ''Knute Rockne got the idea for his four-horsemen backfield shift while watching a burlesque chorus line''! And it's a well-documented fact that the man who invented Velcro first got the idea while trying to remove burrs from his hunting clothes. He spent seventeen years perfecting the product, but he had a hunch he was on to something.

As Agatha Christie's Hercule Poirot said when a clergyman collapsed in front of him after sipping a predinner drink, ''My logic tells me it's not murder, but my instincts keep tapping me on the shoulder.''

Logical Versus Intuitive

By now, most of us are familiar with the right brain/left brain theory of brain functioning. Neurosurgeon Roger W. Sperry won the 1981 Nobel Prize in Medicine and Psychology for proving his ''split-brain'' theory, and the late Dr. Norman Geschwind, a Harvard neurologist, made enormous strides in this area with his studies of stroke patients at Boston's Veteran's Administration Hospital.

This fascinating topic has been the subject of hundreds of

books and papers, and I could not begin to do it justice within the broad study of graphology we are attempting here. Briefly, these studies have found that logical, sequential brain patterning is housed in the left hemisphere of the brain, which governs the right side of the body, and intuitive, spatial functions are a product of the right hemisphere, which governs the left side of the body.

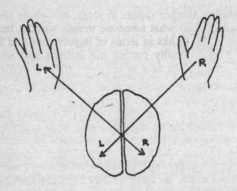

L	R
(governs right hand)	(governs left hand)
logical	intuitive
sequential	emotional
analytical	spontaneous
linear	playful
goal oriented	creative
	thinks in images

Studies have shown that more left-handers adopt printing than right-handers. I find it interesting, since the intuitive side of the brain governs the left hand.

I've often been told, "I'm naturally a lefty, but was forced to write with my right hand as a child. Does this make any difference?" It is believed that using the left hand may enhance right-brain functions, so these naturally intuitive folks may have been blocking their special creative skill for years.

Whether your friends are right- or left-handed, start paying closer attention to how they process information, how they think, then check to see how many intuitive gaps or spaces they have in their writing.

Logical thinkers rarely jump to conclusions. They rely on evidence when making a decision and are usually good at explaining things to others. When solving a problem, they'll systematically try different approaches until they find a solution. They often enjoy puzzles and word games because these are the types of activity where their minds are continually analyzing problems.

The intuitive thinker speaks in ideas, not whole sentences. He can understand what someone means without being able to explain it. He thinks in terms of impressions and feelings, and often has difficulty putting his feelings into words. He deals with a problem as a whole, sifts it through his experience, then puts it on the back burner, allowing the solution to rise to the top.

The intuitive person thinks in terms of visuals. Many common metaphors and visual analogies were created by intuitive people: half-baked ideas, the heart of the city, a landslide victory; "red tape," "seeing red," "blackmail," "green thumb."

Remember Bill and Nicole's unassembled bicycles? The logical thinker studies the diagram, lays out the pieces, and puts the bicycle together step by step. The intuitive thinker "knows" what a finished bike looks like, glances at the picture, and goes to work. He may have a few nuts and bolts left over, but he'll probably use them on another project or store them in the bike pouch and put them wherever they seem to fit when something starts to rattle.

Combination Connected/Disconnected

Most of us fall somewhere in between. We may follow our computer program step by step at work, then at home intuitively know whether Johnny needs a friendly ear or privacy when he closes himself in his room after school.

Jeanie:

> *This is turning out to be a most*
> *Exciting seminar. So very much*
> *opening up. Nan, in particular,*
> *is receiving a great deal — & as*
> *you said — "it's the people that*
> *are the amazing collective"*

Jeanie's writing (shown slightly reduced here) flows with rhythm and energy, breaking occasionally to dot an *i*, cross a *t*, or indulge in a creative flourish (figure-eight *g*). You know from her baseline and spacing that she has the ability to set goals and achieve them, allowing herself time and breathing room for planning and execution. But the energy in the lower zone (physical expressiveness and imagination) coupled with occasional breaks (see in the sample the words *seminar, much, particular, amazing*, etc.) tell us that Jeanie has a creative charm and spontaneity to her spirit.

As an employee, she would have the discipline and motivation to learn the required procedure, yet have the creative imagination to tailor each presentation to the client's needs. Her large middle zone and empathetic slant assist her in "reading" others. Thus her discipline combines with her flashes of intuitive insight to enable her to know when to ask for the sale, recognize disinterest or doubt, and handle each accordingly.

We may use logic and intuition together without even realizing it. How do you shop for a house, perhaps the largest financial investment you'll ever make? It should be a logical decision, right? But is it really?

Let's say I could find you a house in the perfect neighborhood with a good school system. A house convenient to shopping, a hospital, your choice of church, within your price range, and with a fantastic mortgage. Would you buy? Oops, forgot one thing—you can't stand the house. Oh, it's structurally sound, but it has no charm, is not your style, and no matter how much you fixed it up you know it would never feel like home. Logically, however, it has everything on your want list and is an incredible buy. H-m-m-m. Now, how do you really buy? Logically? Intuitively? A bit of both?

I know someone whose writing is totally connected throughout. He bought a house with a buddy because it made good financial sense to do so. He's done a nice job fixing it up, but could leave tomorrow and not look back. He lives there, but it really isn't "home" to him. He says he'll buy the home of his dreams when he finds the woman of his dreams to share it. I wonder if he's shopping for her emotionally or logically . . .

Printscript

"I understand everything you said about connected and disconnected," one student told me, "but I print. Does that mean anything special?" Many people who think they print actually have a combination of printing and writing often referred to as "printscript." Because they can feel the spaces and disconnections, it feels like printing to them.

Once when I asked Jim, a friend of mine, for a sample of his handwriting, he responded, "Well, sometimes I write, and sometimes I print. Which would you like?" I asked for both and here's what I got (again, slightly reduced).

> Many & I just returned from a great weekend in Seattle. We had won a trip for two (hotel & airfone

> MANY & I JUST returned from A GREAT weekend iN Seattle. We had won a trip for two (AIRFARE

Jim has been a firefighter for fourteen years and also happens to be a gourmet cook, author, and television personality in San

Francisco. His writing is open, responsive, rich, and sensual. I'm not surprised that someone who is both a firefighter and a chef is strongly ruled by physical responses and stimuli.

The writing also indicates that Jim is logical and able to respond in an emergency with rational judgment in a disciplined, organized manner. Look at Jim's printing, which he says he uses for directions, instructions, notes, grocery lists, etc. Shouldn't instructions be logically connected? Not necessarily. Printing and printscript are a means of abbreviating, of dispensing with nonessentials and cutting to the heart of the matter. With no frills, no unnecessary links, they are precise and to the point.

I had to chuckle, though, at all the connections in Jim's "printing." I asked him if I could accompany him on his weekly buying trip to Chinatown. Did we zip through the printed grocery list and head back to the firehouse kitchen? No. As we shopped, he gave me lots of little pointers about *why* I should use bok choy and *why* to ask the butcher to cut the chicken *this* way (filling the gaps in my knowledge about cooking, as he filled in the gaps in his printing). Oh, he's an intuitive chef all right, adding a pinch of this and a dash of that "to taste," but he has a logical reason why asparagus spears belong on pizza (the crisp vegetables add a nice counterbalance to the heavy pepperoni and rich tomato). He even places them in logical formation, like spokes in a wheel, providing guidelines for where to cut each slice!

Here's another example of printscript:

meaning to write to you
what you are doing &
ating.

When it comes to problem solving, the printscript writer has the unique facility of coupling logical reasoning with intuitive insight. Depending on the circumstances or problem at hand, he can either research and gather relevant facts to support a sound conclusion or simply zap an answer from his memory bank, reworking solutions applied to analogous problems. His agile, versatile mind can easily shift modes, adopting whichever method is appropriate.

Miss M.B.A.:

not familiar with wha
of services you offer, :

I once knew a highly intuitive and successful female M.B.A. in the banking industry who weakened her proposals in board meetings with declarations about having a "feeling" or "hunch" that a particular strategy would work. Her projects were immediately tossed on the "women's intuition" pile.

With a few shifts in strategy, her programs have obtained full company support and are saving the corporation thousands annually. "I haven't changed my thinking one bit," she confessed happily. "Now that I've taken your class, I merely package it differently. I still rely strongly on my intuition, but instead of acknowledging that it's a hunch, I'll state 'My rationale on this is such and such' and then I list the ideas as they come into my head, in no particular order of importance—just things as I see them. And a table full of executives nods and agrees. It's incredible. Half the time I don't even know what I'm going to say, but as long as I present my thoughts within a structured framework, they buy."

The lady in question, who prefers to remain anonymous, has an unbeaten track record and is highly perceptive in spotting trends and reading people. Please don't envision her as someone who speaks without thinking. She simply cannot always put her finger on *how* she knows—but she knows!

Mind Mapping

To help all those folks who may think like our lady mentioned above, one of the best aids I've run across for the intuitive thinker involves mind mapping, a method of recording thoughts and taking notes developed by Tony Buzan. Its structure allows organization of unrelated ideas.

Imagine for a moment that Nicole is planning her party. Sensual Nicole may plan her theme around a special dish, get a feeling for the atmosphere she wants to create, and only then decide whom she wants to invite, all the extras she'll need, etc. She jots down things as they pop into her head, and her list may look something like this:

beef stroganoff	get nails done	chafing dish
butcher	flowers	fix shade in hall
white rice	ring at jeweler's	polish silver
wild rice	candles	baby carrots
snow peas	rolls	toilet paper
shampoo rug?	Joe—vacation?	blue dress
invitations	salad greens	Joan?
silver pen	Toni—date?	pâté
soda/tonic	cocktail napkins	potluck?
lemons/limes	wine—ask Tom	Bill
dry cleaner	bourbon	

And isn't this the way most of us think? Utilizing a mind map, Nicole could allow her intuitive leaps full range without feeling disorganized or missing any important "connections."

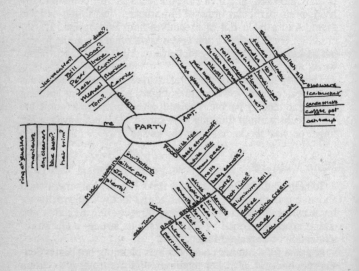

Sham Connections

You may find writing that appears connected but on closer examination turns out not to be. Connecting and doing things the "accepted" way are so important to this writer that he'll block and repress his natural spontaneity and intuition in an effort to preserve the status quo and not appear out of place.

Today at 1:00. I'll be presenting the use of methotrexate in RA. Although I did not prepare it as well as I should. I think I'll do fine on it since I had done some research on it before

The above sample belongs to a pharmacist who must go by the book in his work. Specific state and federal laws govern his behavior. It's interesting to note that when describing a presentation he must make, he states, "I did not prepare it as well as I *should*." He feels he must study and work hard for everything, yet he knows *instinctively* that he'll "do fine." Because he's "done some research on it before," he can now dip into his highly intuitive memory bank for answers.

As for blocking spontaneity: An only child, he was born in Hong Kong and came to the United States nine years ago. At one time he was going to move to Los Angeles to accept a fabulous career offer. His non-English-speaking parents told him he couldn't go, as they couldn't survive on their own without him. A tremendous sense of responsibility coupled with guilt may sustain his need to remain "connected."

Printing

Isn't disconnected writing printing? Yes and no. Printing can be an entire study in itself, and it's wise to know why the writer adopted this style. Many men tell me, "One of my grade-school teachers said she couldn't read my writing. So I started printing, and have used it ever since.''

Whether you learned to print in school, or at an architectural drafting table, or just adopted the style for legibility, it does reveal a preference for quick, intuitive thinking, an ability to appraise a situation quickly and formulate an answer on gut feeling. It also creates a certain amount of emotional isolation. But it's important to know why you chose printing, and why a particular style.

Designer Printing

ALL EXPOSED CONCRETE WALLS
WALLS TO BE PAINTED ~ SEE FIN

Many draftsmen, engineers, and architects use a type of "designer" printing. It conveys a feeling of artistic discipline or aesthetics and may or may not reveal the personality of the writer. (How does he scribble a phone message?)

Printing can also present a stylized façade, useful in achieving anonymity. Once I obtained a handwriting sample from a client that looked something like the first sample below. I requested further samples in one sitting, and the writing relaxed to something like the second sample. The inflated upper zone indicates a need for high visibility and attention (vanity), a trait the scriptor was able to hide in the emotionless, expressionless initial sample.

Sample 1:

I was very interested in your talk
last night on handwriting analysis.
I have always been curious about
why my sister writes like my mother

Sample 2:

This learned S from the shadow
of a tree that to and fro did

All Capital Letters

I HAVE   SEEN YOU   A NUMBE₁
ARE   TALKING ° & HAVE   REALLY
YOU   TALK ON   HANDWRITING ANALY
APPRECIATE   ANY   INFORMATION YOU HAV
TEACH   OR   COURSES BY OTHERS

The writer who chooses to print with all capital letters also is hiding many feelings. This middle-zone writing concentrates and focuses on immediate concerns. Although the writer may be intuitive and aware of others, he is primarily self-involved and isolated in communication. He can seem perceptive and insensitive at the same time.

Studies have often shown that printers feel isolated or lonely. Rather than admit this, they'll adopt an independent, aloof attitude, preferring to accomplish things on their own rather than trying to fit in with a group. Printing effectively hides many subtler aspects of personality and, for this reason, can be one of many signs of evasiveness.

Logic, Intuition, and More . . .

There are many ways to process information. In addition to utilizing logic and intuition, a person can be an investigative thinker and probe analytically, possessing keen comprehension, or gather facts slowly and cumulatively.

Cumulative Thinking

Remember Bill, our satellite tracker from the dinner party?

> when I needed every inch. Whe
> us there was nowhere to go and
>   then a fishing boat app
> line. He towed us all the way
> I waded out to his boat, arms

Even if I were to enlarge Bill's tiny writing to this closer-to-average size, how difficult would it be for you to trace over a line or two of his writing? Would you need to slow down and concentrate to keep all lines flowing in unbroken form? Bill's script follows a logical, sequential thought pattern, but something else is going on here. Can you also sense a feeling of stability and order as you trace over the many smooth, rounded structures?

In much the same way a caterpillar crawls along, inch by inch, Bill's writing slowly progresses letter by letter, in a cumulative pattern, across the page. Forms are carefully shaped and often retraced to add additional stability and strength. Notice as your eye moves along that the "legs" of the letters *m*, *n*, *w*, *h*, etc., are often retraced, rather than standing apart.

Cumulative n: *Open* n:

Cumulative writers are deliberate and thorough, often asking to have things repeated as they plod along, building a strong framework of facts on which to base their decisions. They take time to weigh things carefully, and the firmly rounded and well-structured strokes indicate that they have established a breadth of evidence to support their conclusions. They will not be hurried and may appear slow to others.

a deployment. Before he
our relationship seemed to
going alright. Something he
changed. I would like to

The cumulative writer may arrive at his conclusions a little later, but he'll have all the necessary facts to support his claims. One method of thinking is not superior to another. After all, slow and steady often wins the race (remember the tortoise and the hare?). Thomas Edison was a cumulative thinker and at one time held more patents for inventions than any other man in recorded history. The thousands of experiments he performed to achieve a working incandescent light bulb might well have sent the quick intuitive thinker down the road to look for easier and faster answers. And let us not forget the phonograph and the movie camera. Edison was also known to allow his intuition to surface. After spending several days in experimentation, he would often take a cat nap and awaken with the solution to a difficult problem.

Mary had a little lamb its

fleece was white as snow

and everywhere that Mary went

the lamb was sure to go

Thomas A. Edison

The Investigative, Exploratory Thinker

Earlier this summer, during
they were known as the Pi
Later, they spread panic in

You may notice certain triangular shapes in the writing that seem to form a series of points or wedges. The writing feels strong, aggressive, and energetic. This probing or pushing from the mundane midlevel of writing into the upper zone reflects a searching, questioning spirit that thirsts for deeper, more penetrating answers.

People with this type of writing are investigative, exploratory thinkers, constantly searching, questioning, and examining possibilities. The longer the wedge, the greater the desire to probe and explore. Much like the Doubting Thomas, who needed to prove it for himself, this writer takes nothing on blind faith and delights in uncovering new facts at every turn. Often this style of writing is found among trial lawyers, researchers, and proofreaders, as little escapes their scrutiny. Inventors and explorers often have these formations in their script. Fall and spring usually find the investigative thinkers signing up for another course in whatever happens to fascinate them at the moment.

Don't be offended when the angular writer questions your sources. He isn't necessarily challenging the veracity of your story. He simply finds it so fascinating that he wants to read all the little facts for himself. He may demand of you, "How do you know? Where did you hear that?" But he's just curious. Anyone reading this who has ever raised a "Twenty-Questions Kid" will know exactly what I mean.

Harry Murphy is a graphic designer who questions, probes, and breaks the rules. Long before flex time was considered as an alternative in the workplace, his staff was working ten-hour days, four days a week. Every week they had a three-day weekend, and he got more productivity out of them than most employers ever dream of. Look at his writing.

they were known as the P&s

"Challenge *everything*," exhorts Harry. "If you believe a chair has four legs, then you'll never get to design a Breuer chair." His first job, almost twenty years ago, involved transforming a client's headquarters into a memorable landmark. The nondescript building abutted the freeway and was crowned with a forty-foot concrete footing capped with a hideous water tower that was a paint-peeling eyesore.

Murphy ignored the obvious—the concrete footing—and instead painted the water tower in wild, dazzling geometric patterns. The project was finished in a week, came in $18,000 under budget, was covered by major TV and newspaper media, *and* it gave everyone a "fix" on the building's location. The client who allowed Murphy free rein was Don Fisher, founder of The Gap clothing stores, no slouch on innovation himself.

Notice that Harry's points and wedges not only push upward but also downward into the middle zone. Does that mean anything?

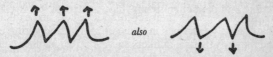

We know that the upper zone is concerned with intangibles, and the middle zone is concerned with reality. There are those who question and probe. Then there are those who question, probe, and analyze, analyze, analyze—bringing the problem home to roost (to the middle zone) while they sift through all the facts in search of the perfect solution.

The Analytical Writer

Envision a funnel. After all the information has been gathered, it must pass one final, "narrow" examination before it is accepted and acted upon.

The natural *v* base joining the strokes in this type of writing is often associated with investigative, exploratory thinking because the desire to investigate leads to analyzing. There are cumulative thinkers as well, who will sift through the broad base of facts they have gathered to formulate a more finalized and refined opinion for an end result. Many attorneys, scientists, researchers, as well as those involved in marketing studies, psychological profiles and evaluations, product development, and forecasting and predicting trends, have analytical "wedges" in their script.

Not only was Harry Murphy investigative, he was extremely analytical, and applied both methodologies when problem solving. Another one of his clients was a seamstress. She needed to convey her versatility and creativity on a shoestring budget. His solution involved designing stationery (letterhead, business cards, invoices, etc.) inexpensively printed in black and white, which Harry then had his client run through her sewing machine! The cards received a stitched line of memorable bright red, the stationery a cheery yellow, and the envelope a welcoming blue. His client could sit down in one evening and stitch up several dozen letterheads and envelopes. After all, sewing *was* her profession. The finished job was unique, creative, and custom tailored to his client. The solution had been analyzed to perfection!

Keen Comprehension

I see myself as a "Senser"
at do you think?
Please send me some

The longer and more incisive the points and wedges, the more penetrating and needle sharp is the person's intellect and understanding. Those whose handwriting resembles a farmer's pitchfork often instantly grasp the gist of the subject matter. Students who assimilate lessons without much study, or salesmen who can think on their feet, adjusting and pinpointing solutions instantly, often have this handwriting style.

Do not assume, however, that lightning comprehension equates with superior intelligence. These writers may be quick, but are not necessarily brilliant. In fact, the quick thinker may become complacent or smug in his world of instant answers and fail to develop his intellectual powers further. Also, many sharp people feel isolated from others, having little patience with those who are slower, and often resort to problem solving alone.

Which "Type" Am I?

When examining your own writing, you may feel that your script's a potpourri jack-of-all-trades. Actually, a variety of connections or formations indicates a certain versatility and, often, fluidity of thought. Do you put the same outfit on every day? Why should you confine your writing to the regimentation of one style? Most of us will have a dominant mode of processing information, but may skip along many different avenues on our way to the main road. On page 195 is the handwriting of a highly creative artist whose script houses a bit of everything, while supporting a deeply analytical substructure.

* * *

Architectural photographer and lighting designer Russell Mac Masters has it all—a logical fluidity of thought that shimmers with glints of intuition, coupled with the keen investigative instincts of a trial lawyer and the analytical skills of an IRS agent. His powerful, rich imagery has graced dozens of issues of *Architectural Digest*, *House and Garden*, *House Beautiful*, and similar publications for the last sixteen years.

So many artists' handwritings I see are vacillating and uninhibited that I was therefore amazed when I saw the structured, analytical undercurrent in Russell's script. "I'm primarily visual," he told me, "and very articulate in visual perception. In my work I'm looking for a delineated and *structured* design, for balance, and composition. Often what looks spontaneous is not. Even in nature, things that appear chaotic have an underlying structure and balance. Every composition that ever was is in nature. She can be chaotic on one hand and totally harmonious on the other. There is a thoughtfulness in design, a spontaneity that is the order of nature.

"I use my intuition, but I'm also very critical, to avoid the obvious. I have to be relentless and overlook nothing. I take into account the lamp cord squiggling across the floor, the seam in the wastebasket.

"Often, I'll manipulate the light to create a mood that doesn't really exist. I can create the visual effect that will evoke the emotional response. Photo-graphy means light writing. I write, I compose, I create with light. I see my work as creating subliminally charged environments, someplace where you feel good. You don't analyze it, *but I do*."

Russell's analytical perception and intuitive insight examine every angle, exhaust every possibility in an effort to achieve perfection. The reason you feel like Cleopatra in the bedroom or Princess Diana in the English garden is that he has carefully analyzed the sight, sound, taste, touch, and smell that rises from every surface. He can light a game room to evoke the aroma of pipes and country tweeds, or elicit heartbeats and furtive smiles from a sultry boudoir.

Russell Mac Masters:

I write just like but faster. — One of the things for me has alwa write anything on paper PHOTOGRAPHY made it

Review

We last left our friends discussing Christmas shopping. "Oh," sighs Toni, "I've got a dilemma worse than any Christmas gift. My boss wants me to come up with a unique and novel idea for showing homes during the holidays. You might think that many people make end-of-the-year purchases, but it's actually our slowest season."

1. Who responded, "How about a house tour complete with Christmas decorations? Intuitively, I know that people often respond as much to cozy feelings as they do to investment facts. A potential buyer in a warm and inviting home might just decide 'This is where I want to be next Christmas.' "

a.

company us as we snake our way to Portage Bay Oster Washington a great fun and I always will th

b.

Thank you for giving
so much time this
afternoon. I am appr

c.

wide and 20-23 miles long, and provid
for a 1000 miles in any direction. We
under cloudy skys and a light breeze
mork on the same side as our camps

2. "It's an interesting angle," muses Toni, "but who has time
for a house tour during Christmas?"
    Who links tours and crowds to fund-raising events and
intuitively responds: "Make it a fund-raising event for the
Children's Orphanage! Holidays kindle the spirit of giving.
Charge a nominal fee, have influential community leaders
serve refreshments, and you've got yourself an event."

a.

I found that with care I could just
to clear the land. Trouble way, the se
for careful sailing and we kept gettin
always towards the beach, and alway
when I needed every inch. When the
us, there was nowhere to go and only

b.

my hand writing in the
shop exhibit. Its okay
to have it and

c.

should be an absolute
Did you know our Isis

3. Which partygoer hopped on the bandwagon suggesting, ''If
it's successful you could repeat it. Perhaps a Valentine's dinner à deux with candlelight table settings. If you plan step
by step, you could showcase the versatility of your offerings
by including one contemporary home, one traditional, one
very large, one 'empty nester.' There are so many *details* to
consider.''

a.

As for me, I've been a
a number of projects
much that I fell

b.

I checked patients in and out, set up
surgery schedules, did medical transcriptions
and occasionally translated for spanish
speaking patients.

c.

accommodations were eleg

was fabulous. Tell Charlie

to the Monte Carlo of

10

Emotional Connections

Garland, Arcade, Angle, Thread

Up until now, we've been concerned with connecting with others *mentally*: Is he quick? Does he think like I do? Does she need a detailed explanation, or will she get it right away? Are they on my wavelength?

Naturally, we connect with others *emotionally* as well: He energizes me! She certainly is a cold fish. That guy is so mysterious.

Many times, of course, the mental and emotional overlap: Am I attracted to this man because I admire the way he thinks and solves problems in the board meeting? Or do I fabricate logical reasons why we should work together because we share a smoldering sexual undercurrent?

We've already examined what happens when a person opts for connections in his writing, or when he prefers to remain detached and works from instincts. Suppose he does wish to connect with others. What's his style? What type of ''bridges'' will he build?

Like people, some handwriting appears open and receptive, while other writing seems stiff and impenetrable. Still other handwriting can look so haphazard you don't know what to think. Much of your feeling about a handwriting stems from responding to its internal structure—how it's put together, how it works. Does it flow harmoniously or does it labor against itself? These inner configurations of handwriting can be categorized into four different styles, expressing how we behave and connect with others.

Garland:

Arcade:

Angle:

Thread:

These four structural shapes are found not only in the strokes that connect the letters together, but within the letter forms as well. You'll probably find it easier to recognize the formations *between* the letters first.

The Garland

An easy and flowing formation to make, the garland resembles an upturned palm—open, warm, inviting, and receptive to the outside world. Garlands remind me of an umbrella turned upside down, ready to catch every penny from heaven. The garland writer is as adaptable and flexible as the "ocean waves" found in his script. These people like to get along with others, avoid conflict, and are usually affable, friendly, and open. Warm and responsive, they react more quickly to feelings and emotions than to facts and figures. Don't stand there telling them how much you care. Give 'em a hug.

Garland writers like to keep the peace and will often compromise to avoid conflict. They might allow an overbearing husband or a stubborn child to win an argument, simply to put an end to the unpleasant atmosphere. In a club or organization, they'll usually agree with the consensus in an effort to preserve harmony, avoid confrontation, and safeguard their feeling of being part of the group. The garland writer sometimes sacrifices individuality for congeniality or safety.

Although he prefers peace and harmony, his need for security is of paramount importance, and he can become possessive or jealous when anything threatens his home, family, or safe, comfortable style of living.

Shallow Garlands

[handwriting sample]

The more shallow the garland, the more shallow the emotional connection. Those who employ a broad, flat stroke don't put much energy into adding depth to personal associations. This easygoing person is inclined to swing and stroll down the path of least resistance, perhaps more through weakness or laziness than through lack of genuine desire to connect with others.

Too Many Garlands

[handwriting sample]

Can you have too much of a good thing? Certainly. In some handwritings the free-flowing garland has been reduced to a mechanical repetition of an artificial form, such as the frozen smile on a beauty queen.

When the script screams "garland" at every junction, the writer is trying too hard to contrive an air of amiability. It seems more like calculated friendliness; an enemy may be greeted with the same warmth as an old friend. Herein lies a twofold danger: Not only will you be unable to "read" the person's true motives, but the writer hides from himself as well, suppressing any emotions counterproductive to his overall image of Mr. Congeniality. He may bury his personality so deep in sham sociability that he loses touch with what he really wants, needs, and feels.

Inflexible Garlands

Dear Ann,

Watched with fascination you fifteen minutes on "People Are Please send information about rates and appointment availabil

When the garlands become retraced, structured, or inflexible, a desire to get along with others has deteriorated to a need, along with an inability to express oneself openly. Perhaps these writers think rocking the boat would threaten their feeling of security, so they try extra hard to go along with anything and everything.

Games People Play

When I examine connective forms in handwriting, I often think of the children's game Red Rover. In playing Red Rover, one stands in front of a group of people whose arms are connected, and waits to be "called over." The easiest way to connect arms is in garland fashion, and indeed it does appear warm, receptive, and friendly.

Imagine what it would feel like if these people suddenly turned their arms upside down, forming arches. Do they appear as friendly and approachable? Might it require a bit more determination for them to maintain this posture? And how quickly could you be assimilated into their pattern if you were to "go over" to their game?

Arcade

The arcade resembles an arch, a strong structural support, which can shelter and protect. Those who easily adopt this formation in their writing are often by nature more guarded and protective.

The garland writer can be compared to a friendly puppy, open and responsive to all who come near. The arcade writer is more like the pup's mother. She stands watch over her brood, providing a buffer and shelter from above. I can open my hand to you, or I can put mine over yours to offer support and protection.

I'm still waiting + goodies from you. ... with only my junk

The arcade writer adopts a controlled approach, as he watches and deliberates. (The garland writer responds first and thinks later.) The arcade writer thinks before he speaks. Sometimes these people are even judged as being stuffy because social mores and customs may be important to them. They are concerned with "doing it right," with appearance and formality.

Because the writing turns inward toward the self (as opposed to being open to outside influences), the writer turns inward for answers and tends to be self-sufficient when solving problems. He is not easily swayed by others' opinions but prefers to examine things for himself.

The arcade writer is often original and innovative. Adaptation to this connective structure involves an enterprising nature with skillful eye-hand coordination and a shrewd sharp mind to match. His disciplined personality and need for structure allow him to concentrate on a goal and follow it through to completion.

Too Many Arcades

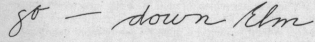

this is the way to go — down Elm to Walnut then right on Main.

An exaggeration of this formal, controlled demeanor would result in too much sheltering or resistance. An inordinate need for protection might reduce the writer to adopting hollow rhetoric. Since he is concerned with appearances, he tells people what they want to hear, and in the process throws a smokescreen over his communication, clouding his true feelings. Stylized or premeditated behavior can isolate the arcade writer from the human contact he may desperately need.

Garlands and arcades can be formed with smooth, rhythmic sweeps of the pen. An angle, however, requires an abrupt change in direction and therefore great discipline and control.

Angle

Steadfast, resolute, and firm, the angular writer is as strong-willed as his script, facing life's challenges with a determined spirit. Disinclined to yield, these folks are usually aggressive, hardworking, and competitive. They may be seen as rugged individuals and nonconformists.

Once his mind is made up, the angular writer is less likely to be influenced by others or deflected from his goal. Often these people do well in their own businesses where they can deal with people and things on their own terms. Despite a certain rigidity in their nature, they make excellent strategists, engineers, and researchers because they analyze from cause to effect, are tenacious, and welcome a challenge.

They may not be the easiest people to get along with. Picture yourself barefoot. Would you rather walk along ocean waves (garland)? Smooth sturdy cobblestones (arcades)? Or on the top of a picket fence (angles)? Ouch! You may encounter resistance to your ideas or projects when presenting them to an angular writer.

Remember the investigative, exploratory thinker? The one who took nothing on blind faith? Recall the angularity in the analytical script.

Exaggerated Angularity

Let's hurry and get there. I don't have alot of time to waste.

Naturally, any exaggeration would intensify these attributes. Excessively angular writing denotes a nature set in its ways, one that cannot easily adapt to new situations or sudden changes in routine. The writing is up and down; the judgment is black and white. The writer is more tense because of the rigidity in his nature. He is not always open and receptive to new ideas and may be skeptical, doubting others' motives. He can be stubborn, obdurate, obstinate, and as hard-edged as his script.

It's fascinating to me to see a certain angularity creep in the handwriting of the elderly. I'm not talking about the rigid neuromuscular contractions forced upon a hand by arthritis. There are some very fluid writers that have adopted a "hardening of the attitudes," refusing to learn a new way, stuck in the lost luster of the good old days. "Don't tell me about computers," they may complain. "You can't teach an old dog new tricks." And in their case, they may be right!

Our dinner companion Joe has many arcades and angles in his writing. We know from his A-slant that he maintains composure, but can still approach others with an affable and gracious manner.

Thank you for giving
so much time this
afternoon. I am appre
of your comments both

Yet his arcades bespeak a need to protect and shelter certain parts of himself from the outside world. The angular supports confirm that he'll tenaciously resist attempts to lift his curtain of privacy without his consent. Joe's rich, heavy pressure tells us that he experiences and feels deeply both physically and emotionally. His writing is also connected, so we know that he does want to connect on some level, and he has logically adopted a style that suits his needs. These sheltering arcades and strong-willed angular formations appear in the middle zone, affecting the area of interpersonal communication.

"I was shy, independent, and somewhat of an individual even as a kid," says Joe. "I do enjoy organizational activity, but I like to be the one to choose when and where I'll participate." When I shared with Joe that he had many protective structures in his writing, he was intrigued, bemused, and receptive all at once.

"There are parts of us that we simply cannot give away," he declared. "I know what's important to me, and in my experience, there aren't many people who are really interested in that. I know they say they are, but they prove something different by their actions. And yet, believe it or not, I find it easy to trust people. It simply takes them a long time to get to know me." He used the analogy of peeling one layer of an onion at a time.

"Getting to know someone is incremental, like daylight becoming darkness. You progress into another phase without being aware of it. It's a gradual and imperceptible experience. People want to enter your life and switch on the lights. Wham! Instant depth, insight, and understanding. I don't think that's possible. Nor do I want it.

"There's a private, cherished, vulnerable part of me that has an untold price. There's no sense giving it away. I'm not as comfortable in personal relationships as those who lay it on the line all at once. You know yourself, Ann, that some people are an easy read. They practically tell you what they're all about before you've had a chance to ask.''

Joe was a soldier in Vietnam and admits that his experiences there have influenced his behavior. ''You give yourself over to other people. You learn to love and accept love from people you might not normally choose to be with. Suddenly, they're gone. In a life-and-death situation, you learn to love very deeply very quickly. You become volatile, sensitive, vulnerable. Sometimes I guess I protect myself with a surrounding membrane. The pain is there, but it's cushioned.

''There's a depth and intensity to my soul that I may not be able to share,'' muses Joe. ''I do give love and total support to those who are special to me. The rest is not as easy to give. I'm not sure I even can.''

Joe's words bring to mind another couple. Don's arcaded writing is very much like Joe's, while Myrna's writing is almost the opposite, full of garlands.

Myrna:

Myrna is constantly giving and sharing herself with others. She says she wishes she could get Don to open up more. ''He knows everything about me,'' she says, ''but when I ask him what he's thinking or feeling I get vague answers that dance around my question. I can tell from his eyes when I'm losing him, when he goes inside and draws the curtains shut. What am I doing wrong? Why doesn't he trust me?''

What Myrna doesn't understand is that Don doesn't trust himself, beyond a certain point. It's not a question of selfishness or unwillingness to share. There is simply a private world within that comes complete with castle walls. Luckily, these folks usually allow others the same privacy and anonymity they require for themselves, knowing what a blessing it can be.

Remember, too, that arcades are one sign of resourcefulness in problem solving. Many artists travel to this deep and secret place within for inspiration.

Michael has been introduced as a bartender at our party; we know he's not only an environmental planner, he's earning a degree in sociology as well. Michael never looks at anything just on the surface. Like Joe, he conceptualizes and internalizes. "I'm interested in how people respond to their environment— to open spaces, to high-rise living. Does it affect how they feel about themselves? How they respond to others? Their creativity? Their communication? How much of our behavior is governed by internal choice, and how much by our environment?"

You'll notice that neither Joe nor Michael seems to have many loops in his writing. In our discussion of zones, we said that upper loops were containers for ideas. Yet both Joe and Michael conceptualize a great deal. Retracing of the loop formation or omission of loops indicates the writer has often chosen to circumvent emotional response and intellectualize his feelings.

A circular, garlanded, looped writing appears more responsive, more receptive. Those loops hold feelings and imagination. Those who favor feeling over fact will often have a "softer"-looking script. The angular writer has chosen to "think" rather than feel and will analyze and structure his responses into reactions that *make sense*.

Thread

Have you even been "struck" with an idea and raced to get it down on paper before you lost it? Did you even take a phone message in a hurry and your writing seemed to dash ahead of your hand? Attempting to keep up with our thoughts, we sometimes sacrifice form in our writing. The script becomes "strung out" like a piece of thread.

Those who hate to be tied down, who go for the broad overview of a project, often have "threaded" writing. They're more concerned with the end result than with how to get there. They can skim along and take in what they need, ignoring the rest. That may sound like an advantage. However, under pressure, those with a sinuous script may miss something important—particularly if they're too quick and operate beyond their optimum capacity. You know the old saying: After learning the tricks of the trade, many of us think we know the trade.

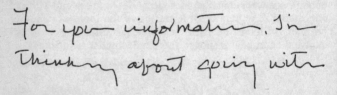

Writers whose word endings tend to evaporate or deteriorate are usually in a rush. Often they're doing one thing while their minds are occupied elsewhere. They may read a book or newspaper while eating a meal (why waste time?) and it's almost certain they've received a speeding ticket or two, as their mind raced beyond the mundane, losing all track of the speedometer.

Just as water takes on the shape of the vessel into which it is poured, threaded writing changes its course at whim. The threaded writer doesn't like to be pinned down or committed to a particular course of action. Flexible and adaptable, he is receptive to outside influences. This sensitivity equips him with certain intuitive insight, enabling him to slide in, assess a situation, and move on. His responsive nature can almost catch the thoughts of another, while he himself remains unfathomable and enigmatic.

Many diplomats, psychologists, and even crooks and swindlers have this in their script. Didn't Brad say he loved me? Or was the answer more accurately, "Honey, you know how I feel about you."

Volatile and unpredictable, the threaded writer can be creative and original or inconsistent and indecisive. You'll need to assess this trait in combination with other aspects of the writing to determine if the quality is positive or negative.

At its best, the writer possesses an intuitive mind and may, like Albert Einstein, be able to grasp the vision of the universe as a whole as his mind skims along, comprehending the big picture.

Albert Einstein:

But didn't we say that disconnected writing is a sign of intuition? True, printscript allows for flashes of intuitive insight to break through. Threaded writing also has high flexibility and adaptability. Unbound by constrictive arcades and angles, or confined to compliant curves, it can streak at whim to any appointed destination or goal. It can assume the formation it needs for the immediate job at hand.

Like the right-hemisphered, intuitive thinker we met earlier, the threaded writer may think in terms of form, having difficulty saying what he is thinking. Einstein said, "Language can limit perception." In the process of discovering the theory of relativity, he envisioned himself "riding on a ray of light." He also said, "Imagination is more important than knowledge. For knowledge is *limited*, whereas imagination embraces the entire world, stimulating progress and giving birth to evolution." I'm not surprised he chose an unrestricted form of handwriting.

Naturally, any exaggeration has its down side. At his worst, the threaded writer is indecisive, evasive, impressionable, and confused. He may hide behind a veneer of pseudo adaptability while failing to communicate on any level.

write something & get together soon.

Before we rejoin our dinner guests, let's take a look at one well-known figure who is a master of diplomacy.

Henry Kissinger:

The heavy pressure suggests the endurance, energy, and drive of a productive personality. The well-formed thread coupled with numerous points and wedges bespeaks the mental alertness of a determined negotiator who takes nothing on blind faith. His ability intuitively to read another while enigmatic himself gives him an edge in rhetorical discourse.

The size of the last name in relation to the first indicates an identification with family heritage and tradition, and that he wants his family to hold him in high regard. Note, too, the loop of creative imagination he has incorporated into the depiction of his self-image. His slant denotes an objectivity in judgment, tempered with a certain degree of compassion. The threaded central core in the writing attests to the fact that he can be impatient with delay or excuses; but this is counterbalanced by other aspects that confirm he is attentive to details.

The singularity of the lower loops reveals a need and desire for isolation and solitude. This, coupled with the thread, indicates that he is a private person. He may be a diplomat, but he relies on his own strength and judgment when executing his tasks.

Obviously, this is a brief description, but it is apparent that there is more to Mr. Kissinger than meets the eye. I have tried to avoid any well-known figures in this book for fear that people will "color" their analyses with preconceived notions and feelings about the person, instead of concentrating on the script itself. The reason I include this sample is that this type of writing, particularly when found in the signature, often evokes the response, ''I can't do anything with that. There's nothing there.'' *Au contraire*.

Common Questions

I have a German friend whose writing is quite angular. She claims that's how she was taught in school. Doesn't training have some influence on the way we write?

We've learned through the study of graphology that our mind, moods, and emotions direct the pen regardless of background. However, it is important to know of a person's original training, not so much because of the final influence it can have, but for the changes and alterations he has made in the master patterns he was taught. We may all have learned a garlanded handwriting style, yet some of us chose to deviate to angles, arcades, or thread. One connotation of continued use of garland would be conformity and adherence to the known, the familiar, the safe.

If a person learned a more angular type of script in school, and has maintained that format, the connotation would also be one of conformity and going by the rules. Could this angularity program the personality to be analytical, strong-willed, or determined in nature? It's possible. Programming the personality through handwriting is called *graphotherapy*, and we'll discuss it at the end of the book.

Here are some common alphabets taught in the United States. Can you spot any instances where your writing has altered, changed, or strayed from what you were taught?

Spencerian:

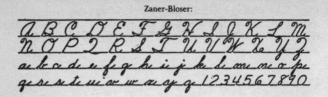

Zaner-Bloser:

Palmer:

Change in Personality/Change in Handwriting

While caring for her elderly father, Joan came across some of her schoolwork that he had saved for over forty years. Notice the almost perfect copybook script with garland connections. Joan still maintains those garland connections, conforming to society's demands in a reliable, dependable manner. She feels it's her duty and responsibility to take care of her aging father and has made many trips across the United States to do so.

Her singular lower loops reveal a desire for more privacy and time to herself. Notice, too, that her once-rounded *m*'s and *n*'s from childhood are now angular. Joan thoroughly researched nursing homes and health-care resources as she lovingly (garland) assisted her father in the difficult transition from private home to nursing facility. Joan's writing is basically receptive garland, but she has some hardworking self-sufficient angles and protective arcades as well.

Joan, 1946:

For amber waves of grain,

Joan, 1986:

when cleaning out my

Combinations

Rarely will you find a handwriting that is entirely garlands, arcades, angles, or thread. Even Kissinger's writing had angles and arcades. Most of our writings contain a combination of formations, just as our personalities contain myriad responses to people, places, and events.

Garland with Angle

Seven and found it interesting and inform

The garland will take the critical edge off the angle, allowing it to be supportive but responsive.

Angle with Thread

Angle with Thread

The decisive angle can add determination to the easygoing thread. This can be a fabulous combination, as the angle prods the keen perception of the threaded writer on to greater things.

Arcade with Angle

Thank you for giving so much time this afternoon. I am appre

As we learned from Joe, the secluded arcade backed by the aggressive angle can stifle social interaction or understanding.

The combinations are endless, and we'll run across a few more in our dinner party. But before we return to our merry friends, let's look at one more thing.

Lack of Connections

You may have noticed that neither Toni's nor Nicole's writing has any connections. The handwriting looks like printing or a form of printscript. So how can we determine how they'll connect with others emotionally?

The writing slant, depth of pressure, overall size, as well as word and letter spacing, will reveal volumes about how they approach their environment and the people in it. Rather than connecting with others at first, they allow themselves some viewing distance, just as they have in their handwriting, taking in the overall picture on many levels.

As with our television-screen analogy, they can listen to one person while picking up clues from across the room. They are neither too susceptible (garlands), missing important clues, nor do they adopt a guarded (arcade) or defiant (angular) approach. Instead, they create a space where they remain available to all surrounding stimuli and input. They absorb messages from all corners of the room and connect when, where, and how they wish.

Notice also that many of Nicole's *r*'s create arcade formations while her *m*, *n*, and *h* formations bespeak a probing intellect. Some of Toni's writing seems threadlike. This could add further definition to her intuitive cast of mind. But the thread is weak and deteriorating and, coupled with a weak pressure pattern, would succumb more easily to a feeling of, Why try? How will all of these connecting patterns affect our dinner party?

Back to the Party

In an earlier review, we learned of a small kitchen fire. The flames have now subsided, everything is back to normal, and Nicole has arranged a beautiful buffet.

This small panic has actually taken any nervous edge off the gathering, as our friends feel less like strangers. Everyone's experienced a sense of excitement, as well as the accompanying relief when it's all over.

They now relax, have another drink, chuckle, and as they move in to dinner they begin to relate similar experiences they've found themselves in.

Toni quickly takes Nicole aside and whispers, "Don't you think we should open a few more windows or light some more candles to clear out this smoke?" "Relax," says Nicole, "we'll be fine."

"But honey, things look so lovely, I just want people to remember this as a *nice* party." Toni sighs. "Trust me," reassures Nicole. "This group is more interested in a good time than a little smoke." Nicole had quickly assessed that this glitch was a blessing in disguise to break the ice for strangers.

Toni:

If Nicole's intuition can pick up on other people's comfort level, why can't Toni? After all, she has intuitive breaks in her script, doesn't she? Check her slant. Toni is first and foremost involved in a world of her own and worried about how people may be judging her. If this were her party, that's what she'd be focused on. She's sometimes too preoccupied with her own self-image to pick up on the responses of others. In this case, her strong backhand slant overshadowed her ability to communicate with them. She is too busy protecting herself, whereas Nicole's levelheaded slant doesn't get in the way.

Because of the size of Nicole's handwriting, she will by nature do a quick once-over and let her intuition take it from there. (At other times, her magnanimity can cause Nicole to overlook things she doesn't want to see. She can still misjudge or get used by people when she ignores that little bell ringing in her head.)

Nicole:

The Art Deco Party on

Although blessed with intuition, Toni doesn't take command of the presence she creates (resourceful, polished, professional). Rarely does she join forces on a new venture (word spacing) nor does she have the emotional energy (pressure) to sustain interest for long. In judging Toni's intuitive breaks, you have to consider that they also symbolize lack of connections with others on a one-to-one basis. Well, then, what about Nicole? She connects from the top down anyway—as a leader—so she has an advantage over Toni in this area.

Nicole's table:

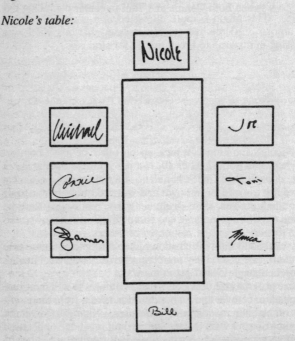

Surprised by the seating arrangements? This is only one solution that came to mind, and I might have arranged things differently had I been in a different mood. Your table may be quite different and that's fine. There is no right or wrong answer.

You may have noticed that people are not spaced evenly by sex—boy/girl/boy/girl. You should know enough about Nicole's confident, decisive script by now to surmise that she's not bound by convention. She'll seat interesting people next to interesting people, regardless of sex. Also, her rich pressure tell us that she's sensually responsive and might enjoy having her man at the other end of the table to provide that special give-and-take male-female energy and sexual undercurrent. With host and hostess anchoring either end of the table, the male-female pattern is broken.

Besides—and Nicole's not even consciously aware of it—this is *her* party and *her* night. Why should she put another woman opposite her in the remaining position of power?

She has seated both Connie and Toni in center positions, but for entirely different reasons.

This central location can be tricky. Have you ever found yourself listening to people on both sides of you engaged in conversation with others while you sat alone? You have more control in a corner chair. Even if the person at the end of the table is engaged in conversation with another, you can easily listen or join in by virtue of your location, making it a threesome. Or you can turn to the person on your other side and initiate a repartee. When you're "stuck" in the middle, you may suddenly find yourself closed out. No problem for Connie, she'll join in a conversation across the table if necessary.

But why would Nicole do this to already shy Toni? Toni is grateful, actually, to be able to sit and observe everyone else and engage in pleasantries on either side of her as the need arises. She's more comfortable here than in a busy corner spot. Besides Connie, directly across from Toni, can come to the rescue if needed.

But what about James? Shouldn't Nicole keep him by her side and entertained, since his reticent attitude won't add much? Enough is enough. She's invited him, but he's not going to monopolize her evening. Let Connie pull hen's teeth in attempting conversation. Connie could converse with a cadaver, so she won't be put off by James's indifference. Besides, Bill promised Nicole he'd talk to James about biking and sailing.

Poor Monica, she was hoping to sit closer to Joe, in hopes of discussing her shopping and design service for his television program. Monica should be thankful for Nicole's keen intuition. Nicole knows that Joe operates best when he's intrigued and curious, when he has to probe for more. She knows that Monica's exuberant nature might give away too much too soon, killing Joe's enthusiasm for the project. Nicole wants them to meet tonight, but negotiate later. Also, Bill and Monica are both detail-oriented people and could enjoy discussing the tiny particulars on almost any subject.

Nicole is intrigued with Joe. She loves the way he approaches others quietly from a distance, making them feel safe and comfortable, as he did with Toni in the kitchen earlier. Yet she senses there's a side no one ever sees. She subtly flirts with him throughout dinner.

She'd kept Michael on her right to unobtrusively feed him information about the others and to allow him to quietly observe the group to gather information for a paper he's writing. With active Connie on one side and Nicole on the other, Michael can remain apart, free to observe and record his observations about human behavior.

In all fairness, Nicole isn't allowing Michael to use her friends as guinea pigs. When she learned about his thesis, she agreed to let him study people at her party, but only if he revealed what he was up to before the evening was over, obtaining consent from those he might want to study further. She's also intrigued by Michael—and by the male species in general. Women she seems to understand; men remain a mystery. They fascinate her, and she enjoys having them on both sides of her at dinner.

"Allow me to join the ranks," says Monica. "I once served Turkey Surprise for Christmas." She proceeds to relate a grand story about an oven on the fritz and her hilarious journey from apartment to apartment before she found a microwave while her guests, stomachs growling, kept singing "Tidings of comfort and joy."

"It happens to everyone," agrees Connie. "I was once caught in a flash rainstorm in West Virginia. We were in the middle of a dark field watching Fourth of July fireworks. In my rush to the car, I tripped and fell face first into a cowpie!" By now the table is in stitches. Notice that garlanded Monica and Connie try to sympathetically "connect" with Nicole's plight. Monica's story is more refined, Connie's matches her free-spirited script.

Monica:

*hey — we all need goals to work towards.
Besides, the end result might determine
one's success or happiness, or both. It depends*

Connie:

*i must close and get back to store
— . Am sorry for the long delay in
of this summer. I'm not sure I even
coffee and T-shirt (which incidentally
who). I've practically worn it out)*

Michael says, "Good company is more important than food any day. Besides, you think of everything, Nicole, even entertainment! There's never a dull moment with you. I propose a toast. To the fiery Nicole Chandler—the ultimate hostess!" Everyone raises a glass in salute.

Nicole turns to Michael and queries, "What if this had happened at the Blue Light Café?" "Well," says Michael, "I'd be stuck behind the bar and probably the last to leave. Guess I'd just seltzer myself down!" Michael's flexible, arcaded printscript suggests fluidity of thought with artistic flair. The zones in his writing flow and interweave in a balanced and adaptable spirit, allowing easy access to the mental, physical, and emotional aspects of his personality.

Michael:

As far me, I've been on
a number of projects
much that I feel the
proverbial juggler
keep several balls' in

"The Blue Light!" yelps Monica. "Isn't that Boz Scaggs's place?" We witness a mild response from James in the form of a raised eyebrow and a mild, "Far out." Apparently Michael has landed smack in the middle of the trendiest night spot in town—*the* watering hole for the avant-garde to see and be seen. People shift in their chairs as they move in to "stroke" the man of the hour. "Are there drugs?" asks saucer-eyed Toni. "I heard he's doing something with George Lucas. What's the deal?" asks Bill. "Yeah? So what rock stars have you met?" queries James. "You know," adds Joe, "we planned to cover the Blue Light in our 'Hot Spot' segment for the morning show. Maybe we could do it from a bartender's point of view." "Fabulous," breaks in Nicole, "you could use the interview in your thesis." The minute she says it she wants to eat her words.

"Thesis?" queries Connie. "What thesis?"

A hushed silence falls. "Well, I . . . ," Michael stammers.

"Let me explain," Nicole steps in. "I think I've just accidentally betrayed a confidence. I'm sorry, Michael. Please, everyone. Let me explain." The guests are all ears. "I met Michael years ago in college. Psychology class. He was earning two degrees, environmental design and psychology. I found him brilliant and fascinating and we became fast friends."

"Well, what do you know," whispers Connie. Bill squirms noticeably, waiting for the other shoe to fall. "I *thought* you were more than a bartender the moment I met you," said Toni.

"I like tending bar," smiles Michael. "It's the best education in human nature I've ever had. I'm working on a study of behavior and environments, and how people interact with one another in certain surroundings." Everyone at the table grows silent.

Note here that Michael received limited attention at cocktails. People were pleasant enough, but what do you say to an aging bartender who could have (should have) done more with his life?

In all fairness to Joe, his logical slant and analytical perceptivity noted everything about Michael earlier, right down to his gourmet cookware and home-grown herbs. Arcaded and protective Joe sensed there was more to arcaded and artistic Michael, and was pleased to find himself seated across from him, even before the "thesis" news surfaced. He felt he had a fairly good handle on Monica's and Connie's outgoing characters from cocktails, knew he could never delve into reticent James in one evening, and would nurture retiring Toni at intervals, but he relished the opportunity to "peel back" the layers of someone he felt possessed hidden depth.

At first people were coolly polite, then showered Michael with the popular attention bestowed on someone featured on a *People* magazine cover. Now that he appears perhaps to know too much, some grow cautious and reserved. The change has taken place not within Michael, but in people's *perception* of him. His level of knowledge, experience, and talent remains the same. The dinner guests themselves have raised or lowered his value in their own minds.

From personal opinions, they made inferences and assumptions. We are all guilty of this type of behavior sometimes. As mentioned earlier, listening experts refer to this behavior as selective response. Eavesdrop sometime when people are discussing religion or politics. They're too busy getting their own point across to listen to the other guy—who they know is wrong anyway. We surround ourselves with facts and people that reinforce our beliefs so that we can feel good about who we are, about our judgments.

Witness the man shopping for a new car. He's open to suggestion as he test-drives various automobiles. Gradually he narrows his choices and selects a Volvo (or other automobile). Once he's made his purchase, or even just his decision, the only other cars he now notices on the road are Volvos. Why? To validate his decision that his judgment is *right*.

The same holds true for our dinner companions. People find what they're looking for, not necessarily what's there. Michael may have volumes to share with them, but many of them selectively screened out the "bartender," assuming they would have nothing in common. If they possessed a knowledge of handwriting, they could have witnessed the depth, artistry, and creative inventive spirit in this individual.

But wouldn't our garlanded writers be open to new experiences? Yes and no. They're receptive, but they also like to be agreeable and not rock the boat. They may just go along with what they already think and believe, rather than question their preconceived notions, which they accept as truth. Someone like angular Joe is more inclined to question what he sees, probing further for validation and facts.

"In this particular project," Michael says, "I'm studying observable signs man uses for expression in his environment. Many are called projective techniques—everything from body language to handwriting analysis. And they all seem to interrelate. It's been a fascinating study!"

"Handwriting analysis?" asks Toni.

"Oh, do mine!" begs Connie. "This sounds like fun!"

"Yeah, sure. Tell her her future," sneers James.

"I felt the same way you do," says Joe, "until we had a graphologist on our show. I have to admit I think there might be something to it."

"Well, Monica, how about you?" flirts Michael. Monica blushes and replies, "I know of a European fashion designer who had a graphologist design her new signature logo. I guess I'm game."

"I read an article about handwriting and corporate hiring in the *Wall Street Journal*," adds Bill. "They claim eighty-eight percent of European companies won't hire without it. Maybe there's something to it."

"What can it tell you?" queries James, a bit less defensively.

"What did you have in mind?" responds Michael playfully.

"Oh, whatever . . . ," James replies, his noncommittal response mirroring his slippery, threaded script.

"Handwriting can reveal whether your life is balanced or overloaded, with too many irons on the fire ["Oh," groans Connie], your energy levels or need for added rest and vitamins ["That's me," nods Toni], your talent for detail work [Bill winks at Nicole], whether you're action-oriented and a go-getter [Nicole straightens in her chair], private or public [Michael gives a short glance of support to Joe], whether you're logical or intuitive, how you connect with others, your sensitivity to criticism, your self-image—oh, a multitude of things, and I'm only a new student!''

''Sounds like you're dissecting people just like they do in biology class,'' protests James.

''On the contrary,'' responds Michael. ''You already unconsciously reveal volumes about yourself every day in the way you dress, walk, talk, and respond to others. We send out signals all the time, but many of them are misread. And, of course, many folks camouflage or intentionally cross signals to throw you off the track. But handwriting reflects the underlying truth. You many assume a man in a business suit with a briefcase to be a rising executive. In actuality, his attaché might be full of 'crack' he's dealing to high school kids. His handwriting could give you a more revealing picture of his true personality. What's great is that you never have to meet the person. You never bias your judgment with personal feelings about his looks, vocabulary, or the fact that he's a janitor.'' Toni blushes.

''For those who wish, I'd be happy to analyze your writing,'' says Michael. ''Is that all right with you, Nicole? It's your party.''

''Certainly,'' says Nicole, ''I think it would be fun.''

''Now remember, I'm new at this,'' says Michael, ''so be patient.'' He pauses for a moment, seeming to collect his thoughts, and Nicole leaves the table to get him a pad and pencil. ''Let's wait until after dinner before we gather handwriting samples,'' says Michael. ''For now, let me ask a question or two, just for my own research to see if your answers will be reflected in your handwriting. You only have to do this if you feel comfortable. Suppose you're on vacation in a mountain cabin for a week. What type of book would you like to read? Or, perhaps you're given a chance to star in a movie. What role would you choose?''

(Here's where you, the reader, have an advantage. You're familiar with our players, so you can assess if the answers given match the handwritings. These are the *actual* answers these folks gave. I didn't change a thing. I merely recorded them. I was as surprised as you may be at some of the results.)

''Oh, Lauren Bacall in *Key Largo*,'' sings Connie. ''You know, lots of *adventure*, smoky cafés, sneaking down hallways, opening and closing doors.'' Notice how her large lower-loop

imagination and rich pressure immediately kicked into gear?
"And my book would be fiction." You didn't expect to keep
Connie entertained with cold, hard facts, did you?

Connie:

> *Shopping and days of walking —*
> *or a new language and foreign c*

"Anything Barbra Streisand was ever in," glows Nicole.
"That's me. Remember when she was singing her heart out on
the deck of the boat in *Funny Girl*? Front and center, thank you.
I'll go for it. My book would be biography." I'm not surprised
Nicole wants to read about famous and interesting people. I
expect her to join the ranks someday herself. Look at Nicole's
ability to eliminate the mundane extras in handwriting and go
right for the spotlight.

Nicole:

> *Hope to see you there*
> *champagne bar, of cours*

"I'll take Gene Wilder's role in *Silver Streak*," prompts Bill.
"Give me a good comic adventure any day. Of course I want to
be the good guy. My book? Definitely a good science fiction by
Isaac Asimov." Mr. Good Guy's writing reflects all the right,
true, moral, and acceptable standard behavior of the hero. And
he doesn't need to slash through a jungle or dangle over a fire
pit, Indiana Jones–style. Those continuous garlands sing: Let's
have fun, keep it light and enjoy the ride as we go. Knowing his
penchant for details and ability to sit for hours devouring ma-

terial at his computer, I'm sure he would love to get lost in a complex sci-fi thriller by Asimov, whose books are technically based.

Bill:

> utes the wind started building, slowly to quickly. The boat started planning into foul weather gear and it began

"Oh, Ginger Rogers and Fred Astaire. That's for me," gushes Monica. "Give me some slapstick, drama, and romance all in one. I would dance and swirl in the most incredible gowns. Novel? Any gothic romance." Monica, like Bill has a script laced with conventional letter formations that floats along on a bed of happy garlands. She, too, would appreciate some good old-fashioned humor. Her slant tells us that she prefers to be "swept up" in a story rather than being halted at every turn with historical facts and figures. Her light pressure bespeaks the stamina of an armchair quarterback who prefers to enjoy a few flings vicariously through a romantic novel rather than drag her emotions through the wringer with every new man she meets.

Monica:

> I've begun looking into a career change. Surprisingly enough, and in contrast to how others perceive me, it's

Since Monica possesses a naturally spontaneous slant, why does her writing appear tight and cramped? Monica carefully protects what limited resources she has, knowing she has a tendency to go overboard when she gets excited about things. Although she seems to travel along in an unbroken pattern, there are a few intuitive gaps and breaks where she stops to listen to the little voice inside that says, "Careful, you're going to wear yourself out." Monica does not have a built-in caution mechanism. She simply responds with the joy in her heart. In doing so, she has sometimes been hurt. Now, she's cautious the only way she knows how to be—by holding back. Rather than stopping to coolly assess the situation as Joe would, her D-slant feelings automatically well up, because that's her nature. Then, when they surface, she puts the brakes on. No wonder she feels drained.

When faced with conflicting signals, you may wonder which characteristic to choose—the outgoing slant, say, or the repressed letter forms. Which one is "right"? The answer is: Both are right, and both exist in the personality. They may exist in conflict and work against each other, but they exist.

"I'd like to play Robert Redford's role in *Out of Africa*," says Joe. "He was a romantic hero of mystery and depth. He challenged the unknown with aviation and big-game hunting, yet he appreciated the beauties that nurture the soul—music, a wonderful library, a loving woman. But no one could ever possess or pin him down. A book? I guess my book would be fiction." I doubt you're surprised that our arcaded writer would want to portray a personality of breadth and depth. And fiction can entice and engross the investigative, inquisitive mind.

Joe:

Thank you for giving
so much time this
afternoon. I am appre

"I don't know," Toni sighs, "there are so many options. And books—well, I'm reading a history of the Napa vintners right now. I've perused one on English gardens, I'm going to read one on financial planning in January in conjunction with a class, and, in fact, I read a book on handwriting analysis years ago." You never know about those F-slant people. Yet Toni doesn't emote pro or con on how she *feels* about the book or the subject.

Toni:

[handwritten] thank you most sincerely all the time and effort you have expended in our

"And what about you, professor?" James asks Michael, before Michael has a chance to ask him.

"Me?" says Michael, taking the turn-around in stride, "I really like *The Thirty-Nine Steps*—the mystery, the intrigue, the fabulous locations. I guess I'd like to be in a remake, probably in a supporting role, and perhaps help with the production as well. I also like mystery books." Note the many layers of the arcaded writer who welcomes the challenge of discovery and intrigue. The pastosity, rhythmic fluidity, artistic fluency, and simplicity of form tell us he's going to be concerned with visual awareness, with scenery, with how things "flow" together, with set production or direction. The arcades tell us that he's intrigued with what happens behind the camera to create the image on screen.

Michael:

[handwritten] proverbial juggler Keep several balls in

"And how about you, James?" responds Michael. "Books? Movies?"

"Read?" quips James. "Better put it on a video for me." Nicole has heard from James's mother that he is a good student, and in fact is drawn to the sciences. She wonders why he is being so evasive, but Michael isn't too surprised. "As for the movies, make me Darth Vader!" James replies.

"Why?" Michael asks.

"He's got the most power and everyone cowers in his presence. I'd rather be the ruler than the good guy," he adds smugly.

James:

This isn't unusual behavior for an adolescent. In our chapter on slants we learned that teenagers who are still dependent financially, but who want to be independent emotionally, often adopt rebellious behavior. Although James is not a child, his parents still speak to him as if he is: "Do this, don't do that." James's threaded, noncommittal, backhanded writing serves him well in his quest for parental separation. He may be under his parents' roof physically, but that's all. Unfortunately, James's position as the detached observer doesn't serve him well in interpersonal relationships with peers.

James feels as alone and alienated from the mainstream of society as any other teenager going through puberty. But his inability to commiserate and share his feelings with a friend or buddy has left him emotionally stranded. (We'll discover in the next chapter that James is sensitive to criticism.) His aloof stance cuts him off from sources of outside support to bolster his image or assuage his fears. He looks to himself as his only resource in times of crisis.

In fact, he enjoys hanging out at Nicole's. He admires her strength and independent spirit, and she doesn't tell him what to do. She's as private as he is and doesn't push; and, of course, she's not his parent and has less "invested" in him. He can hang around unobtrusively and do his own thing. Intuitive Nicole knows how painful it can be to try and "connect" with others. She was once where James is now and turned her feelings of isolation into leadership. She'll leave things the way they are, as long as James feels comfortable with her. If he's ever ready to open up, she'll listen objectively and offer support without becoming too one-sided.

Review

Garland, arcade, angle, thread—rarely will you meet a person who uses only one formation, but sometimes I use exaggerated handwriting samples to help you remember the stroke formation.

1. Henry is one of three asked to design a new marketing strategy to present at the next board meeting. When ready, does he:

   a. Eagerly share ideas with others, seeking feedback and opinions?
   b. Remain guarded, asking to make his presentation last, after he has heard the others?
   c. Propose ideas in a rigid inflexible manner, preferring confrontation to compromise?
   d. Verbally present his plan, intuitively changing, deleting, and adding to his work from the presentations of his colleagues?

Find out be sublest what dit.

2. The masked ball is in ten days. Does Jody:

   a. Eagerly show her costume to friends, chatting about the upcoming fun?
   b. Hide her costume under the bed, saying it still needs a few changes?
   c. Announce that if there are two Marie Antoinettes at the party, heads are going to roll?
   d. Dress in layers, exposing yet another character halfway through the evening?

to start off the Christmas
season! We enjoyed being
with you and your friend
so much yesterday at

11

Personal Self-Image

T *and* D

In one sentence, how would you describe yourself? How would your best friend describe you? What would your worst enemy say about you? There's an old saying that man has three personalities—who he truly is, who he thinks he is, and the man other people see him as. Your own image of yourself—who you *think* you are—will influence your behavior and interaction with others.

You may *act* successful, but if you don't really believe it, then you'll never truly *feel* successful. It will always seem like an "act." Luckily for us, since handwriting stems from the brain, the inner core, it records what we're thinking, regardless of how we act, and accurately assesses our gut-level self-image, even when we're "kidding" ourselves. Through graphology you may understand why the tennis partner suddenly turned defensive, or why the aggressive executive inexplicably refused the promotion.

How we feel about ourselves is reflected in the self-image letters *t* and *d*. They're great barometers of why we do what we do and of any changes that we're going through. They reveal self-concept, both physical and emotional, and measure self-esteem. The *t* monitors feelings or self-confidence and self-assurance, while the *d* discloses our feelings about the physical image we project.

The Whole Versus the Part/Jumping to Conclusions

Up to this point, we've advocated a gestalt approach to handwriting, examining overall patterns (slant, spacing) and styles (angular, threaded). But handwriting can also be divided into specific component parts (letters and strokes). You've now progressed to the point where you're familiar enough with handwriting to begin dissecting the writing letter by letter. But herein lies a danger. Neophytes may go overboard. They'll see one dynamic *t* crossing and shout, "Wow! Look at that enthusiasm. Let's hire him!" Heavens. That would be like marrying the gal in the gorgeous red dress after one meeting, then discovering she wears a housecoat and curlers the other 364 days a year.

Handwriting, like personality, has stable patterns with inconsistent quirks. I'm amazed at the books that state with conviction, this is the *t* (or *d*, or *f*) of someone evasive, hypocritical, masochistic, cunning, alcoholic, and so on. What if we are writing on our laps or on a window sill and are judged by the slip of the pen!

When examining *t*'s and *d*'s take the advice of graphologist Nadya Olyanova: If a letter form appears occasionally, it reveals a tendency; if it appears often, it shows a habit. And "when it is fairly consistent throughout the specimen, it is regarded as an integral part of the character structure." Just like life. You may scream at your spouse once in a blue moon when you're really upset, but if you rant and rave on a daily basis, it denotes a different style of personality, a different temperament. So too, the more often you see the specific *t* or *d* formation, the more pronounced the accompanying personality trait.

There are thousands of combinations of *t*'s, *t* crossings, and *d*'s. For our purpose, we'll cover just the basics. In the letter *t*, we'll be reviewing:

The T *stem:*

The T *crossbar length and width:*

The crossbar position and style:

The *T* Stem

The stem is an integral part of the script and the foundation upon which the crossbar is placed. Since the *t* is located in the middle and upper zone, you may already have a "feel" for how the letter "operates."

The stem personifies the writer's self-image in his immediate environment with regard to self-assurance and self-confidence. The height of the stem is an indication of how far the writer is willing to extend himself to maintain his image—even to the point of vanity.

Retraced T *Stem*

*travel to Sacramento t
visit my aunt.*

Retracing the stem requires discipline and indicates control and a confident self-image. Self-assured, the writer is aware of his own positive strengths and value as an individual. Although he may have down days, it's unlikely that criticism from outside sources can dampen his spirits for long.

Tall T Stem

I'm very interested in having my

    The taller the stem, the harder the person tries to attain high standards. His pride makes him work for approval. Often he will do more than is expected of him. This valuable trait can spur the writer on to work better, accomplish more, and "reach for the stars." His resourcefulness and conviction of his worth as an individual cannot be crushed or destroyed.

Exaggerated Height

I just wanted To talk To her about the positio

    When pride is excessive, the writer becomes overly proud of his achievements. Convinced of his own superiority, he may invite credit before it's due. If your own writing contains this pattern, you know that you're capable of achieving anything you set your mind to. But take care that a lofty self-esteem doesn't lead to the trap of thinking that there are only two ways to do things—your way or the wrong way. Make allowances for folks who may not possess your self-confidence. Consider helping them to your level instead of associating only with those of your caliber. It can be lonely at the top!

    Here's a tip for people who work with or are married to someone with vanity in his/her handwriting. How do you cope with this excessive pride? It may kill you to do it, but you must hang on this person's every word. Act as if they are the world's greatest authority and praise their every decision. Why in the world would I suggest that you do this if the individual is already vain? Because they will think that you're a genius for recognizing their great superiority, and you can usually wind up having whatever you want. Personally, I've never been able to bite my tongue long enough to pull this one off, but I know for a fact it's one effective way to deal with vain people. And about the only way, too, since they have no intention of changing. (If I have offended any NOW members with this description, please accept my apology, but rational methodologies don't always work with irrational people. This works!)

If your child or teenager has vanity in his writing, however, that's a different story. Those who think they know it all, particularly at an early age, are on a fast downhill track. Why? Cohorts in school or business soon recognize that "you can't tell him anything," so they stop offering advice, suggestions, and criticism, knowing that it will not be heeded. The person has too much invested in being right.

Short T *Stem*

already written. Thank for non-smear felt-.

The writer with a short *t* stem (when the rest of the upper zone is balanced) is independent and doesn't lean on others for advice or opinions. Although he may appear to be a conformist, inwardly he chafes at social restraints and is not bound by custom.

Looped T *Stem*

I enjoyed listen too you, with nd Rosa. On the T.V. program

If a retraced stem indicates control, a looped stem indicates slackness. In our discussion of zones, we learned that loops are containers of ideas. The writer adds space for imaginative ideas where they don't belong—in the self-image. His mind works overtime imagining what others are thinking or saying about him. He may become overly susceptible to criticism. If the writer allows negative comments to take root and grow, doubt and fear will chip away at self-confidence, affecting relationships and performance. Think of criticism as being like an injection at the doctor's office. Try to concentrate on the benefits, instead of the fact that you're going to get "needled."

James is sensitive to criticism and is apt to take negative comments too personally. With his habit for threading, he can also skim along the surface of painful events, ignoring the lesson to be learned, failing to assimilate constructive advice.

Inflated Loop in T *Stem*

When the loop "balloons" out of proportion, imagination stretches to the point of paranoia. The more thin-skinned a balloon becomes, the less it can withstand outside pressure, and the slightest touch can burst it. People with this trait are so sensitive, they'll misinterpret the meaning of another's glance. They take everything to heart and exaggerate statements out of proportion. They even become suspicious of another's motives. Psychiatrist Jerome Frank, of Johns Hopkins University, claims that stress is not related to events in our lives, but rather is derived from "the patient's *interpretation* of events."

The writer worries: Why is that woman looking at me like that? What did he mean by that remark? The person becomes so preoccupied with his own self-image that he cannot get a true perspective on the greater picture. It's difficult to see the picture when you're inside the frame.

Single Stroke T *Stem*

Take iT at the portico earliesT opportunity. Ther

Those who've adopted a simple downstroke for the *t* stem often devise shortcuts in other areas of their lives and are able to get right to the point. They dislike long phone conversations or dissertations that seem to lead nowhere, and they don't like to be kept waiting. Many writers eliminate the upstroke on a *t* when beginning a word, but the connotation of efficiency carries more weight when this simplified form is found midstream in the writing.

Tent-Shaped T *Stem*

Athank Pamela and Todd everything they have dor

A tent-stem *t* has both feet firmly planted on the ground and isn't about to budge without a good reason. Often this is evidence of stubbornness. When analyzing the writing of a "mule ears" personality, I often say, "My, you certainly have the *courage of your convictions*. You must be presented with a good reason, before you'll change your opinion." What if you are married to or work with someone stubborn? Never put him in a position where the answer is yes or no. Once such a person has said no, he may refuse to reconsider, even if he sees the error of his ways. You must allow the person to think it's his idea if you want to get your proposal passed.

my handwriting.

Martha's husband had several tent-stem *t*'s in his writing. When they added a master bedroom and bath to their home, she desperately wanted a whirlpool spa. She had broken her back in an accident years earlier, and her husband himself had a weak knee and had undergone foot surgery. They were both over sixty, and she felt it was about time they took care of themselves.

Martha was afraid he might think the spa an extravagant idea and knew that once he had said no, that was it. She studied, shopped, and found exactly what she wanted, then took her brochures and questions to a neighbor who had a pool with adjacent spa, to discuss the pros and cons. A few weeks later when they were invited to the neighbor's for a picnic and swim, she made sure her husband sat and relaxed his tired body in the spa. He thought it was great. At that point, the neighbor produced Martha's brochures, which she had left there weeks earlier. Her husband studied them and said, "Honey, I think we should get one of these. They're great, and they would add to the value of the house." He thought the whole thing was *his* idea.

T Crossbar

When writing the *t*, the writer must interrupt his rhythmic flow of up, down, and around, to execute a completely separate horizontal stroke for the crossbar. This requires control. The pressure exerted in the crossbar indicates strength and willpower; the length indicates enthusiasm and endurance.

Weight of Crossing

A strong crossing indicates willpower. The depth of pressure, of course, conveys depth of energy. If you were crossing a stream, would you rather inch along on a thin sapling, or step confidently across on a thick wooden plank?

Length of Crossing

The length of the crossing indicates spirit, enthusiasm, charm, and charisma. A person who extends his line will extend his sphere of influence, will "push out" the walls to go after what he wants.

Short, Heavy Crossing

t

example of my handwriting which isn't to rot.

The short *t* crossing would indicate strength, but not of long duration. The energy and determination might be limited to personal projects or immediate events.

Long, Heavy Crossing

t

and Bob and I think that we can venture into a little more

A long, thick crossing indicates a forceful will, plus the energy and determination to carry out plans and goals. These people can sweep others along with them in their enthusiastic plans.

Long, Thin Crossing

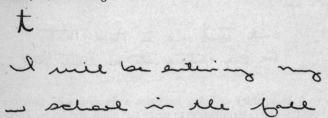

A long, thin *t* crossing indicates enthusiasm, but without the strength to back it up. This is the crossing of the well-intentioned volunteer who agrees to organize the bake sale or write the new computer manual but runs out of steam halfway through. If only his energy equalled his enthusiasm!

Short, Thin Crossing

There is neither the energy nor the drive to sustain much effort with this type of writing. If 50 percent or more of the crossbars are this way, do not expect much from the writer in the way of physical or emotional energy. A person who has just been fired from his job can have *t* crossings like this.

Position and Style of *T* Crossbar

How high or low you place your crossbar will indicate how high you're willing to set your goals—how far you'll rise above the everyday mundane (middle zone) and reach for the stars.

Average Height

t

·ely loves and cares about
Ken or is he just being.
truthful person or not.

Traditional copybooks teach a *t* crossing that rises two thirds of the way up the stem. If crossings are placed in this position, the writer will strive and reach for what he knows he can accomplish. He has an honest evaluation of his talents and what he can do. He is comfortable and secure knowing what is expected of him and would rather work and progress at an expected pace than go racing ahead and fall flat on his face. Never underestimate realistic goals; these writers are reliable and steadfast and know where they are going and how they're going to get there.

I've been occupied with

Michael has only average *t* crossings? That's fine. With his energetic, artistic script, I'd hate to see him chasing rainbows and blue-sky plans. Michael is going to achieve whatever he sets out to do—and with flair and style. He's both impatient and realistic. He values shortcuts, but knows that nothing worthwhile is ever achieved without effort. He's willing to work for what he wants and reap rewards in time. When his writing gets crowded, the crossings have a tendency to be reduced in strength. He's learned to pace himself.

High T *Crossing*

t

me pleae let me know - all (
are gratefully accepted.

These folks reach to the future for dreams and goals. This writer is ambitious, enjoys hearing success stories, and speculates about how far he could go. He'll put plans into action and rise above the pack to realize hopes and desires. Forward thinking, he probably has a good idea where he'd like to be five years from now.

Bill, our satellite tracker, has a high *t* crossing. He's already purchased a home and is completing his M.B.A. at night. He's also on a rigorous training program for the Olympics, although they're a few years away. Bill's script is very connected, and in his own words he will "follow through regardless of what it takes. Sometimes I don't always do things the easiest way but I never give up!" With those willpower *t* crossings, I'm sure of it.

I found that with care I could just ~
to clear the land. Trouble way, the sea

Floating T *Crossing*

t

I have been interested in

handwriting analysis fo

It's fine to have your head in the clouds, as long as you have one foot on terra firma, but the writer who loses touch with his far-flung ambitions may wind up chasing rainbows. If the handwriting is forceful and laced with leadership, the person may accomplish his goals if he has a support staff of practical individuals.

Low T Crossing

t

been very interested, for a long time
about getting my handwriting an

The more the person crouches and returns to the mundane events of day-to-day activity, the more immediate and short-range his goals. The writer may need encouragement from outside sources, as he tends to undervalue his own importance. He would rather remain where he is and feel safe than face an unknown challenge and risk failure. He needs to think about stretching and growing without comparing himself negatively to others. A lack of faith in himself blocks the learning process.

Many writers with low *t* crossings argue with me that they're well aware of their strengths and weaknesses and are merely being realistic. When I ask them about their three-, five-, and ten-year plans, they tell me, "Life deals you a certain hand, and you play it." I've learned from experience that these writers haven't assessed their talents, but instead have taken the easy way out, often finding themselves restless, bored, or quietly depressed without knowing why. "Yeah, sure, I'd like recognition," claimed one man, "but what for? I'd have to win the lottery or something." He was placing his possible achievements on outside sources—luck or chance—rather than drawing on something from within.

Toni's average-to-low *t* crossing is short and weak, indicating short-lived energy behind her willpower.

thank you most sincerely
all the time and effort

Bow T *Crossing*

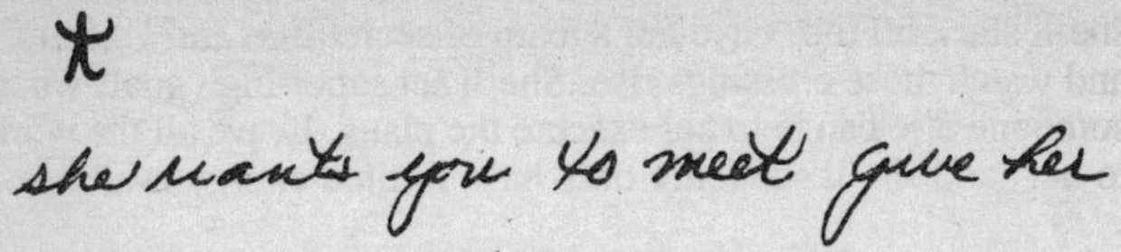

[handwritten: she wants you to meet give her]

Being receptive is one thing (garland formations), but when the willpower becomes limp and pliable, the writer lazily reaches for his goals. Unlike the low *t*-crosser who feels unworthy, this person is aware of his abilities but lacks the will to do his best. He may like to play victim, indulging his whims and desires. ("Gosh, I'd like to accomplish more, if only. . . .") He'll invent excuses for why things can't be done. He can adopt a self-indulgent attitude.

Writers who have these formations get furious with me when they hear this and list all sorts of hardships in their lives that prevent them from achieving their goals. Curiously enough, when I offer to resolve their problems so that they can get on with their lives (I'll loan you the money, I'll help you find the job), they struggle to invent *more* excuses for why they can't get off the dime.

For those bowed *t*-crossers ready to throw this book across the room, let me acknowledge that when I'm feeling lazy, sorry for myself, overwhelmed, or want to play the martyr, my writing looks like this too.

Connie and Nicole have some bowed *t* crossings. But be careful that you don't misjudge *t* crossings found in *th* formations. Many writers link *t* and *h* together for simplicity's sake. It's faster. And the *t* crossing takes a "dip" as it fluidly swoops down to include the *h*. This symbolizes fluidity of thought, linking everyday activity with future plans and dreams. It's true that Connie does have a few lazy strokes and so does Nicole. But I'm not surprised. Connie plans far too much for a twenty-four-hour day. Something's bound to curtail her energy supply.

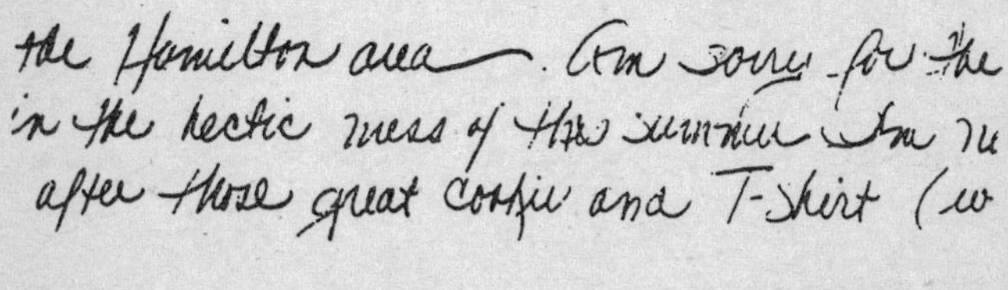

[handwritten: the Hamilton area — Am sorry for the in the hectic mess of this summer I'm m after those great coffee and T-shirt (w]

Remember "big picture" Nicole? Drown her in details and she'll slack off too. Give her a team of secretaries and "gofers" and watch those crossings rise. She'll set super-high goals when someone else can help her execute the plans. Leave all the work to her, and she'll suddenly only have limited energy available.

I todc Thursday +
to attend my brothe

Umbrella T Crossing

I recently spoke with a wor
who attended your workshop o
hemisphericity. I am interested

Those who are trying to literally "bend" their willpower and bring it under control will have an umbrella *t* crossing. These people are usually on a self-improvement program. They strive to curb their enthusiasm and channel strong passion into productive effort.

Crossing to the Left of the Stem

I'm really not ready
for them - I think

When the willpower, energy, enthusiasm, and force stop short of completion, we're looking at the procrastinator. Have you ever heard the saying: Hard work is the accumulation of simple tasks you didn't do when you should have? If your writing looks like this you have a tendency to drag your heels when it comes to something you fear or dislike doing. You first need to examine what you procrastinate about and why before attempting to rectify the situation.

Once, before I even analyzed his handwriting, a client assured me, "It's procrastination. That's my downfall. It's been that way all my life." There wasn't a trace of procrastination in the writing! But it was laced with fear of failure. He wasn't a lazy procrastinator, he was scared to death. Once we worked on his fear of failure, the procrastination vanished.

Crossing to the Right of the Stem

Much like the slanted writing that seems to rush headlong into the fray, this writer responds quickly to his environment. Sometimes designated the "temper *t*," the writer usually knows his mind and speaks it. Responsive and impulsive, he's restless and intolerant of the slowpoke who stands in his way. Many who write hastily will fail to cross thoroughly the *t* stem in a controlled and disciplined manner.

I would not judge the outspokenness of impulsivity as harshly in a hastily written script as I would in slow writing, where the writer has deliberately chosen to respond in a reactive and uncontrolled manner. I have more compassion for the man who pushes me aside in an effort to escape a Doberman than I do for the dowager who dresses me down for accidentally dropping a canapé on the carpet.

Hasty script:

This is a sample of
Writing - & I would
appreciate four

Slow script:

tell me more about myself

than agitated as is my future.

Arrowlike T *Bar*

✝

for the police to be Requested
to make immediate Contact
with their post at the bridge
at Zanypuram to check the

When the crossing appears to have been slashed with a knife, the writer is capable of blistering outbursts. The thickness of the stroke will indicate the force behind the feeling, while the length will record the duration of the expression. Temper and anger are strong emotions and are expressions of impatience at having to consider others' feelings.

Remember, psychologists claim teasing is a form of anger. Anyone who undermines your self-image, even in a teasing manner, must resort to subversive tactics to express his true feelings.

Fading T Crossing

t

Of the task I am a

At work today phon.

After a tiring day, even the most enthusiastic salesman will need to recoup his energy. Many of us experience this whisper of fatigue midway through a demanding project. Take note of your dwindling enthusiasm and change your focus or pace, allowing your reserves to rebuild.

Descending T Crossing

t

about the party

until today.

Just as some fail to control their willpower, like the right-tending crossers mentioned earlier, others have too much control!

Those who are able to direct and force their will toward others can develop a domineering or overly aggressive spirit. The downward slanted *t* crossing can indicate a person who is anywhere from pushy to autocratic. The heavier the crossing, the more forceful the energy. The longer the crossing, the more persuasive the personality. These people can persuade others to aid them in accomplishing their goals.

Ascending T *Crossing*

t

*unfortunately I
much of your most inter
interview on "Look Whos Talk
This morning,— the*

An ascending slant connotes enthusiasm and an uplifted spirit. Those who allow their enthusiasm free reign in the world of dreams and hopes for the future exhibit this characteristic *t*. One caution: Any exaggeration of a characteristic will throw the writing off balance. There *is* such a thing as having too much enthusiasm for a project. The enthusiastic dieter can jog herself into a wisp of smoke or the dedicated zealot donate his next mortgage payment to a political candidate when his enthusiasm knows no bounds.

Hooks on T *Crossing*

t t

*very good at creative
writing. from my collection*

Often those who write quickly already have their hand and pen in motion when they sweep into the act of writing. In an effort to maintain momentum, these writers are also reluctant to pick up their pen and leave the page. They may gently drag the pen in final flourishes. The pen can leave hooks or drag marks. These hooks have been described as the tenacious trademark of those who refuse to let go, refuse to give up. Speculation has it that the writer may be hooking into new ideas in the upper zone.

Sometimes these marks have been referred to as irritation hooks because impatient personalities incorporate them in their script. It seems logical that those who write and think quickly might be irritated when interrupted or asked to slow down.

Efficiency T *Crossing*

perfect accomplishment of mission in this present

Those who connect a confident self-image with willpower exhibit in one swift motion resourcefulness that relishes expedient results. The homemaker who makes her shopping list while driving through the car wash, the executive who listens to tapes of the board meeting while jogging, the high school quarterback who devises new football strategies for his psychology term paper, love to kill two birds with one stone. A car phone is not a luxury for these people. They hate to sit idle at the red light when they could be accomplishing something.

Left-Tending T *Crossing*

information about y October Work shop at

When a forward-tending stroke turns inward, the writer returns to the past for encouragement and support. He exhibits a lack of self-confidence and may need pep talks and encouragement before he can "return" and meet the challenges of his environment. These people feel doubtful, or emotionally starved. All of this happens, of course, on a subconscious level. This behavior may surface as subtle nagging self-doubt or worry.

Regressive Crossing with a Return

I had the pleasure
I would like to know
Respectfully
Sir

Notice how the *t* crossing returns to the self before projecting forward to the future? Those who initially turn inward, revert to inner resources and a sense of past accomplishments to bolster their self-image. They then carry forward images of self-confidence and strength to face the future, generally developing a feeling of assurance as they go along.

Because the writer looks back, he may also torture himself with thoughts of things he should have done. Much of his present energy is spent bemoaning neglected opportunities. He'll be attending a dynamic class or informative board meeting and instead of giving it his full attention, his mind will wander to: "I should write Aunt Phoebe a thank-you for my birthday sweater." He may remind himself repeatedly in the next week that he "should" write Aunt Phoebe. Had he spent his "if only" time writing, the note would be in the mail by now.

Note, too, that "should" is a form of judgment, implying that you somehow slipped up. I "should" feels very different from I "will." It implies right and wrong, lost opportunity, a retracing of steps (just as the *t* crossing regresses and retraces itself). The writer is still carrying around old habits from childhood (and that's where he's returned for guidance!).

Tied T *Crossing*

I don't understand how
she can stay such a posi
thinker under the circum

If the return ties itself in a knot, this is evidence of persistence and tenacity. He may have to turn inward to give himself a little pep talk now and then, but he will hang in there and get the job done.

Flair T *Crossing*

will appreciate you
sending me this
information

There are those whose enthusiasm just naturally exhibits itself with a certain flair and flamboyancy. Indeed, those who exhibit flourishes in their script often approach all of life with a bit of dash, panache, ingenuity, style, fun, and freedom. In ill-formed or ostentatious writing, the writer may bore others to death as he hogs the limelight to showcase his self-appraised cleverness and style.

Physical Self-Image: The *D*

Once you understand the letter *t*, confidently retraced or openly vulnerable, the letter *d* falls into place right behind. The *d* records our visual, physical self-concept and how we project this image to others.

Retraced D *Stem*

d

they gathered around to toast Grandfather on

If the stem is disciplined and retraced in form, the writer fortifies a confident and self-assured attitude. Comfortable with his appearance, the writer is unaffected by slights or wise-cracking comments, be he in or out of fashion. The taller the *d* stem, the more pride and dignity the person brings to his self-image and demeanor.

Very Tall D *Stem*

d

so much into handwriting but we laughed because we

An exaggerated pride in physical appearance leads to vanity. The writer may become arrogant or conceited when consumed with his own self-aggrandizement, falling victim to flattery or hollow praise. A writer who equates self-worth with self-image will naturally fall prey to loss of self-esteem when his looks begin to fade.

Short D Stem

d

"doing a handwriting
doesn't distort The
I often write this la

The writer with a short, strong, confident *d* stem possesses an independent spirit. He will usually frequent many different clothing establishments and put together a look of his own. Disregarding present-day fashion, he may adopt a particular style and keep it for years; one thinks of Katharine Hepburn's hairstyle.

Looped D Stem

d

and handwriting analysis
sessions. I am presently
in theraphy and am some

A person with a weakened self-image may feel self-conscious about his physical appearance. He may feel uneasy speaking up in public, sensing that all eyes are "on him." He could be a fabulous dresser, possessing a poised and polished demeanor, but it does little for his self-confidence. Remember, the larger the loop, the more vulnerable and sensitive the person is to criticism.

Karen, our gourmet dieter with the sensuous pressure, has

looped *t* and *d* stems coupled with low *t* crossings, reflecting a
low self-image sensitive to criticism.

was to elude my grasp
— knows I've been courted
Doing men. I feel as
im always chasing rainbows
find the rain!

Karen said she had once been forty pounds overweight. She
said she felt unloved when fat and determined never to be that
way again. Too bad Karen had not learned to love herself fat or
thin. Often those with low self-image are very hard on themselves. They'll criticize their short-comings before you have a
chance to, thus avoiding the pain of outside judgment or con-
demnation.

Note that vanity in this script may be a defense mechanism
used to counterbalance feelings of inferiority.

Inflated D *Loop*

𝒬

Could you please send in ion our Handwriting and also, How does one get. be a "Certified graphology.

It is important to remember that our self-image comes from *within*, from right between our own ears. I've seen the writing of a New York model that has the exaggerated looped *d* stems of an ugly duckling. This woman, not a beauty in the classic sense, is stunning and exotic, with a smoldering intensity. Her photos vibrate with sensuality and passion. She is reed thin and even had her back teeth pulled to give her cheeks a more sunken look. No matter how you photograph her, all she sees is "too short [she's five foot nine], too old, too angular, not pretty," etc. Little five-foot-five me reminded her that there will *always* be someone younger, taller, blonder, etc. They're being born every day. It's a fact. But it doesn't take away from her grandeur and presence.

People with oversensitivity often feel unloved and unwanted, and can literally program themselves for failure. Often they'll have a low *t* crossing as well and may even overeat or overdrink on their path to self-destruction in order to validate their feelings of unworthiness.

For example, a newlywed wife may feel that she's bright, attractive, charming, and competent. If the man she worships and adores tells her that she's clumsy, homely, and stupid, she may begin to act "as if" it were true. But why would a self-confident individual allow this to happen? Well, it's pretty easy to fall victim to the trap when you're only five years old (or three or two, etc.) and that's usually when our programming begins. Suppose you make a terrific mud pie for Mom and Dad with just the right number of pebbles, dirt, and dead bugs. You proudly carry your creation into the kitchen envisioning the groundswell of praise and what do you hear? "You stupid child, get that mess out of here *at once*."

As an adult, she may experience the same feelings in a board meeting when an impatient boss snaps, "Sit down, Carole. Anyone with half a brain knows that won't fly with our new budget." She feels like a fool, and automatically, like Pavlov's dog, Daddy's tape kicks on "stupid, stupid," reinforcing what she's been trying to run away from all these years.

Remember, handwriting records the patterns in our brain—what *really* runs our behavior—not the pep talks we fool ourselves with after a day of positive-thinking rallys.

Lyric or Literary D

The literary or Greek *d* bespeaks an appreciation for cultural, literary, or poetic avenues of thought and study. Many writers, artists, and those with an aesthetic nature incorporate this formation with a lyrical rhythm into their script.

Something else interesting about these people—many of them also adhere to the "law of the written word." In other words, they may be skeptical of anything they see or hear, but give credence to what they read. They may hear about or actually witness a news event, but will believe that the best account of the incident is what they read about the incident.

Why is this information valuable? Suppose you're in negotiations with a "literary *d*" fellow. Rather than spending hours in dialogue and discussion, hand him a pad and pencil and let him write out the important points. Somehow things seem more valid if they're in writing, particularly if he's doing the writing! Even if you dictate the list—"Here, Charlie, let's cover our main points"—then hand him a pencil as you vocalize your concerns, he's more inclined to carefully consider and agree with what he sees in print. Quirky, but true nonetheless.

Review

1. You're a personnel manager in a large corporation reviewing a series of work performance evaluations. It's time to meet with the employees for personal interviews and discussions.

- Which employee needs to set higher goals?
- Which employee is unduly upset by criticism?
- Which employee appreciates an honest evaluation of his efforts?

a.

At the last minute the
asked me to hostess th
party for the teenagers
thirty of them!

b.

today I got a card from Donal
but he didn't say he missed m
or that he cared at all.

c.

When the going gets
tough the tough get going
I can't think of anything to
write on this paper.

2. You need to set up a decorations committee for the annual
   Shriners' dinner. This involves preparation of fifty center-
   pieces that employ the Shriners' motto and logo.

- Which person would make the best chairman?
- Who has more enthusiasm than stamina?
- Whose personal pride in appearance might prompt him to
  add the last "finishing touch" to each piece?

a.

you a note & we wou
hear from you –
   I listen to that progra
every day – Its great –
Learn lots g good things

b.

I enjoyed your presentation very much.
I think handwriting analysis is somethin
children and parents should explore as a
family. Taking classes and trying to impro

c.

Let's get these results into the first quarter report.

3. You need volunteer models for the fashion show fund-raiser.
   It's time for tryouts.

- What glamorous gal would just as soon work behind the
  scenes?
- Who would arrive perfectly groomed after having eaten nothing but apples for a week?
- Who would rather not walk the ramp with all the other beauties, but will at least remark about her heavy thighs before
  the judges have a chance?

a.

discusses different methods of dividing the work load today.

b.

Donald's determination to diet developed good health habits

c.

experiment. I am 72 yrs old and have sold stereos for 3½ yrs, am unemployed and

12

Me, Myself, and I

The Personal Pronoun *I*

"No man is an island," wrote John Donne, but tell that to the executive who just made a fool of himself at the board meeting, or the woman in a strapless dress at a party where everyone else is in casual sweaters and jeans, or the "Mr. Everything" bachelor who just had his marriage proposal turned down. Ever had your pants rip in public? Or your shirt catch in the door of a bus? You can certainly feel as though you're out there all alone sometimes, with all eyes on *you*.

Some speculate that our self-image (as revealed in the letters *t* and *d*) seems more like reactive behavior in response to how others treat us rather than a record of how we actually feel about ourselves. Helen felt sexy and elegant, ready for a grand summer party, until she found everyone else dressed for volleyball and burgers.

Still, there are those who are confident and self-assured regardless of circumstances. Those with a sensitive self-image are more susceptible to outside influences. A person's actions, feelings, behavior, and accomplishments are *always consistent* with his self-image.

The personal pronoun *I* encapsulates in a single letter the writer's self-concept and ego. Here, isolated and alone, we exhibit our persona on stage for all to see.

This is the course you traverse when forming the personal pronoun *I*:

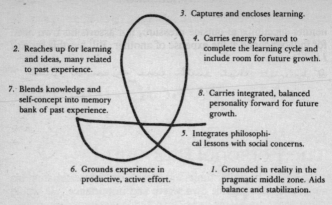

3. Captures and encloses learning.

4. Carries energy forward to complete the learning cycle and include room for future growth.

2. Reaches up for learning and ideas, many related to past experience.

7. Blends knowledge and self-concept into memory bank of past experience.

8. Carries integrated, balanced personality forward for future growth.

5. Integrates philosophical lessons with social concerns.

6. Grounds experience in productive, active effort.

1. Grounded in reality in the pragmatic middle zone. Aids balance and stabilization.

As with all letters in handwriting, the personal pronoun *I* needs its own height, width, and expression. The *height* of the letter reflects the writer's need for high visibility, for ego gratification. The *width* of the letter reflects his ability to open up and relax. He can spread out and take all the space it needs. In graphological terminology, the height of a letter is equated to ego and need for feelings of high self-esteem, the width is equated to relaxation and self-confidence.

A personal pronoun *I* that has a height proportionate to the other upper zone letters (*b,d,f,k,l,t*) would indicate a confident personality unafraid of other's judgment. If the width is comfortably proportionate to the rest of the writing, we witness someone with a sense of personal self-worth, someone open and receptive to people and events in his environment.

Variations in Size of the Personal Pronoun *I*

Average Size I

*happy I sent away
n analysis. I really*

There is a nice balance to the personality that leaves the writer neither timid nor headstrong. He is comfortable with himself and his peers, easily able to give and take. He is able to volunteer ideas and suggestions without infringing on another's space. He neither succumbs to outside pressure, nor asserts his own need for independence at the expense of another. Bill has this type of *I* in his script.

I found that with care I could just r

Small I

say I am considering it

At times, the writer limits his growth by underestimating his abilities or denying his own worth and importance. He would rather blend in with the crowd than be subject to public scrutiny. Modest and unassuming about his accomplishments, he may find it difficult to recognize and accept his good qualities. When faced with a new challenge, he must first overcome self-doubt. Lack of faith in himself may limit his ability to achieve. A person with a low self-image can still do well at work as long as he is doing something he knows well, and with which he feels comfortable.

Large I

I would like to see

Relaxed and open, the writer with a large personal pronoun *I* has a strong self-image and is not too concerned with others' opinions of him. His self-confidence allows him a spontaneity in relationships, and he's not afraid to ask for what he wants. Others usually recognize and respect his high degree of visibility, which further solidifies his position.

Inflated I

I'm interested in

Any exaggeration in handwriting is an exaggeration in personality, so watch for conversation peppered with *I, I, I,* as the writer is most concerned for himself and the image he projects. But just as Shakespeare admonished that "the lady doth protest too much," so too, be wary of this tower of power who may be standing on feet of clay. Those who need to be noticed and grab the spotlight may be reaching for more than they have earned.

When a large personal pronoun *I* appears in naturally grand magnanimous writing, the energy and power of the surrounding script support the accomplishments of a strong ego. But when the pronoun jumps up or "screams" for attention, we may be witnessing pride, vanity, or bluff if the remainder of the handwriting does not lend credence to such exaggeration.

Variations in Style of the *I*

Reversed I

when I used to to spe. letters to feel companion I can only say that.

You may need a magnifying glass or strong daylight to spot this one because you'll have to look for ink flow to determine the direction of the pen. (Check for a high point on the left side of the lower loop or heavier pressure on the left side of the upper loop.) Those who adopt a stance "counter" to the norm are exhibiting a rebellious spirit. The writer views himself as unique. If the formation is harmonious with the rest of the script, he may be a quiet individualist, making his mark in subtle and creative ways. This person usually has many original ideas, which he seldom hesitates to act upon. If the form appears squeezed, repressed, malformed, etc., the person may be experiencing social conflict and practice overt rebellion.

Retraced I

J

mail.   If done by mail
I would like to know the

When a person puts "the squeeze" on his self-image, he limits spontaneous expression. He limits his feelings of self-worth and may feel unsure, tense, or inhibited. He may not be open to accepting criticism, but instead continues to defend his narrow self-concept, resorting to caution and withdrawal in the face of change, limiting future growth.

A person's mental health depends on his feelings about himself. You need to see yourself as likable and accepted by others in order to feel "worthy" of another's praise.

We also tend to judge others by the same yardstick we use to judge ourselves. If you can accept yourself, with all your strengths and weaknesses, you'll be more likely to accept others unequivocally as well. Even if others accept you, if you do not feel "worthy" of their attention, you'll foil their attempts at communication or meaningful relationships.

Printed I

I

I just saw you on TV

A single line is the most direct, economical way to express the ego. The writer who dispenses with elaboration shows an independent personality "stripped bare" of nonessential adornments. Selective and discriminating, these people prefer to go it alone, unencumbered by endless rules and societal demands. A person of conviction, the writer prefers to stand on his own, relishing the feeling of satisfaction and accomplishment that self-motivation brings.

The writer needs license in decision making and requires enough leeway to exercise self-direction. Many free-lancers have this in their script. A clarity and simplicity of thought allow the writer a keen perceptivity in stripping problems to their bare essentials. They appreciate the simplicity of pure form and are often culturally inclined. Both Joe and Michael have this formation.

I am appreciative

I've been occupied

Printed I *with Serifs*

I

ay — or I cut them away like
I don't want to look back, but

When a person underscores and "tops off" his self-image, he adds conviction to his belief that independence is the best course of action. These supportive strokes signify willpower and reinforce his Lone Ranger image. When a printed formation such as this is found in cursive writing, this suggests that the writer does not wish to be known intimately. He prefers not to rely on others for social or emotional support. Nicole and Toni have this formation in their script.

?ny I MISSED youR

Betty and I should like
thank you most sincerely

Left-Tending I

I
there, I made some new of
Is the thought of lossin

If the self-image withdraws toward the safety of the past, the writer is expressing a desire for self-protection and privacy. These people often withdraw to "size things up" before sharing who they are with others. Teenagers who need to separate themselves from convention and tradition often adopt this idiosyncrasy in their script. A self-image that "curls" back upon itself exhibits feelings of isolation.

Reticent James has this in his script. Some students question, "But how can you judge this trait when the writing itself has a backward slant?" Note that James's personal pronoun *I* formation is also squeezed and repressed as it hooks over itself in an embryonic sheltering form. This ego projection of his self-image guards itself as carefully as does his signature image.

my handwriting in the
shop exhibit. Its okay

Right-Tending I

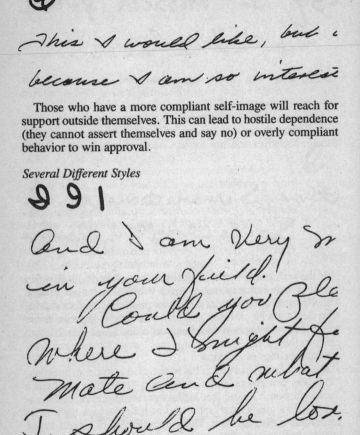

Those who have a more compliant self-image will reach for support outside themselves. This can lead to hostile dependence (they cannot assert themselves and say no) or overly compliant behavior to win approval.

Several Different Styles

The writer who adopts many forms may adopt many different personas in an attempt to find out who he is. He may be fiercely independent one day, and conservative the next. Check the *t*'s and *d*'s for feelings of self-confidence. Also check for threadlike letterforms or connections indicative of one who shifts allegiance and opinions at whim.

Upper Loop Only

g

I just felt I had to.

The writer who emphasizes thought and imagination in his self-image often adopts a creative, imaginative, and simplified style of self-expression.

When you find this formation in a person's script, try to ascertain the penmanship training of the individual, as many European countries and the Sacre Coeur schools here teach this personal pronoun *I* formation. Adherence to a school model in this instance would indicate conformity.

According to graphologist Jane Nugent Green, author of *You and Your Private I*, British writers often adhere to the "Upper Loop" school model or adopt some form of a straight-line formation. These simplified forms indicate creativity and individuality. She claims, "Choosing to write in a very simple manner is quite often done by rather complex personalities."

Since the upper zone "relates to intellectual thought, philosophical considerations, and idealism," says Green, "the writer places special emphasis on abstract values that he has created or encountered." Although the form appears simple, it contains the garland, the arcade, and the angle, signifying a mind capable of absorbing from a variety of sources.

Lower-case Personal Pronoun I

i

i don't know

When a writer is too unsure of himself to "take a stand" he may resort to a disappearing act, burying his ego within the body of the writing. You must search for his self-concept, as he fails to project himself into his environment. Many adolescents or those with an immature ego adopt this stance.

Be sure to analyze this form in conjunction with the rest of the writing. Often the *i* will be strongly formed and even call attention to itself with a circular dot formation. In this instance, we are witnessing false humility: The writer goes out of his way to draw attention to poor little humble me.

i

i love meeting people. i have tw

sisters. i like the out of doors and t

Your Self-Image: Is It Consistent?

Most interesting for the graphologist is to see the personal pronoun *I* in conjunction with the rest of the script.

Ted has a strong decisive script indicating self-confidence. Yet his personal pronoun *I* is small and constricted. Ted can initiate projects with gusto and motivation. Inside, however, he may experience self-doubt and fear. He projects more confidence than he actually feels. Analyzing the script as a whole can help you deal with all of Ted's feelings about himself, judging when to praise and when to offer constructive criticism.

Ted:

I've just recently started my business and I think this

Jamie has a tall, confident personal pronoun *I*, which indicates faith in herself and her abilities. Her middle zone, however (area of communication), is tense and retraced. Inwardly, Jamie feels uncertain. She's a fireball when working on her own, but when forced into teamwork situations, she becomes fearful and frustrated. Knowing Jamie's ideal work requirements, you can lay the groundwork for positive self-enhancement, rather than fostering an atmosphere of tension and worry.

Jamie:

I'm sure I can make it to
Thursday's meeting. I'll give you

Your self-concept is a blend of all those images and feelings you have about yourself. You don't think of yourself in just one way. In certain situations, you'll feel confident and self-assured; in others you may feel tense or nervous.

Check the expansion and constriction in your writing. Those who allow themselves the space and breathing room they need will have an open and relaxed (expansive) handwriting. Every positive experience teaches us to "relax" a little, reconfirming a positive self-image. Failures prompt us to "pull back" and hide behind feelings of doubt, distrusting our abilities. Those who restrict their egos may have felt a restricted sense of self-worth earlier on in life.

Mom, Dad, and the Personal Pronoun *I*

Part of our feelings of self-worth may be tied to how others treat us. There is no denying that parents and other nurturing figures played significant roles in molding our self-concept. Psychologist Alfred Adler believes that the infant's relationship with its mother is its first introduction to social contact, to acceptance or rejection.

(When I use the terms mother and father, I'm referring to male and female role models in the early formative years. You may have been raised by an aunt, grandmother, etc., or possibly be an orphan. A child often adopts a coach, teacher, older brother or sister, etc., in the absence of a parent.)

Psychoanalyst Dr. Karen Horney's optimistic theory is that man naturally works toward *positive* self-realization. Given half a chance, she reasons, every child will try to develop to his optimum positive potential. She also believes environment can play a role in our development. Naturally, environment is not totally responsible, but in certain instances, it can certainly play a part. She relates scenarios in which parents are seen as indifferent, intimidating, partial to other siblings, hypocritical, overprotective, and so on.

Think back for a moment. Can you recall a time when a parent seemed disappointed or impatient with you, yet you had no idea what you had done wrong? Now an adult yourself, you realize Mom or Dad was probably just having a bad day and simply responding to the pressure and responsibility of adulthood. But the scars of rejection are there just the same.

No one expects a tender seedling to survive when forever pelted by harsh storms or continually crushed underfoot. All people need acceptance, understanding, and love. When our adult relationships lack these qualities, we may leave the marriage, or quit the job, etc., for sheer survival. Children too young to make it on their own can feel trapped and helpless in what Dr. Horney calls "a potentially hostile world." The feeling of not being good enough, not accepted for who we are, can produce extreme anxiety.

Trying to find a way to cope, the child may develop one of three strategies: cling to the most powerful authority figure (mom or dad); rebel; or withdraw altogether. These coping mechanisms become an unconscious part of our behavior and are *carried into adulthood.*

We all adopt coping mechanisms to get through the unpleasantries of life, and often these responses are so ingrained, we aren't even aware of them. And don't fool yourself into thinking you can change your behavior overnight. Witness the cypress tree that has learned to adapt to the windy seashore. Its trunk is literally twisted and contorted in resistance to the wind until it cannot stand upright. It has adapted to its environment in order to survive. If you transplanted the cypress to a sheltered spot, could it suddenly "untwist" itself?

If a man has been paying lip service to his mother for forty years to keep her at bay—"Yes, Mother. Whatever you say, Mother"—do you honestly believe he's going to suddenly change and stand up to her because he's living with you?

So, too, understanding Mom's or Dad's "games" (comparing siblings, etc.) doesn't mean we can automatically change our behavior. We may still unconsciously respond with our old parent/child patterns out of habit.

Here's a case in point. I once interviewed a group of men as to why they drove sports cars. (The automobile can be *very* tied to the self-image for some people.) The responses contained the usual—feelings of power, makes me feel sexy, I like the speed, etc., but what amazed me was how many grown men confronted me with an air of little boy protest, declaring, "I decided that when I *grew up* I was going to drive exactly what *I* wanted."

Roy is six foot four and frankly looked uncomfortable in his little Europa. "Wouldn't you be more comfortable in something a bit larger?" I suggested. His chest swelled as he smugly replied, "My mother *hates* this car! She thinks it's dangerous. Every time she visits I roar into the driveway and stand her hair on end." I'll never forget thinking, as I watched him curl his body like a snail into his car, "Gee, he's actually driving that car for his mother, not for himself!"

The personal pronoun *I* not only records your own self-image, but also reflects the parental sources that helped form this image. Hundreds of case histories, counseling sessions, and follow-up questionnaires have verified that indeed the parental influence is intrinsically contained within the handwritten self-image.

Mother's Influence on Self-Image

The upper loop reflects the influence of mother on our self-image. The sheltering arcade rises above the mundane daily routine to protect, shelter, and guide us. It encases ideas and ideals associated with growth and future dreams. The loop then turns downward, to bring ideas and learning down to the world of reality and social concerns. Mother shows how to apply lessons to daily living—you share your toys with others, you don't hit someone when you are angry. The stroke is rooted in the give and take of social interaction (the middle zone).

Father's Influence on Self-Image

"Just wait 'til your father gets home!" "My dad can beat your dad." Action, power, results—here and now—the traditional image of male influence has been to take command and show by action and example. Mother shelters; father defends.

When the self-image stroke returns to the baseline, the home-front, the sphere of activity, it turns to the father figure for influence and support. This formation also reaches to the past, the source of family rules and regulations, integrating past experience with present activity. The stroke sharply angles and thrusts forward to meet the challenges of the future head on. This decisive and determined stroke (echoing the willpower of the *t* crossing) counterbalances the large influential sphere of mother. The formations meet, commingle, and balance one another. Note the father image combines curved support with angular discipline and will.

Parental Power

When it comes to independence versus family conditioning, there are certain decisions that may be strongly influenced by family ties. You might select a certain career, mate, buy a home in a particular neighborhood or price range, etc., in an effort to please or avoid displeasing Mom or Dad. These emotional chords stifle freedom. Through family conditioning we repeat patterns from childhood that may no longer serve us.

Strong Maternal Influence

naturally, I felt I

Remember Roy contorting his body into a sports car Mom hated? Guess who's controlling *his* self-image? The area of handwriting that receives the most emphasis is the area that has the most influential hold over the writer. On some level, Roy's decisions are still made in an effort to try to "show" mother.

Keep in mind that most of this influence became ingrained before the age of thirteen. Herein lies the danger. Often young children cannot distinguish truth from falsehood, fantasy from fact. They believe in the Easter Bunny, Santa Claus, and Mom and Dad. These figures are bigger than life to a child. Thus if a parent tells Johnny that he's stupid, lazy, or slow, on some level he'll accept it as true because it seems to come from a very powerful source. He may feel differently about himself, but he's only a child and has little trust in his own judgment. Before he can assess the situation from an adult perspective, he absorbs this information and accepts it as fact.

Later, as an adult, no matter how many positive self-help books he reads, when he enters the board meeting and is criticized by the boss, those old images resurface and once again he hears, ''You'll never amount to anything.'' Sure enough—Dad was right! And the childhood image persists . . . Interestingly, interviews with successful people often include stories about a parent who told the subject as a child ''You can do or be anything you want to be. You are special and unique.'' And the child goes on to fulfill the prophecy.

Strong Paternal Influence

I have just seen you

One client of mine had inherited a grand old manor that had become a financial burden. Yet Franklin wouldn't dream of selling it. At fifty-seven, he was a successful real estate salesman, but poured tons of money into a thirty-two-room stone monster he didn't need. If anyone could have found the right buyer for this estate, it was Frank, yet he remained tied to this financial albatross. ''Why, Frank, for heaven's sake, why not sell?'' I demanded. ''My father would turn over in his grave. I couldn't. He'd kill me.'' Frank was firmly convinced that his father would view him as a failure and traitor for selling the family estate. His father had passed away thirteen years ago. Poor Frank. Until he let go of Dad, he couldn't let go of the house . . .

Lower Loop Cut Off

if I can change myself is to change. Also I would how I can go about it.

In some scripts, the father figure seems to end abruptly, almost as if the influence had been literally "cut off." This is exactly the case. This often shows up in the writing of children who have actually lost a father, or whose fathers were away a great deal or preoccupied for some reason, and they felt they were cut off from his influence.

I know of a young teenage girl who had this in her writing. She had been sexually molested by her father since the age of nine. They existed physically under the same roof, but emotionally she had *severed all ties*. He didn't exist for her. (This graphological clue assisted a psychologist in asking the right questions that eventually led the girl to revealing the incidents.)

I know of another young man who had been "cut off" by his father after he disclosed the fact that he was homosexual. His writing also carried this information.

Lower Loop Ungrounded

I am a left-handed (
Incidentally I was not

A person whose personal pronoun *I* takes on this attitudinal structure often lacks a sense of security where the father figure is concerned. What happens to a person is important, but what he *feels* about what happens to him is even more significant. The father may have been right there with the family the entire time, but for some reason (domineering mother, sibling rivalry, etc.) the person did not feel that he had the strong backing and support of a male role model.

Lack of Lower Loop

I

I was born in Cincinnati
here all my life. I like it be

If the lower loop is absent, either the father did not aid in establishing direction, or the writer rejected the father's example. In either case, the person has "let go" of his male role model.

Space Between the Loops

I

I would like to say – In so f
the sunshine again. I will hei

When the male and female influences are not "joined" within the self-image, the writer experiences a separation in their influence. The parents may be divorced, or if living under the same roof, in a constant state of disagreement or tension. I know of one young woman's writing with this formation who has the happiest marriage you've ever seen. I met the rest of her family at her wedding and later remarked on how close they seemed to be. "Are you kidding?" exclaimed Betty. "My parents fought constantly when I was a kid. I used to go in my room and shut the door to try and get away from all the yelling. I guess they love each other, but I promised myself that I would never have a marriage like that. If we can't talk it out, I just wait until we've both cooled down. Sure marriage is a challenge, but I *will not* have my children experiencing what I went through. It's just selfish and self-serving." Docile Betty's eyes were shooting sparks, and I realized the family disharmony had a deep and lasting impact on her.

What we're also talking about here is a separate influence, separate power. Let's say you want to borrow the car or spend the night at a friend's house. Would you ask permission from your mother or father?

"My dad," quickly responded one student. "I could wrap him around my little finger. Mom was a different story." "See what I mean?" I prompted. "If you saw your parents working as a team, you would have witnessed them both abiding by the same decision."

Is this important? You bet it is. Why? Let's say you did want to borrow the car. Mom says no. Dad says yes. They argue, Dad wins, and you get the car. What else happened here? *Mom lost.* You come to view marriage as a win/lose situation rather than a partnership. What happens? This puts you in a win/lose frame of mind when handling power or relationships.

Additional Loops to the Personal Pronoun I

With the addition of loops to either or both the upper and lower personal pronoun *I* formations, the writer adds an extra bit of imagination with regard to the parental figure. He may elaborate on some idea he has of parental authority that shaped his perception of male and female.

Figure A:

Figure A is the writing of a young man who idolized his father, a heart surgeon. He was convinced of the man's superiority, wouldn't tolerate any negative criticism of him, and devotedly followed in his footsteps in the same profession.

Figure B:

> *I don't know if your travels even take you to Washington D.C., but if they do I'd love to meet you.*

Figure B is the writing of a young professional woman in banking. She is the fifth and youngest child in a family of all boys. Although her parents' greatest joy would be to see her married and "taken care of," she has chosen an independent route to establish her self-image and worth as a female. She is strongly tied to her father's approval and hopes to win his praise for her independent accomplishments and not just because she's daddy's little girl.

Hooks on Personal Pronoun I

> *I cannot describe the sensati*

Hooks signify grasping and holding onto something. Writing that hooks and curves toward the past expresses a reluctance to achieve independence.

Interestingly enough, the hooks in the sample below do not seem to be able to grasp and hold onto anything to bolster the ego and self-image. This formation has often been found in the writing of those described as emotional orphans. It may belong to an actual orphan or to someone who simply feels isolated or alone, without anyone to cling to.

> *I will always be ther and that I'm not an*

The Bigger Picture

Naturally, the pronoun *I* must be analyzed in conjunction with the rest of the writing. We do not exist independently of our environment anymore than a letter of our script can stand alone.

A psychologist who works with high school truants agrees that it's not the behavior itself, but the person behind the behavior, that needs to be studied. A girl who only believes she can be loved if she engages in promiscuity has a lot invested in retaining this behavior. The forger who has won the admiration of his peers for his cleverness will resist efforts to extinguish this image; in fact, he'll expend great effort to promote it. The behavior may be negative, but the image is positive. And that's what graphology helps the psychologist determine—self-worth and self-image. There are just as many lawbreakers who have a pride in accomplishment as there are criminals who feel worthless and unloved.

Review

1. You're a junior high school counselor assisting students to achieve a positive self-image. Which student:

- Turns regressively inward in a protective shell, unable to assimilate the benefits of counseling and support?
- Presents a confident demeanor, backed by a wholesome self-image of who he is and where he's going?
- If encouraged to focus on subjects in which he is already successful, might experience positive reinforcement, expanding his confidence?

a. *I guess I'll stop writing*

b. *name is Cindy I am years old. I will be*

c.

> *I know I am capabl*

2. Marlene sabotages long-term relationships with men, claiming, "They're all alike. One day they get bored with you and
   just walk out. I've seen it happen. I'd rather cut my losses
   early than be abandoned in the long run. But it sure gets
   lonely sometimes." Which handwriting is laced with experiences that would foster this type of thinking?

a.

> *de down. Therefore,*
> *any folks are surprised*
> *hen they learn I am*

b.

> *ere to apply for this*
> *ilar field? I am especially*
> *sted in working with*

c.

I would love to h

trip also. I would

3. "No I won't," exclaimed one fourteen-year-old as I analyzed handwriting at a private prep school. "But you
come from three generations of the finest lawyers on the
eastern seaboard," protested the headmaster. "What will
your family think?" "That's their problem," he replied.
"I'm going to be a rock star." I knew his tradition-bound
family was in for a scrappy time with this independent
headstrong youth.

a.

The only old sample
I could find (so you can
write when not being se
about it) was a copy of c
of a business letter I wrote

b.

If I treat myself as I t
I appear to be, I ma
myself less than I an
But if I treat myself

c.

at Sunrise Mall, I
for a florist, but I
find one. I wanted

Part Three

Putting It All Together

13

The Analysis

When we last joined the dinner party, our characters were busy connecting (and disconnecting) with one another. Michael had offered to analyze everyone's handwriting. Some now eagerly and some reluctantly participate.

"Do me, do me!" begs Connie, and Nicole interrupts. "Why don't we take our dessert in by the fire and make ourselves comfortable. This could take a while." "Whatever you like," responds Michael politely, "but I really need to speak with each person privately. You can compare notes later." Joe watches Toni's shoulders relax and he gives her a little smile. "It's all right," encourages Connie. "I have nothing to hide. You can say whatever you want in front of everyone."

Professionalism

People in a group situation often respond as Connie did. Often they think graphology is just a game and won't reveal anything of depth. Michael may seem overly cautious, but he's very wise.

I strongly recommend that you do handwriting analysis one on one, in a spirit of professionalism and privacy. Believe me, you'll be glad you did. You will find that people have no idea how deeply you can probe with handwriting. They're amazed—and sometimes embarrassed—at what you discover.

There will always be one spoilsport in the crowd who'll deny your findings, even if they're accurate, casting aspersions on your newfound knowledge.

I always try and verify my findings afterward, especially when I've encountered a vehement protester. Family and friends may then tell me, "You were right on target, Ann, but Terrence will never admit it. He can't even admit to himself that he has trouble with anger" (or whatever).

Often-Raised Questions

Conflicting Results

You may have had your handwriting analyzed by two competent graphologists and received conflicting reports. How can this be? There can be many reasons. A great deal of the accuracy depends upon the handwriting sample provided.

I myself am a morning person and an early-bird sample from me would definitely project more energy than one taken at 3:00 P.M. Many students collect samples at parties, where people feel more open, relaxed, and willing to submit a sample. But parties often include alcohol, which acts as a depressant on the nervous system and will surface in the script as depression.

Also remember that any area of study involving human beings is bound to be affected by the individual providing the opinion. As objective as we try to be, we all color things with our own personality and feelings. As in other professions, there are good and bad handwriting analysts; their work will reflect their insight, experience, years in the field, courses of study mastered, etc. (Why do you often go for a second opinion after visiting a doctor or a lawyer?)

Finally, you are now aware that there are often several conflicting personality traits within the same individual—short temper with humor, gregariousness with a desire for privacy, etc. One day Mom burns breakfast and Dad huffs out of the house; another morning he thinks her snafu is newlywed adorable. As Walt Whitman said, "Do I contradict myself? . . . I contain multitudes. . . ." Perhaps different graphologists picked up on different aspects of the same personality.

So Which Type Am I?

So many people today have allowed themselves to be pigeon-holed and categorized, through sociological tests, personal color charts, or the like, that they assume graphology will do the same. Yes, handwriting can reveal your strengths and weaknesses, but that doesn't mean you should nosedive into a stereotyped profession that showcases these talents: I'm artistic, therefore, I'll be an artist.

Dictionaries of occupational traits and endless aptitude exams will tell you that those successful in banking are good with figures, detail oriented, disciplined, and that artists are expansive, creative, etc. But wait. One of the most successful bankers I know is extremely creative with loans and money. His handwriting is bold, dynamic, and imaginative. I also know a talented artist who is the most meticulous, mathematical, precise guy you'll ever meet.

If we were to go by tests, education, or personality types, who would have hired Thomas Edison (three months of formal schooling) or Henry Ford (didn't finish the eighth grade) or Apple cofounder Steve Wozniack, considered an oddball and social recluse in high school. Handwriting can and does reflect those untapped potentials hidden deep within us. It can help you channel them into areas of strength and growth, be it banking, the arts, or landing on the moon.

And, as you also know, the whole is *always* greater than the sum of its parts. Remember Trudy at the supermarket? She is certainly much more than a woman in a soiled raincoat. She happens to run her own catering business, appears in television commercials, skis like a demon, and is a mystery buff. The coat, I'm told, came from a wardrobe friend from "The Streets of San Francisco" and used to be worn by Michael Douglas. So much for trench-coat Trudy!

A Living Science

As with any living science the possibilities are endless and may change as variables change. A drug that alleviated your arthritic pain last year may be altered in effectiveness by your change in diet today. The circumstances of your life may alter in a thousand ways. Life is movement. Handwriting is life.

Does this mean that handwriting cannot be analyzed because it may shift and change? Certainly not. It's very mutability endows it with the capacity for instant up-to-the-minute accurate evaluation. Psychologists studying diaries of patients can often determine not only when a problem started but what brought it on by reviewing a collection of journal entries that change throughout the months and years. Remember, too, that we all go through mood swings and temperament changes, while our basic, underlying nature remains steady and sound. You still recognize the handwriting on the envelope as your mother's, whether she happened to be happy or depressed that day. When you *do* notice changes, you are then prepared to act upon them.

Fitting the Pieces Together

Each chapter in this book merely adds one more ingredient to the recipe. After all, what makes a lemon cake? "The lemon!" you'll argue. Really? Take away the flour, sugar, eggs, baking soda, etc., and what's left? Just lemon. What good is an ability to recognize heavy pressure in handwriting, if you can't determine how the person is going to use it? Does it thrust itself on the world in angular force or sweep through with garlanded receptivity?

So how do you group all these character traits together? Which one has more significance? Which one cancels the others out? Jean Hippolyte Michon, the founder of European graphology, believed, "One sign does not cancel the significance of another sign; the counterweight of the opposing sign must always be considered. The human being is a complex unit, therefore it is necessary to examine every little element lest we forget the wonderful unity of the entire being."

Adequate Sample

Like any other profession, handwriting analysis needs adequate material to obtain accurate results. Some folks ask that I analyze an illegible scrawl on the back of an envelope or a faint photocopy of a signature. You wouldn't stand twelve feet outside the doctor's office fully clothed and shout, "Guess what hurts?" would you? Yet some folks expect graphologists to be psychics or miracle workers.

Try and have your subjects give you at least a page of writing on unlined paper, thus allowing them to regulate the spacing. Ballpoint pens help to reveal a wider range of pressure patterns, but if they have a favorite pen, as Joe did, let them use it, as this too will reveal something of the personality.

When doing an in-depth analysis, more than the one sample is always helpful. If samples are taken from different days, so much the better. This can assist you in determining a range of personality and temperament. Also ask for age, as this is not revealed in the script (one reason personnel departments favor its nondiscriminatory status). Any other pertinent information (physical disabilities, handicaps) should be recorded as well.

Content

"But don't I give myself away in the subject of my writing?" people ask. Not really. Some graphologists claim they never read the content of the sample, in order to remain completely objective and impartial. This, I think, is short-sighted, as everything about the writing can give you further clues. I always base my *first* impression on energy level and visual patterns only, saving the content for later. Some folks may deliberately fabricate information in an attempt to throw you off. But don't worry; handwriting always reveals the truth in the end.

Others try and produce an "anonymous" sample, devoid of any personal feeling. One man's sample read, "The sky is blue today, the same color as my sweater. I had corn flakes for breakfast." In reality, he was going through a great deal of pain with regard to a breakup with his wife. I did see a great deal of disturbance and "blocking" in his writing, which he quickly denied. Later in our session, he admitted to the terrible conflict he was experiencing. He didn't want to write about it, however, as he thought that if I were *any good*, I would be able to guess it! His communication with his wife was as blocked as his communication with me. He wanted me to read his mind. I had actually seen great fear and caution in his writing, and he admitted that he was afraid of me and what I might find.

Handwriting can show you when a person is hiding from himself, but you may not know the reason why. True, the analyst need not work directly with the content of the writing, but content and energy often go hand in hand.

One woman wrote, "My husband left me for my best friend. At first, of course, I was angry and hurt, but that was four years ago. Now all is forgiven and we are friends again." That's what the *words said*, but they analyzed: hostility, resentment from the past, low self-image, and jealousy. So, yes, it was important that she wrote about something meaningful to her. But what she was telling herself and what was true for her were two different things.

First Things First

Initially, place the writing in front of you and simply "absorb" impressions. Does the writing seem energetic, cautious, placid, frenzied? Try not to concentrate on any specific characteristics, and try not to associate it with other writing you have seen. Keep an open mind, as though you were meeting this person for the first time—which, in a sense, you are, even if you've known him all your life!

Once you've gleaned an initial impression, allow your eye to roam through the spaces and patterns to catch specific formations that give the writing character, flavor, and personality. Now you can begin your analysis.

Help!

Once students have an overall impression of the writing, they often feel lost or overwhelmed at the prospect of putting it all together. They're unsure of where to begin, so they resort to the "hunt and peck" method, picking out those things they most easily remember and ignoring the rest.

Try this. Review what you've learned by asking yourself a few simple questions. Remember, *you know more than you think you know.*

1. What is your overall impression of the writer's energy level? And what effect might this depth of energy have on his emotional responses? his physical appetites? (*pressure*)

2. Is the energy controlled in a disciplined, organized manner? (*spacing*) Is it dispensed with initiative and perseverance? (*margins*)

3. Can this person stay on target to achieve his goals? (*baseline*) Does he prefer to tackle projects from the outside in, working with the bigger picture, or the inside out, assessing all the details from a comfortable and personal perspective? (*size*)

4. How does he express and release this energy outward in his everyday environment? (*slant*)

5. Can the writer balance and distribute his time and energy

equally among all spheres—physical, emotional, and intellectual? Is one area emphasized at the expense of the others? (*zones*)

6. How does the writer wish others to view him? (*signature*) Is this consistent with his true personality?

7. When presented with a problem or a stimulating challenge, how will his mind go to work on a solution? (*thought processes*)

8. What is his style in connecting with others? (*connections*)

9. How would you describe this person's internal image of himself and what effect will this have on his behavior? (*t*'s and *d*'s)

10. When it comes to total self-image, does the writer operate from a concept that is important to him alone? Does he have a balanced, wholesome self-concept? Is he influenced by past memory pictures of what others thought of him? (Personal Pronoun *I*)

11. How well do you feel you can get to know this person from preliminary social contact? Does his inner core, his private self-image add to, detract from, or conflict with your first impressions? Can you see how private feelings influence public behavior? (Part One versus Part Two of the book)

I realize there are hundreds of ways to analyze handwriting, but if you can write a simple sentence or two in answer to each one of these questions, you've just written an analysis.

Go for It

On the following pages are handwriting samples from our eight dinner companions for you to analyze. Follow the above questions and see how you do. Later, you can read Michael's analyses and compare notes. Your analysis may read quite differently from Michael's, and that's fine, as long as you've covered the basics. Have fun!

You probably have a pretty good handle on Nicole and Bill, so why not start with them.

Nicole:

The Art Deco Party (

should be an absolute !

Did you know our frien

modelling # 3-5 millio

worth of estate jewel

     Hope to see you the

The champagne bar, of co

Bill:

Every 30 or 40 seconds we'd get s
I found that with care I could just
to clear the land. Trouble way, the se
for careful sailing and we kept gettin
always towards the beach, and alway
when I needed every inch. When the
us there was nowhere to go and only
Then a fishing boat appeared
line. He towed us all the way back
I waded out to his boat, arms full o
a thank you gesture, the fisherman

Joe:

Thank you for giving
so much time this
afternoon. I am appre
of your comments both
personal and professi
Really looking forward
your appearance on P

James:

my handwriting in the
shop exhibit. Its okay
to have it analy

Thank you very much

Toni:

Betty and I should like
thank you most sincerely
all the time and effort
you have expended in ou
and that of the hotel

Monica:

relish

in the thought of sketching hoards of
my own personal creations, hand selecting
from the finest silks, wools, etc all
over the world, and having my very own
personal dress designer deal with the
finishing touches.

Connie:

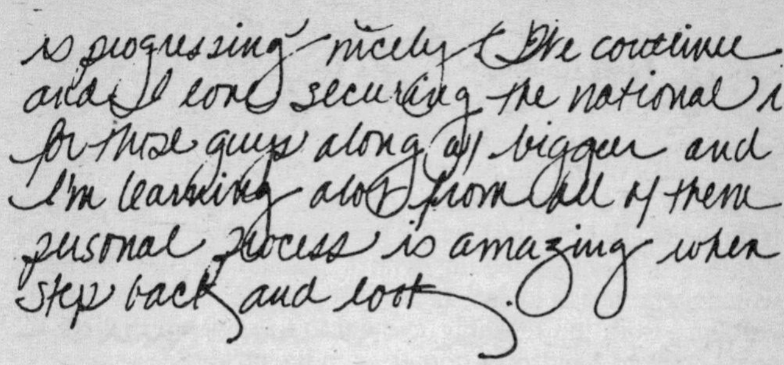
is progressing nicely. The continue
and I are securing the national
for those guys along w/ bigger and
I'm learning a lot from all of them
personal process is amazing when
step back and look.

Michael:

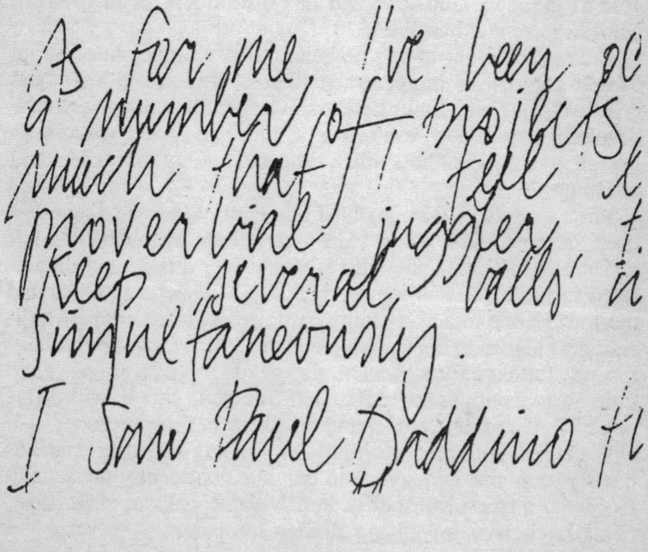
As for me, I've been on
a number of projects,
much that I feel
proverbial juggler
keep several 'balls' in
simultaneously.
I saw Paul Daddino

Michael is a beginner, just like you, so he took a deep breath and remembered to *keep it simple*. Also, I may step in once in a while to help him out, or explain to you how he reached his conclusions.

Nicole

should be an absolute

Michael's overall impression of Nicole's handwriting is one of energy and expansiveness operating within an organized framework. Her medium-heavy pressure coupled with pastosity signifies a depth of feeling with a passion for life. She is a woman who needs to see, hear, taste, and touch life at all four corners—from the crashing cymbals in symphony hall to the cold, cracked hand of a homeless indigent—little escapes Nicole's sensual nature.

Her large, commanding script with well-formed letters reveals a confident, enthusiastic risk taker. Nicole enjoys being highly visible and seeks responsibility and leadership. She is able to influence and lead and has little doubt as to her own abilities (size and baseline).

The upright slant in this magnanimous yet disciplined script further confirms a temperament that is cool, controlled, and practical—one who looks before she leaps. She's not one to rush headlong into a new venture or emotional appeal without an overall awareness of how much time and energy the project will consume.

Michael notices that much of this energy seems to manifest itself in the middle zone. Here is a person in touch with her social environment, one who is expansive, direct, and uncluttered (printing) in her communication. Michael also notes that the lower zone is active (loops) yet selective (no loops), indicating a balance in needs. Nicole wants to see tangible results—rewards for her efforts. Yet she also needs solitude, privacy, and time away from the spotlight. Self-directed, Nicole will determine when and where to spend *and limit* her resources.

We know from prior reading that Nicole's signature matches her script in size and style and that she confidently presents to the world a true picture of herself without walls or subterfuge. (This holds true for all our dinner companions, so we won't repeat it again.)

Michael is at first surprised to see the lack of connections in Nicole's script. He always felt that he and Nicole "connected" very well in thought and action. Then he slowly smiles to himself. Of course, he chuckles to himself, Nicole was "connecting" *with me*; I'm not sure I ever really connected with her. We always seemed to be on the same wavelength, but that's probably because she was *on mine*. Sure, the large middle zone belies a need for social interaction, but she was holding the reins all the time. Nicole's separated (printscript) writing allows her to "open" and "tune in" to others. She's always been a superb negotiator. Now Michael understands why. Her intuition "senses" when to back off and when to move in to close the sale.

Michael sees an unusual comingling of capital and lowercase letterforms. They are balanced and harmonious, yet have a unique and individual pattern. This reinforces fluidity of thought.

Not one to utilize tried-and-true methods, Nicole typifies the personality that can "borrow" an idea from a totally unrelated field (science, engineering, nutrition), churn it through her conceptualizing machine, and arrive at a new formula or solution to serve her own unique purposes—much as Teflon no-stick cookware made its roundabout entrance through the space program.

Michael also notes that many of Nicole's *r*'s and *a*'s form arcades. Resourceful and self-sufficient, Nicole does turn inward for answers, and a certain formalism pervades her actions as she quietly calculates the benefits of any proposition (arcade plus A-slant).

Michael now understands why Nicole's *t* crossings fall into an average or slightly higher position. Yes, she has the confidence of a leader (size, style). But she calculates and weighs her options carefully (slant, word, and line spacing). She's not going to burn the candle at both ends or run off to New York to head a corporation and work eighty-hour weeks. Nicole looks after number one (MZ emphasis) and will set average goals that she can accomplish within the overall framework of the life-style she has chosen for herself. Better to be a big fish in a small pond (size, visibility), she reasons. Nicole is excellent at what she does, but her goals (work) are tributaries that feed into the mainstream of life—enjoying the present moment, living life to the fullest here and now (expansive MZ). They are not rivers of high ambition that flood their banks, leaving the owner exhausted and spent.

Nicole's personal self-image (personal pronoun *I*) is selective, discriminating, and stands on its own. She relishes the satisfaction that self-motivation brings and there is a clarity and simplicity to her nature.

Overall, Michael sees Nicole as confident and versatile, energetic and self-assured, popular and gregarious, bold and self-reliant, a survivor with endurance, a natural leader who brings order out of chaos.

Buzzwords

Were Michael to tell Nicole about her pressure, she might think he was referring to anything from her blood pressure to the pressure in her job. Be sure to remove graphological jargon and buzzwords from your vocabulary before giving your final analysis. Throughout the remainder of the analyses, Michael will indicate features he based his analyses on (zones, baselines, etc.). You'll know when and where to remove the words that might confuse your client—words such as pressure, arcades, etc.

Bill

> I found that with care I could just n
> to clear the land. Trouble way, the sea

"Whew!" exclaims Michael, moving closer to the lamp, "I'll need a good light to see all the details in this one!" Michael's overall impression of Bill's writing is that of a disciplined and detail-oriented person (size, preciseness, spacing). Bill's capacity for energy, drive, and endurance seems in keeping with the norm (pressure). Thank heavens, thinks Michael. If he put any more energy into this meticulous script, he'd be wound up like an eight-day clock! Bill can obviously stay on target to achieve his goals (baseline). And those goals will probably be more personal and self-motivated, as he isn't a person who seeks the limelight (size). Michael surmises that Bill is probably comfortable working by himself, and his naturally introspective nature, coupled with his talent for detail and organization, allows this self-motivated individual to pursue any avenue of interest with confidence (tracking satellites, sailing).

Coupled with a logical slant (A-slant), Bill approaches things in a calm, cool, and deliberate manner. He's objective and practical (spacing). No dry Christmas trees in the apartment while Nicole's away! Bill has the ability to stand back and appraise the situation (spacing) and then use discernment in doing the "right thing.'' Michael noticed that although Bill seemed to feel more comfortable roaming around at cocktails (A-slant) he moved to the couch with Monica, creating a conversation center and helping to get Nicole's party off on the right foot—the logical thing to do.

Bill has a good balance of zones in his script. We know that he's inquisitive, enjoys a mental challenge, and delights in expanding his storehouse of knowledge (upper zone). He likes social exchange and feedback (middle zone) and can draw on past learning to assist him with future successes (lower zone). Like Nicole, he enjoys seeing tangible results for his efforts (lower zone).

The connected pattern of his writing confirms a deliberate, constructive reasoning process—cause to effect—and he will often attempt to slow others down as he ''fills in the gaps'' for them. He'll tackle a project start to finish but can sometimes get locked into repetitive patterns (overly connected writing).

When assessing a situation, Bill is deliberate and thorough. Before reaching a decision, he constructs a framework of facts; he builds a broad base of evidence that lends stability and strength to his reasoning process to support his conclusions (cumulative as well as logical thought process).

Bill has an honest evaluation of his talents. He knows what he can and cannot do. He's practical and realistic in his goal setting, and he's reliable, steadfast, and dependable (*t* stem and crossing).

He's comfortable with himself and his peers and he does not assert his own need for independence at the expense of another (personal pronoun *I*). Bill needs no great ego stroking. He's attentive, adaptable, and hospitable to his fellow man (garlands).

Although he's a bit too slow and thorough for Michael's taste, Michael views Bill as an all-around ''nice guy''— adaptable, diplomatic, responsible, logical, stable, courteous, and sincere.

Even arcaded Joe told you quite a few secrets throughout the book, so let's do him next.

Joe

> Thank you for giving
> so much time this
> afternoon. I am appre

Michael lets out a long low whistle. No one's going to read *this* guy like a book! Michael's overall impression is of a strong, resourceful, highly disciplined, organized professional (medium-heavy pressure, regimented left margin, spacing, angularity). Well, here's a guy with enough sensuality and passion to match Nicole's, Michael thinks to himself (pressure, pastosity), but he sure keeps it under wraps (slant, rigidity).

From the broad margins and generous spacing, Michael can sense that Joe is discriminating and poised, allowing himself room to pause, reflect, stand back, and take in the whole picture. His talent for organization prompts Joe to catalogue his impressions, then later return to analyze their emotional depth and origin.

Joe's logical slant (A-slant) reinforces his objective discernment. He doesn't need to be managed or directed by others; *he* is in control. Emotional appeals fall on deaf ears to one who accepts total responsibility for his actions and feels you should do the same.

Joe's strong active middle zone tells us that he likes to get involved and that he enjoys a variety of personal encounters and experiences. He can be direct, giving you his undivided attention, but he still needs to be in control of when and where this happens (arcades, slant). His well-defined lower zone denotes a resourceful nature that draws on past learning to assist him with future successes. Like Nicole, he's a pragmatic, get-to-the-point person who is interested in producing results (efficient upper zone shows *planning*, active lower zone indicates *doing*).

Joe's keen insight and probing intellect are part and parcel of his analytical nature. He takes nothing on blind faith. He silently watches Michael like a hawk to see if he formulates opinions and reaches conclusions through carefully applying his knowledge of graphology or through some innate skill in "reading" other people. "I wouldn't expect you to put any credence in this science," Michael tells Joe, "until you've proven it for yourself." "What, me study graphology?" asks Joe. "Well, one of us will have to pass your test," replies Michael, "either me or graphology. If you don't have time to study the science, then you'll study me. You'll have to believe in me before you'll believe in what I say." The two men silently exchange knowing smiles.

Joe's many angles and arcades support a protective and controlled personality who watches and waits, often turning inward for answers. True, the arcade formations can assist Joe in original and innovative thinking. But the angles signify a strong-willed personality who will not adapt to the new until it has been proven. He also tenaciously resists attempts to lift his curtain of privacy.

Joe is selective and discriminating, standing on his own two feet, and relishes the satisfaction self-motivation brings. He needs license in decision making and he'll perform tasks with clarity and simplicity (personal pronoun *I*).

It's obvious to Michael from the guarded arcades, rigid angles, and self-contained slant that it takes time to get to know Joe. Yet the rich pressure and pastosity, coupled with an aesthetic refinement, confirm that it's worth the effort expended to learn more. Michael is intrigued.

Michael sees Joe as shrewd and observant, dignified and discreet, persevering and resourceful. He'll work long hours without tiring and expects a great deal from others. He doesn't suffer fools gladly, and he'll dispense with time wasters swiftly but chivalrously. The artistry and depth of passion will surface for those patient enough to stand his test of time. Rome (and friendship) wasn't built in a day.

Time to challenge our skills. Let's try James.

James

You can include this Sam
my handwriting in the
shop exhibit. Its okay

Michael's overall impression of James's writing is of a person a bit isolated and defiant on one level, yet passionate and wanting to "connect" underneath. James is a prime example of the wary skeptic. Don't fall into the trap of defending yourself to this type of person. Simply tell the truth, as Michael did, and say, "Your naturally skeptical nature will not allow you to accept on blind faith what I'm about to say. I'm aware of that, but here are my findings. . . ."

James's medium-heavy, pastose script tells us that he feels things very deeply. Couple that with looped *t* and *d* stems that underscore sensitivity to criticism and we're going to have to tiptoe through his analysis. He may tune us out as soon as we hit a soft spot. Writers with a left-tending slant and sensitivity traits often act as if other people's opinion of them isn't important, but it is. Michael sees all this going in (left-tending embryonic personal pronoun *I* and signature), so he proceeds cautiously. In fact, Michael sensed internal conflict at first glance. Wisely, he mentions this to avoid having James conflict with him while he's in mid-sentence. "Well, James, this is really interesting," says Michael. "There seems to be a lot of push and pull in your writing. Some conflict. You may feel one way one minute and just the opposite the next. I'll try and clarify what I mean as I go along." With any luck, James may hold his fire for a moment and give Michael a chance to explain his findings.

James, like Nicole, is a person of passion and excitement. He has a rich, full-bodied pressure that overflows into dark pools of pastosity throughout the script. Unlike Toni's quietly controlled backhand slant, James's writing seems to be pulling at the reins, straining to break free. We sense the effort expended in damming this flow of emotions—emotions that seem to lurk just beneath the surface, ready to break free at any moment.

The extra-wide margins and wide letter spacing confirm that James is cautious, reserved, and distances himself from the needs of others. Yet the erratic baseline suggests that he is indeed swayed by circumstances in his environment that prevent him from adhering to a steady course. His slant reconfirms a desire to keep to himself, to maintain a vantage point of control.

The cut-off lower zone corroborates a desire to limit his activities to a select circle of friends (peers?). The fact that it fails to return to the baseline of reality also confirms that he does not incorporate past experience into his present-day reality, thus making it difficult for him to learn from past mistakes. Couple that with a leftward slant that indicates he tends to hold people at arm's length emotionally and you see how difficult it would be for James to take advice from others or seek outside counsel. Coupled with vanity in the *t* and *d*, James succeeds in his effort to remain apart from others.

Notice the vacillating size of the middle-zone letters ("include," "sample," "analyze"). At times, James has bursts of self-confidence and enthusiasm, the next moment, he experiences tension and self-doubt. He's like a fly on a hot stove, susceptible to outside pressures (the "heat") at the slightest provocation. James's threaded script portrays a nature that is flexible, adaptable, hates to be tied down, and is receptive to outside influence. Formless, it remains evasive and indecisive.

Michael takes note of, but does *not* verbalize to James, that his vanity provokes him to take too much to heart and he is overly sensitive to criticism (*t* and *d* height and looped stems). The *t*'s and *d*'s also exhibit a stubbornness that requires James to defend his ego (tent stem). The self-image (personal pronoun *I* and signature) is tense and inhibited, limiting spontaneity of expression and reconfirming a lack of faith in himself. James must overcome self-doubt before he will allow his writing to "venture forth" and tackle the unfamiliar. He is guarded and defiant.

Michael sees James as one who fears that he won't be accepted. In order to avoid rejection, he rejects others first, pulling back in self-protection. He hides his fear of criticism behind a smokescreen of bluff, bravado, and a seeming unconcern for the opinions of others. He feels things very deeply and is restless and confused, desperately needing to be understood, all the while pushing away those who might answer his needs. Boy! How is Michael going to approach him with this information? Perhaps he could adopt my "same side of the desk" trick. Whenever I'm sitting across the desk from someone (doctor, lawyer), I always feel as though they are in the position of power. There I sit in the little guest chair at the feet of the master. Depending on the size of the master's desk, it can really be intimidating! When I'm working with certain clients, I'll often step from behind my desk and sit *beside* them in the other "guest" chair. This puts me on *their* level, as an equal sharing information, not as a master dispensing wisdom. Michael might gently suggest in a kind and nonthreatening manner that James's desire to build walls is not only successfully keeping others out but also keeping himself locked in, so that no one will ever get to know what a neat guy he really is. If Michael can get James to see that the only person judging James is James himself, he might relax his vigilance for a moment: It's important that Michael lets James know that he accepts him totally, just the way he is, and isn't asking him to change a thing (no judgment). He's merely relating the situation as he sees it, and is putting it out there for James to think about.

And what about enigmatic Toni?

Toni

In deference to the dignified handwriting placed before him, Michael adjusts his posture to something a bit more refined. The script is expansive yet private, strong yet delicate. The overall appearance seems to embody more the quiet diplomat than an aggressive real estate salesperson. Hmmm, muses Michael, here are a few more mixed messages. The narrow margins bespeak a personality that seeks involvement and participation, yet the regimentation of the margins, line, and letter spacing support a cautious, controlled demeanor. Toni appears to be a woman who knows her own mind yet is reluctant to express her opinion.

Michael can see that she can stay on target to achieve her goals (baseline) and is good with details (size, organization). He can see how others would respect her cool judgment (slant) and air of authority (tall upper zone).

In a much more adult way, Toni is a bit like James. She finds it difficult to warm up to others at first, so she holds them safely at arm's length (slant) and studies them intellectually (light pressure) to see if she can get a handle on them, then determines the appropriate emotional response (Should I be chatty? Professional?). Toni appears cautious, careful, a good listener, but slow to respond.

A personal friend might view her as a bit aloof, wishing that she'd ooh and aah along with their latest venture. Her clients, on the other hand, often appreciate her reserved demeanor, feeling that she is carefully assessing their needs and wants (location, schools, sunny kitchen) and not just dragging them to every open house in town.

Toni has good zonal balance, and her overall execution is one of crisp economy devoid of frills. She's efficient, realistic, values productivity, and cuts her losses with the nonserious shopper expediently.

She is able to be a shrewd and critical observer, selective and decisive in her thought processes (slant, economy of style). She intuitively knows what will and won't work (lack of connections), is able to plan ahead (zonal balance), utilize her time well (spacing), and present her proposal in an intelligent, clear-sighted manner. She is calm and reflective (slant, light pressure), relying on impressions and observations (intuition), with the ability to appraise a situation quickly (points and wedges). Michael knows that the lack of connections in her writing indicates that Toni can probably intuitively "read" the needs of a buyer.

Oddly enough, Toni can seem perceptive yet insensitive at the same time. How? The same disconnections and standoffish slant that allows her to distance herself from others emotionally and tune in intellectually can distance her from her own feelings, leaving her feeling isolated and alone.

Toni's goal setting is well suited to her short-lived energy (light pressure) that lies behind her strong willpower (disciplined style, baseline). Toni knows all too well that she can tire quickly from too much of anything (clients, travel, paperwork) and, like Nicole, she looks after number one (slant) and paces herself (spacing).

Michael sees that her strong personal pronoun *I* attests to her willpower, and to her desire to maintain an independent spirit. Michael senses that, as with James, he must be on the "same side of the desk" with Toni, but in a very professional, discreet manner. He can corroborate that her life, like her script, is dignified but lonely, much like the life of a royal personage who must maintain a certain distance and decorum. Speaking from his psychological background, Michael can also let Toni know that he totally supports her. Unfortunately for Toni, so many of her professional contacts come from personal associations *and* so many friendships are formed through professional organizations that she may feel she needs to be all things to all people and "on her guard" (slant, spacing) all the time. Toni was worried about the torched hors d'oeuvres; she didn't want it to reflect on Nicole, on her competency in other areas. Nicole realized that it only made her "human" and set the tone for a relaxed party. Toni's writing is dignified but devoid of feeling. Michael may be able to persuade her that holding back (from others' judgment) will also hold her back from life.

Toni is intelligent, clear-sighted, a good listener, practical, calm, and reflective. If she can begin to trust Michael, to feel that he is "on her side" and nonjudgmental, she may allow herself to reflect on this analysis, perhaps approaching him at a later date for further information and insight.

See how this works? Once a stranger came up to me after a television show, protesting, "I can see how this stuff really works, but I wouldn't *want* to know everybody's faults. I wouldn't have any friends left." On the contrary. First, we're not looking for "faults," but for greater insight and understanding. And the better you know someone, the more compassion you'll have when dealing with them. Do you think Michael is "judging" Toni? He's just trying to get to know her better. And Toni could use a friend with whom she can be totally spontaneous (and totally accepted). With his background and training, Michael might just be that friend.

Both Toni and Monica seem to have the same energy level (pressure), but they certainly operate differently.

Monica

> in the thought of sketching hoards of
> my own personal creations, hand selecting
> from the finest silks, wools, etc all

An overall impression of Monica's writing presents quite a different story. The slant and pastosity alone bespeak a lively, impulsive, and stimulating personality. The forward angle of the slant further supports a character that's compassionate, responsive, restless, and quite possibly gullible and naïve, as she rushes headlong into every endeavor.

Like Toni, Monica's energies will be quickly spent, and she needs her rest. Her pastosity (love of life, sensuality, rich spirit) may deplete her supplies much sooner than she expects, and she may become moody or feel "Why try?" when things suddenly seem too overwhelming.

It seems unfair, thinks Michael to himself, that a person with this much enthusiasm has to use up her reserves so fast. Then he remembers all the positives of light pressure and realizes that Monica also possesses the spirit of a gentle romantic, a dreamer. Thank heavens she has this softness, or she might burn herself out. Nature forces her body to rest while her mind still hums along. With any more energy, she'd be running *ahead of* her dreams.

Her spacing and margins document a need for involvement and participation, yet the disciplined, adequately spaced lines tell us Monica is in control of her time.

The size of her writing corroborates an attention to detail. When questioned about her new business, Monica replies, "I know what I'm doing and I can prove it with my *research*." Like Bill, she wants her work to provide personal satisfaction; she'll quietly work alone for long hours (size) to accomplish her goals. But she's so vibrant and enthusiastic. Wouldn't she seek high visibility, like Nicole? Not really. She could become just as enthused about a popular cause and work anonymously without acknowledgment.

Like Nicole, however, she wants to see tangible results (lower zone). Her active upper zone tells us that she does enjoy planning and considering the possibilities. But the zones are in balance, and after she's theorized for a while, she wants to make her dream a reality. At first Michael thought the middle zone appeared a bit small, but taken in the context of the overall size of her script he decides that Monica has a strong, independent ego, capable of concentration and able to set strong personal goals. The lower zone is active and balances the writing, but seems a bit narrow. Michael surmises that Monica selectively chooses what past events contain important lessons for the present. Monica feels in control when doing things her own way and has chosen a select framework in which to operate (size, narrow lower zone). The impulsive slant verifies that she operates from likes and dislikes and that she is impatient and wants to see results *now*.

Luckily, notes Michael, her writing appears to be quite connected, preventing her restless spirit from jumping to conclusions. Monica wants to rely on logical evidence to support her theories. She will systematically try different approaches until she finds the proper solution. Monica's a bit like the person who makes a list of all her requirements for the perfect house (size, detail-oriented), then wants to rush out and find it *today* (slant, narrow margins); but she'll hunt for months if necessary until the right one appears (size, connections, balanced zones). Of course, with her pressure, Monica may need a few mini-vacations along the way.

Michael has to deliberate about the middle-zone size before he finally concludes that indeed it is in balance with the size of the overall script. One reason the letters appear so dwarfed is that they're standing in the shadow of a very tall upper zone. Vanity? Monica? You bet. But is this some frilly feminine ego blown out of proportion? Hardly. Monica's ego stems from a rigid self-discipline and demanding attention to detail. Couple that with a repressed script and we have a person who may be a harsh critic, judging herself by demanding, rigid standards. See how she seems almost to hold herself back? She wants it to be perfect, meticulously accurate down to the last detail. Her abilities are tied into her self-image, and she demands as much of her ego as she does of her disciplined handwriting. Often when people put restrictions on themselves (compressed writing), they have a lot of judgment, a lot of "shoulds" in their life. With "shoulds" come right and wrong. When you set yourself up to be right or wrong, you'll set up your ego to come to the rescue. It will have to stand up tall and proud (tall upper zone) to defend all these "shoulds" and judgments in your life. Although Monica appears to set average goals, you can infer from her disciplined, organized script that "average" is probably pretty demanding by her standards.

Monica has a few conflicts in her script. She truly wants to operate from a concept that is important to her alone (size), yet she needs to connect with others (connections, slant) and at times is dependent on their approval (dependent slant, large ego). Michael feels that Monica may sometimes get in her own way because she is so anxious to see results. He sees her as entertaining, stimulating, impulsive, compassionate, gentle, romantic, sensual, restless, self-critical, and one who depletes her energies. Michael tells her, "You are so gifted, so special, so creative, so soft yet strong. I wish you could just stop and appreciate all your fine qualities—your gentleness, your enthusiasm. I actually think you would accomplish more if you could slow down. I can see that you have a million ideas, and probably get thirty new ones daily." "Fifty!" Monica nods and laughs. "Well, put them in a journal, along with sketches, pictures, dreams, and why not record your feelings while you're at it? Stop and think about how you might like your whole life to *flow*. Many of these ideas may be sidetracking you from one of your goals—peace of mind, a family . . ." Monica silently nods.

"You're an artist and a dreamer with the spirit of a child and the critical drive of an executive. Let's see if we can't make all this work for you instead of having the executive constantly curbing the child and exhausting the artist!"

Time Out

Well, what do you know. Michael has saved Connie for last. She wanted to go first, yet he left her in the living room to "entertain the troops" while he quietly saw the others one by one in the library. Why?

Sometimes it's wise to take your first volunteer; they're enthusiastic, eager, and probably not as skeptical as some. But often the most defiant will volunteer first to prove that "there's nothing to it"—attempting to sabotage your credibility. I once learned from a professional platform speaker that the first person to ask you a question after a speech will always challenge you or have a negative comment to make. In fact, he may not have heard the last half of your speech. Once you've "pushed his button" all he could think of from then on was his retaliatory question. This is not the case with Connie, but I just wanted to alert you to be on the lookout for the "spoiler." You need all the support you can get when you're just beginning.

Back to Connie. Michael instinctively felt that gregarious Connie (with *nothing* to hide) would rush back to the living room and tell everyone everything. Michael knew he might risk losing Toni or James if they heard too much too soon, so he satiated Connie's curiosity by allowing her to quiz others as they were finished. "I'm sorry to have kept you waiting," Michael smiles at Connie, "but I wanted to save the best for last." He winks and everyone applauds as Connie marches into the library.

Connie

is progressing nicely (I've continued and I can securing the national for those guys along w/ bigger and I'm learning alot from all of them

Michael's overall impression of Connie's writing rings true with her character—busy, exuberant, fun, and "overbooked." The energy is certainly there. Relatively stable baselines and controlled margins tell him that on the whole she is capable of accomplishing desired goals. That is, until her flamboyant and overly active imagination entices her down the garden path of new adventure (inflated lower zone).

Her forthright slant confirms a personality who moves forward to meet challenges in her environment. Connie certainly isn't someone to cheer others on from the sidelines—not when she could quarterback the plays herself.

The overall size verifies an ego that is practical, adaptable, and balanced. Connie is neither a scene stealer nor a meek mouse. Connie seems to be a take-charge person, like Nicole. Only to the untrained observer, however. Connie's exuberance (slant and pressure) and imaginative love of life (lower zone) automatically give her high visibility. But in command of the total situation? Hmmm. I think I'll leave my bet at Nicole's window, thank you, says Michael to himself. True, Connie is extroverted and demonstrative. She's also sensitive and malleable to outside circumstances that may trigger her responses, good or bad. Michael knows that Connie's emotions color her decisions, and she'll often tackle the project she likes to do first—choosing new slipcover fabric, for instance, rather than finishing the income taxes (slant).

Is Michael being unfair to attribute so much emotionalism to Connie's slant? Not if evaluated in combination with her zones. Let's see where Connie gets out of "balance." The lower zone— activity and imagination—is overpowering the rest of her script. Connie's strong suit is also her Achilles' heel. This inspiration and drive must be focused and harnessed into productive effort. Otherwise, loss of concentration and dissipation of energies will result, as Connie tries to pursue every new idea that comes her way. Gratefully, Michael concedes, her disciplined baseline and margins have helped her incorporate this whirlwind lifestyle into a somewhat manageable pattern.

Although Connie's writing at first appears connected, on closer inspection Michael notes several breaks and gaps. Connie has a bit of printscript, allowing her to assess situations with both logical reasoning and intuitive insight. There are enough connections to make her want to support impressions and feelings with facts and figures. She likes to have a feeling of continuity, of flow in her thinking, supported by a framework of background research (connections and lower zone). Intuitively, Connie deals with problems as a whole, only later stopping to fill in the gaps.

Michael senses from Connie's garlanded script that she enjoys connecting with others. She's affable, receptive, warm, and responsive. Do all these garlands mean she might sometimes sacrifice her own individuality for the sake of "belonging"? Perhaps. But Michael's not worried about Connie becoming a pushover. She has enough arcades to protect and defend her interests; they provide a good counterbalance for her gregarious, eager script. No one's going to walk all over affable Connie. She's receptive because she *enjoys* working with others, sharing ideas and energy. After all, she's got ideas to burn (lower zone)!

Like the others, Connie's signature is in keeping with the rest of her script in size and style, and her *t* crossings are of average height. Once again, we have a person comfortable with who she is, aware of her capabilities, and realistic in setting her goals. Her positive, clear, honest self-assessment allows her to present to the world who she really is, embellished a bit here and there when her imagination gets out of hand (lower zone). The personal pronoun *I* expansively takes up all the space it needs (visibility) but discreetly tells you little if anything about the author (retraced). Connie would prefer you to focus your attention on activities and projects in her outside world (lower zone) than on the internal whys and wherefores that make her tick (partially retraced personal pronoun *I*).

Does Connie operate from a concept that is important to her alone? Yes and no. By nature, Connie must answer the call of her own wild imagination. In doing so, she often exhausts her energies but exhilarates her spirit. She would never be content in a routine job, no matter whom she was trying to please. It's important to her to have the goodwill of others because she truly loves and embraces the spirit of mankind and humanity. She longs to feel part of something she recognizes as greater than herself, a worldwide "oneness" of life. Victory, to Connie, is sweeter when shared. To sacrifice camaraderie in pursuit of an elusive private goal (be it scientific, spiritual, or whatever) diminishes the triumph. Yes, Connie is her own person, introspective and reflective (arcades, lack of connections), perceptive and inquisitive (points and wedges), energetic and driven (pressure, baseline, lower zone). But she's a child of the universe (garlands and imagination), eager to share her joys, risks, and sorrows. With Connie, you never get a pale Xerox copy. Even on a bad day, she reaches from the depths (lower zone) to give you the real McCoy.

Michael sees Connie as confident, adaptable, creative, imaginative, inquisitive, perceptive, and energetic. Slow her down? Ever try and stop a freight train? Let her hitch her wagon to a star, thinks Michael; she'll probably get there! Knowing her penchant for producing tangible results, Michael chides Connie that she'll probably be the first to turn that adage into a reality. "Well, I *have* applied to NASA for a Volunteers in Space project," confirms Connie. Michael shakes his head and smiles.

Did I say Connie was last? What about Michael's writing? I volunteered to do Michael's write-up (through the eyes of a beginner) to assure objectivity and impartiality. Not only might Michael be blind to his own faults, he might also be a bit reluctant to toot his own horn.

Michael

My overall impression of Michael's script is one of artistry, creativity, and imagination. It appears restless, unbound by rules and restrictions. At first glance, it reminds me of a photo of Einstein's desk—organized clutter. But on closer inspection I realize the writing is quite minimalist, unencumbered by unnecessary loops and swirls. Its "frantic" quality comes from the *movement*, not the internal structure. It's like watching a powerful dancer unleash his energy across the stage. The movement may overwhelm you at first, but as you adjust to the rhythm, you discover it arises from disciplined patterns, from organized strength, unwilling to confine itself to conformity.

Can Michael stay on target? When he clears his calendar of unnecessary clutter he can. "Clutter?" objects Michael. He views his life-style as quite simple, really, pared of nonessentials. He doesn't even own a TV set. "I don't have time to watch it." Most free evenings you'll usually find him at a concert, play, or coffee house. Don't misunderstand. He's neither a dilettante nor a pseudo-intellectual. He's simply more interested in active participation than in vicarious learning. Like Connie, Michael has a full life. There'll be a book in his backpack, a French tape on his morning run. He's another one whose pastosity (rich pressure) leads him to sample the banquet of life. Although lower-zone interference distracts from overall organization, the strokes do not strongly demand attention. I think he'll be able to achieve his goals—although not as many as he would like to at one time!

The overall size of his writing tells us that Michael likes to tackle projects from the outside in, to see the overall scope of the project in its entirety so he can plan accordingly. And with his intuitive, inductive thought process, he can formulate answers from impressions without first needing access to all the facts (lack of connections). He has the ability to think in conceptual terms and appraise a situation quickly (size). He has little need for conformity in thinking, or for bouncing ideas off others (unique printscript style, lack of connections).

In fact, Michael often turns inward for answers, and is resourceful and self-sufficient in problem solving (arcades). When he does "bounce ideas," it's more for criticism or confirmation of a conclusion he's reached on his own than an attempt at "think tank" mentality (wide word spacing). True, others' ideas stimulate and challenge him, prompting him to question or discard old beliefs (analytical, investigative wedges). Michael accepts nothing on blind faith. Even the graphology he *seems* to embrace he is still practicing and proving for himself.

Because Michael's upper and lower zones have been pared to the efficient minimum, his middle zone assumes a dominant role. Size alone commands our attention. Michael has little doubt as to his own abilities. And the expansive, comfortable sweep with which his writing is executed confirms an ability to influence and lead if he so chooses. Mankind intrigues him. He's an observer of life.

His slant is fairly upright, telling us that he has control of his emotions, and can be logical and objective. But it also leans slightly forward as his heart reaches out to hear the story of another. He can empathetically put himself in another person's shoes. We might initially be drawn to Michael's friendly nature (B-slant, large middle zone), but it wouldn't be long before his piercing intellect would remind us that he has little patience for laziness or tapioca personalities (points and wedges). Michael's strong middle zone moves forward at a fast clip. He's alive, aware, in touch with his environment, and his script is expansive, clear, and direct.

The active lower zone reflects a pragmatic, get-to-the-point nature. Yet you may also notice that many loops seem unfinished. Is this because we are viewing printscript? Or is Michael sometimes reluctant to learn from past mistakes? It's a bit of both, actually. Because he's a doer who enjoys getting on with life, Michael is not one to dwell on the past. Operating intuitively, seldom will he need to work things out in a laborious, step-by-step process (lack of connections). Rather than conscientiously drag every little loop back to the baseline (let's look at how they've done it in the past), he prefers to wing it and move on. This doesn't mean that he *can't* conform, he simply chooses creativity and innovation over the tried and true whenever he can. He doesn't need to study how you did it (past history) because he doesn't intend to copy you.

Here's a personal observation. Notice how Michael's mind is *constantly* working—probing, restless, questioning (angles, angles, angles). I have a hunch that this sensitive, intuitive man sometimes feels *too* ''tuned in''—*too* aware of people and events in his environment. I think he may withdraw (word spacing, arcades), not only from others, but from his own perceptivity, to save his sanity. I'm a bit relieved that Michael can let go of his lower zone, perhaps dropping old memory pictures. He thinks too much as it is!

Michael sets practical goals. His efficient *t* formation values shortcuts in its economy of style and is realistic in its objective placement of the *t* bar. His personal self-image (personal pronoun *I*) dispenses with elaboration, is selective and discriminating, and can stand on its own.

Michael's writing appears original and intelligent, creative and restless. It seems strong yet gentle, playful and free-spirited yet disciplined and demanding. As with Joe, it will take you years to know the many layers of Michael. He's charismatic yet enigmatic.

* * *

There! You've done it. And wasn't it easy? Eventually, this information will become so second nature that you'll be able to use it from memory without having to refer back to the text. Hopefully graphology can become part and parcel of your daily living as it is for me.

A Final Note of Caution

Whether new to handwriting or an old pro, you'll sometimes find a personality trait in handwriting that seems to conflict with the person you know standing in front of you. *Trust the handwriting.* I know this sounds a bit presumptuous if you're new to the science, but it will prove right every time. For example, I once dated a man who seemed very kind and attentive. When I saw his handwriting, I was shocked, as it showed evidence of a very short temper and meanness. But I know Tom, I argued with myself. Here's one instance where the handwriting must be off somehow. Ignoring signals (love is blind), I proceeded headlong into a relationship with a man who indeed turned out to have a very ugly temper.

If the trait surfaces in the handwriting, whether you see it in the personality or not, it definitely is there. It may not surface right away, but the *potential* and capacity are there.

Also, and this is very important—a person can have traits that do not surface in the handwriting. I had four samples of Tom's handwriting. There was no evidence of temper in the first two samples. Luckily, he kept sending cards, and I got the total picture before long. What if I had only one sample, and temper was not evident in the handwriting? Does this mean the person doesn't have a temper? Of course not. When analyzing handwriting, you can only glean from the sample what is there. Everything may not "surface" at one sitting. That's why it's always preferable to have two or more samples.

Just like meeting Trudy in the supermarket in curlers and a dirty raincoat, you're seeing only a part of Trudy. At a black-tie dinner, you might see Trudy in a totally different light. To judge her solely from one appearance would be shortsighted. If Trudy were perfectly groomed and presented handwriting that appeared somewhat rushed and scattered, would you be fooled? Wouldn't you realize it was a very real part of Trudy? What if you met her in curlers and she handed you an organized, fluid sample. You might be surprised, but you would realize that Trudy was capable of that type of behavior as well. So, too, when you see temper (or anything else), realize the capacity is there. Likewise, don't assume every handwriting sample is complete. There may be other personality traits that might surface at another time. That's why it's so important to get as much writing as you can. (At least two pages would be ideal.) People can rarely maintain a facade for long.

14

A Final Word

The Challenge

My greatest challenge in writing this book has been to impart some simple basic guidelines to enable you to grasp the essentials of graphology while simultaneously conveying to you that it is in fact much more complex than it may seem at first. Graphology ordinarily correlates with basic principles of human nature, and so you can acquire a rudimentary background fairly easily. On the other hand, the science of graphology has been developing over many centuries and now incorporates psychology, sociology, psychiatry, medicine, the study of educational dysfunctions, learning aptitudes, and a host of other areas of expertise.

Because most of us learned to write at a very early age, that skill has become "second nature" to us, and we've forgotten the intricate and complex learning process we went through initially. The extraordinary process of writing involves split-second coordination between our physical and mental abilities. Scientific studies of brain function are a bit beyond our scope here, but they too attest to the tremendous effort involved in learning how to write. *Nothing* else compares in challenging every aspect of brain and body coordination. Children will unconsciously curl their feet and legs around their chairs, the tips of their tongues protruding, as they concentrate on this complicated learning process involving the entire neuromuscular system!

Another challenge I faced was to provide you with enough to get you started without inundating you with facts and figures that would leave you confused and overwhelmed. The scope of the field of graphology is enormous, but no matter how valuable the totality may be, without a knowledge of the basics you'd be wasting your time in an advanced class.

Tip of the Iceberg

Handwriting analysis is exciting, and, yes, it can change your life, but we've only just begun. "Well, at least I know about pressure!" prompted one student. True, you have the basics, but there is primary pressure, secondary pressure, grip pressure, displaced pressure, directional pressure, as well as pressure patterns that reveal physical ailments.

Each formation reveals further and further secrets about the individual. Don't get discouraged. If I tried to give it all to you at once, you'd walk away with nothing. (Ready for calculus? Oops, you forgot algebra. . . .)

But you do now have a firm foundation and a solid groundwork for understanding the whys and wherefores behind human behavior that are revealed in handwriting. There are no limits to where you can go from here. Further applications and volumes of study have been devoted to such advanced areas as memory, musical and mathematical aptitude, hidden talents, honesty and dishonesty, acquisitiveness and greed, childrens' handwritings, learning disabilities, handwriting and hiring, even sexuality, alcoholism and drug abuse, anorexia and bulimia, jealousy and resentment, sadism and masochism, forgery and fraud, schizophrenia and psychopathy. Handwriting is nothing more than a release of your energy patterns. If they are disturbed or altered (including physically), this, too, will be revealed.

Growth and Change

What if you see traits revealed in your own writing that you'd rather change? "I can discover facts, Watson, but I cannot change them," said Sherlock Holmes. Luckily for us, we can change things about ourselves we aren't happy with. And not just by putting on an act and hoping our new attitudes will somehow work their way inside. Through handwriting, you can program new thoughts and feelings into your psyche by physical and emotional pathways instead of through the intellect. In effect you are changing from the inside out. The method, called graphotherapy, has been utilized in European schools for years. It involves more than just changing a loop or a swirl, and so to play with a few sample exercises here would not do it justice. I only mention it so that you may know that once you grasp and understand the power of handwriting, you can also appreciate the valuable implications of this vital pathway to the brain for change and growth.

Be patient. It has taken me fourteen years to decipher the complexities and assemble them into a useful, simplified form. For now, absorb what you've been given and practice, practice, *practice*. Then when further aspects of handwriting are revealed to you, you'll understand how the pieces fit. Inevitably, after a beginner's class, there will be one student clamoring for more. He wants to know everything *now*. He reminds me of the young lady who spent all her money on tennis lessons—beginning, intermediate and advanced—but never touched her racket between classes. Her buddy took a series of ten lessons and practiced regularly twice a week for two years. When time came for the tournament, guess who won? If you faithfully absorb the information you've been given so far, you'll be miles ahead of the pack!

Remember, analyzing handwriting is much like analyzing a person sitting in front of you. It's challenging and intriguing; but he's just another person much like you, so relax! At the same time, it's a powerful doorway that leads straight to the subconscious. Accept the challenge. Open it.

If you would like further information about graphology and its many applications, you can write to me at P.O. Box 3218, San Francisco, CA 94119.

Answers to Reviews

Chapter 3
1. b,a,c
2. Medium
   Light
3. Phyllis

Chapter 4
1. a,b,c,
2. a
3. a,b

Chapter 5
1. c,d,a,b
2. a = Marge,b = Sally

Chapter 6
1. b,d,a,c,f,e
2. c,a,b
3. c,b,a

Chapter 7
1. c
2. b
3. c
4. Although Connie knows of every good place to go, her restless energy might exhaust you the first day. Nicole could easily fill each day to the brim, but knows how to pace herself (spacing) so that tomorrow can be just as enjoyable. Living for the now, she might treat herself to a massage back at the hotel to wind down her day.

Michael could be great fun as well, with a full middle zone

that embraces each new experience, and upper and lower zones that balance "planning" with "doing." If it's only three days, and depending on where we're going, I myself might choose Connie and let her wear me out because it's so much fun to be with her imaginative free-wheeling spirit.

Chapter 8
1. b
2. c
3. d
4. c

Chapter 9
1. a
2. c
3. b

Chapter 10
1. d
2. a

Chapter 11
1. b,c,a
2. c,a,b
e. a,c,b

Chapter 12
1. b,c,a
2. b
3. c

Index

About the Author

ANN MAHONY is a lecturer and author on the science of graphology who has been practicing for over seventeen years. She has covered the entire spectrum of handwriting analysis from forgery and fraud to corporate hiring, and is one of the few analysts in the country recognized as professional by business, government and education. She has appeared as an expert witness in both federal and superior court.

Ms. Mahony resides in San Francisco, California.